WU CHANGSHUO

A POLYMATHIC MAESTRO OF CHINESE ARTS

Compiled by Shanghai Wu Changshuo
Art Museum

ACC ART BOOKS

Contents

Preface

Wu Changshuo Art Museum, situated at No.15 East Lujiazui Road, Shanghai, functions as a critical cultural centre and museum, invested in and operated by the municipal government. Surrounded by Lujiazui Central Green, Wu Changshuo Art Museum has retained the characteristics of late Qing-dynasty architecture through multiple refurbishment projects over a period of 34 years, brought about by the reform and opening-up policy. This 110-year-old building, designed to house and protect cultural relics, is testament to the success of the reform and opening-up in the Lujiazui area and indirectly epitomises how Shanghai has been active in preserving, respecting and promoting the culture of this great city alongside its economic hypergrowth. In early 2022, the government launched a new architectural project called Meet-the-World Lounge in Shanghai. At the same time, the Culture, Sports and Tourism Administration of Pudong New Area revamped the nearby museum to make optimal use of its space and function. Throughout 2024, on the occasion of the 180th anniversary of Wu Changshuo's birth, the Shanghai Wu Changshuo Art Museum has put on exhibitions of original works, forums, and academic research events, mainly focusing on the theme of Wu Changshuo's artistic legacy. Over 80 featured collections from Wu Changshuo Art Museum have been specially compiled to create this book, illustrating how skillful and versatile this most benevolent, dedicated and receptive man was. With the debut of the all-English publications of Wu Changshuo's artworks, we endeavour to bring a better understanding of Shanghai and China to the rest of the world through not only Wu Changshuo's work but also his noble personality. In particular, we hope that viewers can appreciate the cultural spirit that has brought about the evolution of and is embedded in Pudong New Area, as well as its profound broad-mindedness and resolution to exchange and communicate with global culture. As we would say in China: 'The sea is fed by all rivers; it is vast because of its capacity.'

Operation Leader of Shanghai Wu Changshuo Art Museum
August 2024

1

THE PAST AND PRESENT OF SHANGHAI WU CHANGSHUO ART MUSEUM

The Yingchuan Villa

Jiang Jiehong

In the last four decades, China has seen the most extraordinary economic growth, fuelled by rapid urban development, the scale and speed of which are unprecedented in human history, particularly with regard to the increase in construction projects and urban population.[1] Buildings, architectural complexes, streets, and even whole cities can be transitory, leaving little trace of what has gone before. Many scholars have rightly referred to the recent urban transformation of China as an 'urban revolution'.[2] At the same time, more attention should be given to the intangible processes of transformation: for instance, how individual urban residents experience and perceive their changing cities through cultural means for a more holistic and multifaceted understanding of urban aspiration and its consequences in China and beyond. From a historical perspective, the spirit behind the urban construction in contemporary China can be traced back to the early days of the People's Republic, when urban spaces, residential areas and working zones, sometimes combined as *danwei* (work unit[s]), were rearranged for both practical and ideological reasons. The changes continue all the way through the revolutions in the last century, and through the acceleration of economic and urban development since the Open Door Policy (1978), shaping a moving reality, one that is almost surreal, beyond the normal and perceptible daily experience.

As one of the largest cities in the world, with a population of more than 25 million people, Shanghai has indisputably become a global financial centre, and a representative materialisation of the 'China Dream'. In Shanghai, the Pudong district was established as one of the state-level new areas (*xinqu*), with special economic and development support from the government since 1990. It has been primarily represented by the image of its Central Business District, Lujiazui – a peninsula formed by a bend in the Huangpu River – featuring the Oriental Pearl Tower, as well as the Jinmao Tower, the Shanghai World Financial Centre, and the Shanghai Tower. Among the forest of skyscrapers in Lujiazui, there is a large, detached house in a traditional style of Chinese architecture, which is currently called the Wu Changshuo Art Museum (WAM). In comparison with all the modernised (or Westernised) high-rise buildings that populate the area – with their minimalistic glossy or matt structures, their neon lights and giant LED screens and façades – it appears to be antiquated, solitary, and isolated from everyday life. As one of the oldest

1
For further discussions see, for example, Friedmann, John (2005), *China's Urban Transition*, Minneapolis: University of Minnesota Press; Wu, Fulong (2007), *China's Emerging Cities: The Making of New Urbanism*, New York: Routledge; Hsing, You-tien (2010), *The Great Urban Transformation: Politics of Land and Property in China*, London: Oxford University Press.

2
For instance, Campanella, Thomas J. (2008), *The Concrete Dragon: China's Urban Revolution and What It Means for the World*, New York: Princeton Architectural Press.

existing buildings in the city, it has survived the turbulence of wars and political movements of the past century, and it has witnessed the dramatic urban transformations in post-Mao China. To understand the country's revolutionary urbanisation and its social and cultural impacts, this project focuses on this unique building of national heritage in Shanghai.

Originally, the Yingchuan Villa (as WMH was previously known) was privately owned by the successful entrepreneur Chen Guichun (1873–1925). With his self-taught English, Chen started a career in overseas transportation, mainly between China and Britain. By monopolising the supply of railway sleepers and coal for the Shanghai-Nanjing and Shanghai-Hangzhou railroads, he built up the family fortune, and further developed the business into the real estate market alongside the Huangpu River. In addition to his acclaimed success in commerce, Chen passionately served the public by establishing hospitals and schools and making donations to charities.[3] In 1920, for example, with support from his friends, such as Yu Qiaqing (1867–1945), a powerful tycoon, and Wang Yiting (1867–1938), a prominent businessman and celebrated artist, Chen led the fundraising campaign to establish one of the earliest hospitals in the country – the Pudong Hospital.[4]

Starting in 1914, the construction of the Yingchuan Villa was completed in 1917, at which point it was one of the most luxurious mansions of its time. The location had been chosen in what was then the area of the so-called 'muddy pier' (*lannidu*), present-day Lujiazui in Pudong; in the owner's words, 'to view the wildness of the Jiangnan [the regions south of the Yangtze River landscape] during the days, and to hear the sound of the wave of the Huangpu River in the nights'.[5] The name of the Yingchuan Villa (Yingchuan xiaozhu) came from an ancient county in Henan Province in the Qin Dynasty (221–206 BC), the origin of the Chen clan. The family's philosophy was engraved on the top of the three ceremonial gates (*yimen*): the one at the main entrance leading into the courtyard reads *shude wuzi* (endeavour to always help others), and the two on the sides are *juren* (dwell in benevolence) on the east side and *youyi* (walk in the path of righteousness) on the west.[6] Chen's Yingchuan Villa became a gathering place for celebrated Shanghai artists and intellectuals, including Wu Changshuo, one of the leading figures of the Shanghai School.

3
Chen Jijian and Fan Guixiang, Chen Guichun's great grandson and his wife, voice recording provided by Chen Yin, Chen Guichun's great granddaughter.

4
Chen Guichun became the inaugural president of the Pudong Hospital, succeeded by Wang Yiting, and Du Yuesheng (1888–1951), an influential underworld leader in Shanghai, as the second and third presidents. The name of the hospital was changed to the Oriental Hospital in 1993. See Wang Qisen, *Minzu banyi jianxinlu* (The Hardship of Nationalists Establishing the Hospital), *Xinmin Evening News*, 19 December 2010, p. B13.

5
Couplet by Chen Guichun, dates unknown.

6
The inscriptions of *shude wuzi* and *juren youyi* are quoted from teachings in the Chinese classics, respectively, *Book of Documents* and *Mencius*.

After Chen Guichun passed away in 1925, his business declined.[7] According to his youngest granddaughter Chen Juying (b. 1933) – the only grandchild who is still alive – family members fled from the house in terror after Japanese forces began the Battle of Shanghai in August 1937, when she was four years old.[8] The Yingchuan Villa was occupied by Japanese troops and turned into the headquarters of the Japanese Military Police during the Second Sino-Japanese War (1937–45), and then by the Nationalist Party as the National Garrison Command up until 1949. When the family members were allowed to return, numerous dead bodies – killed or tortured to death – were excavated in the garden: no one wanted to live there anymore.[9] After the founding of the People's Republic of China, there was a series of political campaigns, including the abolition of private ownership via the socialist transformation of industry and commerce in 1953, whereby the government would become, in effect, the major partner.[10]Private merchants and capitalists, including Chen Yuzhang (1895–1958), the eldest son of Chen Guichun, were asked to 'volunteer' their enterprises for transformation into the new 'joint state–private ownership' (*gongsi heying*). The Yingchuan Villa was then used for different purposes: as a printer's premises, as a tanning workshop, and as a tax revenue office. During the first few decades of the new regime, responding to government policy that encouraged procreation, the population surged. In February 1959, the property was taken over by Dongchang Housing Management Station (*Fangguan suo*).[11] It was reconstructed, with existing rooms partitioned and allocated to local people. Although the physicality of the house as a whole remained, its original purposefully designed structure and functionality were annihilated.

Since the late twentieth century, with Pudong having been identified as the focus of an urban development strategy and was to be transformed into Asia's new financial centre, demonstrating China's ambition to become a major world economic power in the 21st century.[12] As a result, the fate of the Yingchuan Villa changed yet again. The original complex consisted of four sections in the main building with a large garden at the front and two annexes on either side to accommodate the family's servants. Because of the urban planning in Lujiazui, the garden and the first section were bulldozed in the early 1990s to widen the road in front of the house (East Lujiazui Road), while the annexes were removed to

7
According to Chen Yin, Chen Guichun was murdered, possibly by his business competitors. Interview with Chen Yin, online, 7 July 2023. All interviews in this book are conducted by the author, unless otherwise stated.

8
Starting on 13 August 1937, the Battle of Shanghai was fought between the National Revolutionary Army of the Republic of China and the Imperial Japanese Army of the Empire of Japan at the beginning of the Second Sino-Japanese War, a conflict of three months that involved one million troops and constituted one of the bloodiest battles of the Second World War.

9
Interview with Chen Juying, the youngest granddaughter of Chen Guichun, online, 10 August 2023.

10
So, Bennis Wai-yip, 'Private Ownership in the Early 1950s: Findings from New Material', *The China Quarterly*, No. 171, September 2002, pp. 682–703.

11
Fangguan suo is a particular administrative department of the Chinese government responsible for public housing management, maintenance and rental and sales arrangement.

12
Wu, Victoria, 'The Pudong Development Zone and China's Economic Reforms', *Planning Perspectives*, Vol. 13, No. 2, 1998, pp. 133–65.

give way to a public park. The remaining body of the Yingchuan Villa experienced two further reconstruction processes, as part of being preserved as one of the city's surviving architectural heritages. First, in 1996, following a decision by the Pudong government, the building was repurposed as the Showroom of Lujiazui Development (*Lujiazui fazhan chenlieguan*) to promote the latest achievement in the area. It was planned to open to the public on 1 July 1997 as a present for the anniversary of the Chinese Communist Party, and to celebrate the return of Hong Kong to China. While reconstruction work was taking place, inevitably the entire building – which then housed approximately 80 homes, with residents including families with children – had to be vacated. The initial reconstruction was primarily to change the functionality of the building – from residential dwellings to office and exhibition spaces. The second round of renovations began in 2008, directed by a group of experts in traditional architecture and professionals led by Cao Yongkang, and focused on the details of repair and renovation, aiming to restore the house to its original state. The building had been left in a poor condition due to the lack of professional conservation over the years: in addition to the loss of its first main section, some carved wooden windows and doors were damaged or missing. With few textual or visual references of the original building available at that time, part of the restoration, reproduction and replacement of the components was done in consultation with research into another surviving house of a similar style but on a smaller scale, Yang's Residence (*Yangshi minzhai*) in Pudong.[13] In 2010, the villa was repurposed once again as today's WMH, not only to commemorate Master Wu Changshuo and to celebrate his influential achievement, but also to showcase Chinese arts and culture to an international audience. In actual fact, in his lifetime, the artist Wu Changshuo only stayed in the building as a guest for a few days.[14]

The Yingchuan Villa followed the style of the *jiaoquan fangzi* (ring house), which features rooms all around, usually built symmetrically, leaving a courtyard in the middle. Similar to the courtyard house (*siheyuan*) in Northern China, the entire building looks visually like a rice funnel to symbolise an endless flow of wealth for the resident family. Today, the building has three sections: the first and the third respectively include five more or less identical rooms, with a main hall in the middle of each section, flanked by four smaller rooms; the second

13
Interview with Cao Yongkang, online, 29 July 2023. Yang's Residence was built in the 1930s by Yang Hongsheng (1884–1966).

14
According to Lin Wei, the current Director of WMH, it was only possible to protect the building from being demolished by renaming it with the name of Wu Changshuo, utilising the fame of his artistic legacy. Interview with Lin Wei, 23 October 2023, Being Art Museum, Shanghai. On 4 April 2014, the building was listed as a 'Cultural Relic in Shanghai.

section of 'wing' rooms in between the two sides connect the sections together as an enclosed residence.

With both traditional craftsmanship and advanced (as it would have been back then) technology, the building features a combination of Eastern and Western aesthetics. For example, there are traditional Chinese interiors and decoration in the living rooms, bedrooms and studies, and European-styled details, such as plaster mouldings, in the dining rooms, tea rooms and bathrooms.[15] The building was constructed primarily in wood, using inherited structural techniques from traditional Chinese architecture. It features classic flying eaves and black-and-red brick walls, while also embracing Western aesthetics and materials, such as geometric-patterned floor tiles and dark-green glazed wall tiles, as well as coloured window glass that would receive attention for its decorative quality even in the West.[16] Taking advantage of Chen Guichun's overseas trade, some architectural materials, facilities and accessories for the house were imported from Britain in the 1910s,[17] hence its Western taste reflects the late Victorian and Art Nouveau styles, moving towards Art Deco.[18] When Shanghai prospered and became a global metropolis at that time, Art Deco would have been introduced as one of the most popular styles to be incorporated into the city's architecture and design and, possibly, influenced the architecture of the Yingchuan Villa.

There would almost certainly have been numerous attractive and expensive items of furniture in the rooms, too, but all have vanished. However, we can still appreciate the high quality of living through the observation of what has been left or restored in the building. Most significantly, the villa houses the most exquisite carved-wood decorations, which appear prevalently throughout the building – on doors and windows, beams, purlins, pillars and railings – and have earned it its reputation as the 'Pudong Mansion of Carved Patterns' (*diaohualou*). Some wood carvings involve hybrid patterns with Western decorative elements and visual formats, while some have inherited the recurring motifs of plants, animals and mythological creatures of Chinese tradition, such as plum blossom, orchid, bamboo and chrysanthemum, known as the 'Four Gentlemen', representing virtues such as morality, purity, modesty and persistence. What has made the building exceptional are not only those symbolic patterns, but also the

15
The information about the Chinese and Western styles of the building varies, with no accurate record before the residential building was renovated as a showroom in 1996. For example, see Cao Yongkang, *Pudong chuantong minju yanjiu* (Research on Traditional Residential Buildings in Pudong), Beijing: Zhongguo jianzhu gongye chubanshe, 2019, p. 89.

16
Forsyth, Michael, and White, Lisa, *Interior Finishes and Fittings for Historic Building Conservation*, Hoboken, NJ: Wiley-Blackwell, 2011, pp. 132–33.

17
Interview with Chen and Fan, op. cit.

18
Following its advent in France in the 1910s, the new style of design known as Art Deco flourished in Europe and the United States during the 1920s. For example, see Jean-Paul Bouillon (1989), *Art Deco 1903–1940*, New York: Rizzoli; and Patricia Bayer (1990), *Art Deco Interiors: Decoration and Design Classics of the 1920s and 1930s*, London: Thames & Hudson.

idiomatic narratives and folk tales produced in the form of wood carving. Among numerous carvings, it is believed that there is a complete set depicting the story of the *Romance of the Three Kingdoms* (*Sanguo yanyi*), including well-known accounts from this Chinese classical novel.[19] However, no credible archival material or any obvious evidence has been found to support this claim; the figures in the wood carvings, dressed in various costumes and depicted in a range of scenes, very possibly represent many more (or other) stories than just those told in the *Three Kingdoms*. These stories have been reproduced in other visual forms of Chinese crafts as well as performed through the genres of traditional opera, plays and storytelling. Placed (if not hidden) on the beams high above, those most exquisitely carved narratives remain largely obscured by distance. Indeed, to the former residents, they were seen as fixed performances, whether from radio or theatre, staging 'one play after another'.[20]

Today, cities come and go, with all the necessary appurtenances travelling alongside as part of the globalisation process. Through this process, the term 'Shanghai' is no longer singular, but plural, in the way that it represents multiple cultures and desires, in its ever-changing self. The city Shanghai is proud or humiliated, peaceful or turbulent, idealistic or distressed, while the Yingchuan Villa has become a theatre to stage all these changes.

* Jiang Jiehong, Professor and Director of the Centre for Chinese Visual Arts, Birmingham City University; Principal Editor, *Journal of Contemporary Chinese Art.*

* This article is excerpted from *Shanghai: The Sleepless Theatre*, originally published in November 2023 by Shanghai People's Fine Arts Publishing House.

19
Cao, op. cit., p. 89. *Romance of the Three Kingdoms* is a 14th-century novel, attributed to Luo Guanzhong (c.1330–1400), and recounting the dramatised story of the Three Kingdoms (220–80), Wei, Shu and Eastern Wu, the tripartite division of China among the dynastic states.

20
Interview with Tang Ai'xin (b. 1924), September 2015, conducted by Yao Mengxi. Tang Ai'xin and her husband moved into the Yingchuan Villa in 1952 and left in 1996.

Rejuvenating an Ancient Mansion – Introduction to Shanghai Wu Changshuo Art Museum (originally the former residence of Chen Guichun)

Shanghai Wu Changshuo Art Museum

A centenary-old historical mansion established in 1914 is situated on the south of Lujiazui Central Green. With an approximately 1,103 ㎡ floor space, it was built by the wealthy merchant Chen Guichun at considerable cost, making it one of the few luxury mansions in Shanghai of that period.

A perfect marriage of Chinese and Western styles, the mansion is of custom design and craftsmanship, blending the most advanced construction engineering at that time with premium building materials such as Chinese cedar for the roof truss and the graceful carvings on the structural surface, all of which have earned the mansion the mantle of a 'carved mansion in the Pudong New Area'.

Following the typical quadrangle (Siheyuan) structuring of ancient China, this fully symmetrical mansion, with a total of eight halls and six side rooms, was built using a 'penetrating and interlocking' framework. The main hall is tall and spacious and was built using the bracket system with nine small blocks (San Dou) and one capital block (Lu Dou), a system rarely used in residences. The Western-styled triangular pediment with differing heights and bare brick walls is lined with red brick on the façade, and the majority of doors and windows are traditional Chinese-style wooden partitions. Additionally,

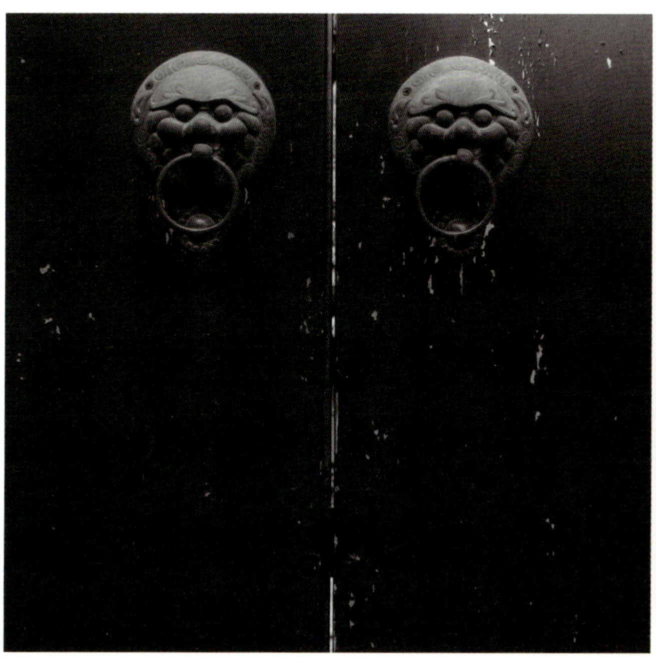

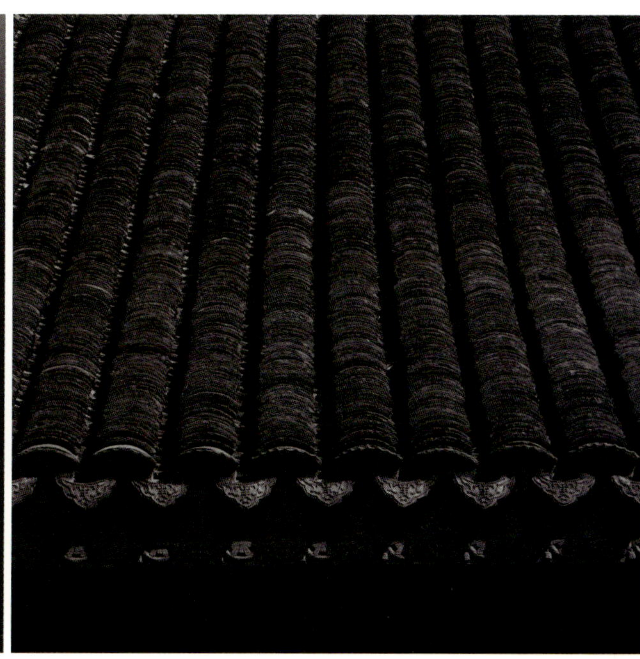

complex scroll designs are used for the interior overdoor of the Shikumen-styled secondary gate.

The most advanced finishing techniques and materials of glass, patterned tiles, and glazed-tile dados, and the Western-style wood trim and fireplaces were applied in a number of spots – a cutting-edge design and construction for that time.

All the roof trusses, doors and windows were elaborately sculpted, and the beams, cross beams, and lintels were carved with patterns of flowers and birds. Flowers favoured by Westerners such as lilies, tulips and roses were carved using traditional Chinese wood carving techniques, along with the 'Vase with Three Halberds' (平升三级) design, and paintings such as *Eight Horses* (八骏图) and *Romance of the Three Kingdoms* (三国演义). This illustrious fusion of Western and Chinese architectural styles continues to attract attention today.

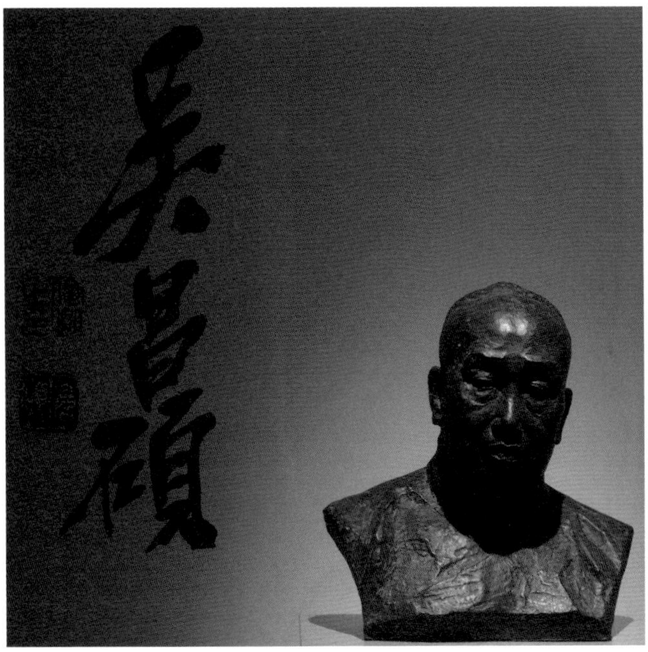

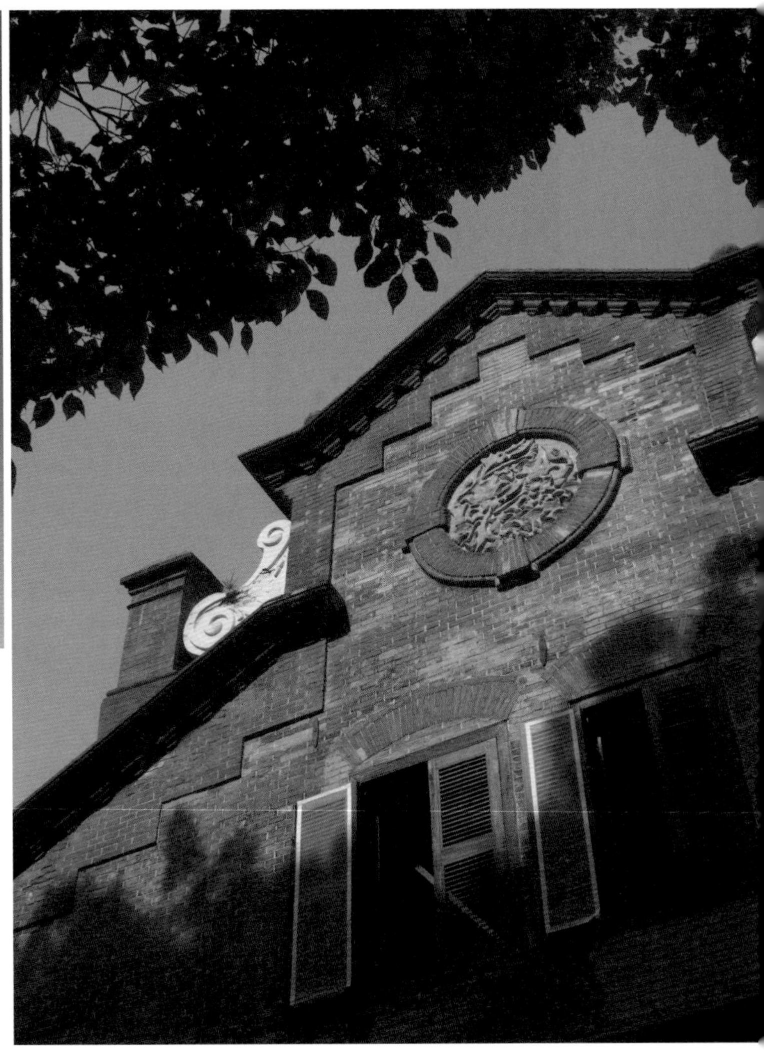

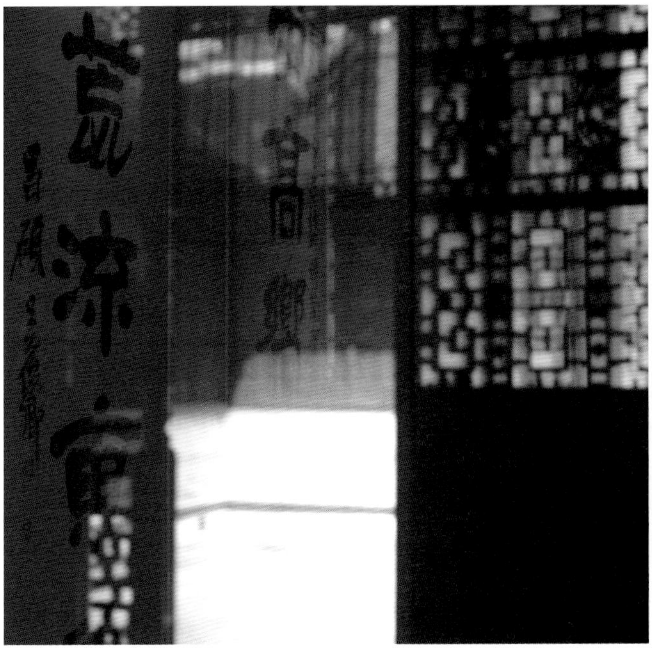

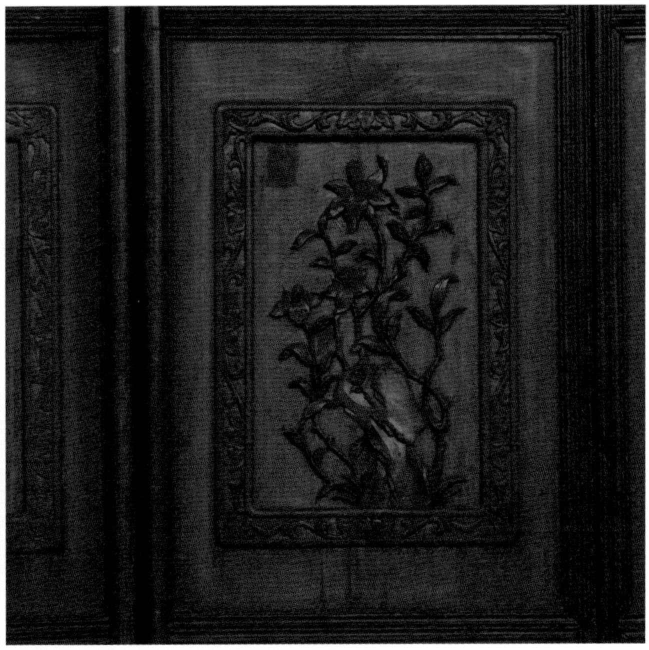

This historical mansion has borne witness to a century of changes as Lujiazui has transformed from a rural area with crisscrossing country paths to a world-class financial hub. During this time, the mansion has gone from being the private property of an affluent country gentleman to becoming the Wu Changshuo Art Museum, which houses Chinese art and history and public artefacts. Listed as one of the major historical and cultural sites protected at the provincial level in Shanghai in 2014, the mansion stands out as an exclusive example of classical tradition and culture among the trendy high-rises in Lujiazui.

Based on in-depth research and an examination of the cultural landscape of the Lujiazui area, the brand-new Wu Changshuo Art Museum in Shanghai is dedicated to functioning as an international art and cultural exchange platform, perfectly combining Oriental and Western attractions over three spaces:

I. The Shanghai School art exhibition area with Wu Changshuo's works at its core provides the public with immersive displays of the Shanghai School artistic accomplishments with digital interactive content. In addition, it provides a viewing space for the public, and there are organised routes for security checks, fire protection, registration, etc.

II. The exhibition hall for the original Shanghai School artworks, the display hall for exhibiting contemporary artworks in their cultural context, and the Shanghai-lifestyle art shop.

III. Three functional areas: exhibition halls for seal engraving, inscriptions and epigraphs, with historical sections of related literature and academic studies.

The Wu Changshuo Art Museum in Shanghai endeavours to draw on existing Shanghai cultural resources and explore new ground. By connecting public cultural services to those in creative industries, and by publicising relevant cultural and educational public events, it is hoped that an artistic essence will be unleashed, giving a sense of cultural belonging to citizens in its real sense.

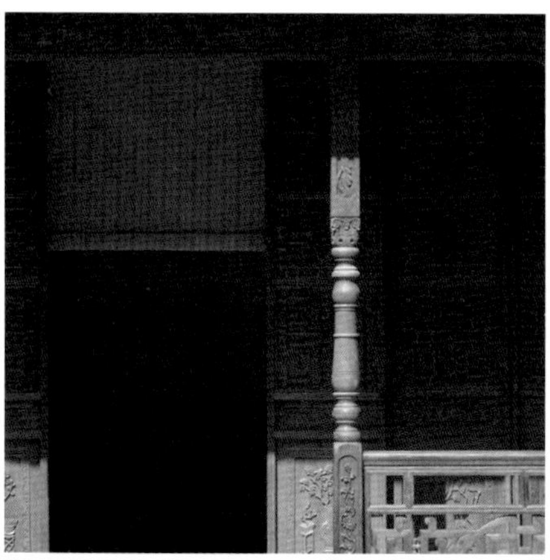

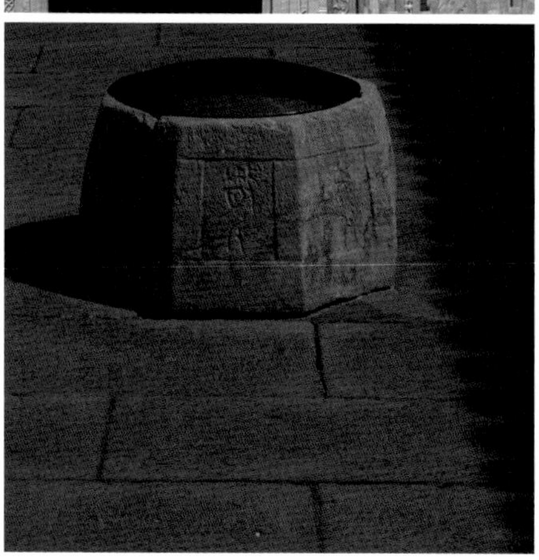

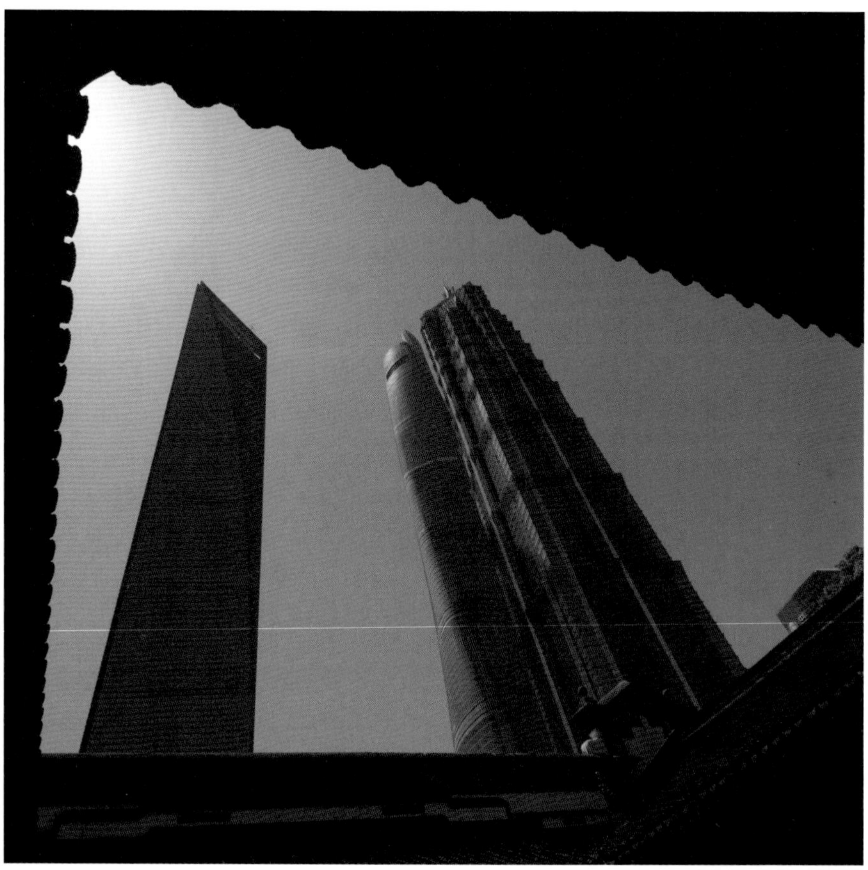

2

MASTERPIECES AND COLLABORATIONS: WU CHANGSHUO AND FELLOW ARTISTS

Artist Relationship Map

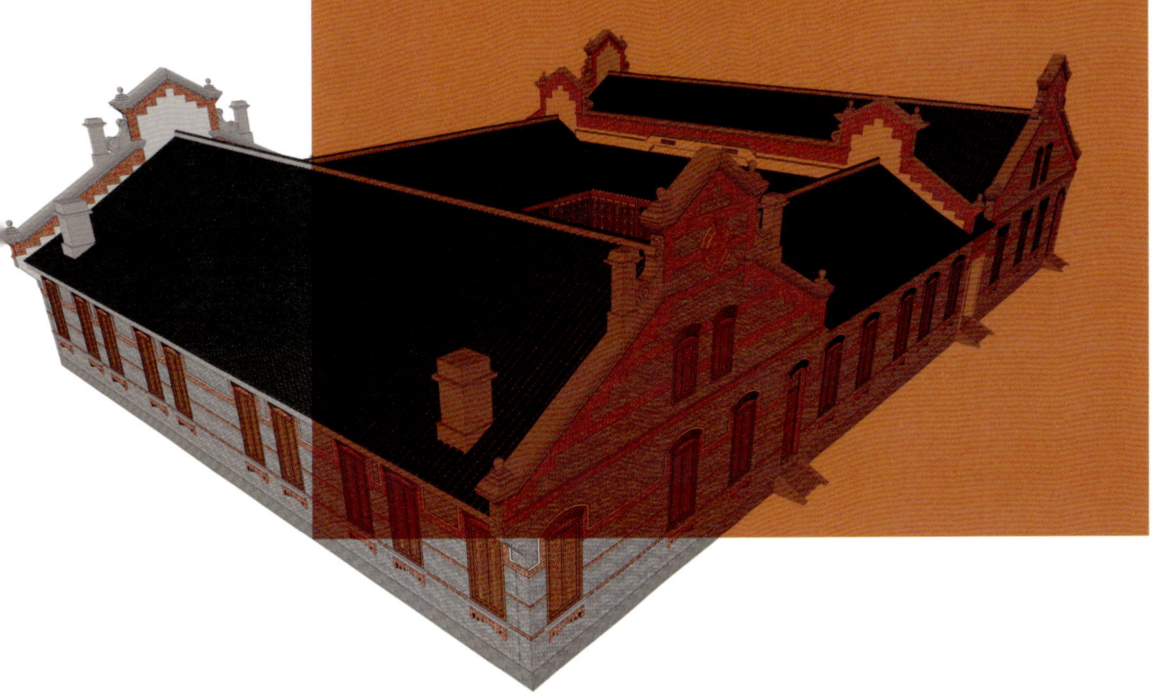

Wu Changshuo's Story: His Life Journey and Artistic Accomplishments

Wu Changye

The rich artistic legacy built by Wu Changshuo has proven its time-honoured presence in China, as well as countries and regions globally, and continues to achieve a profound appreciation right up to the present day.

Wu Changshuo was born in an impoverished mountainous area of Zhangwu Village, Anji County, Zhejiang Province, in the late Qing dynasty on 12 September 1844 (the first day of August on the Chinese calendar). His father Wu Xinjia was selected to sit the provincial-level imperial examination, though didn't go on to launch an official career. His mother Wan (her surname) gave birth to three sons and one daughter, with Wu Junqing (as he was initially named) the second born. In the face of the ravages of war, he left the village with his father and styled himself as Cangshi in memory of surviving the dangers in Shicangwu, another mountainous area near Zhangwu Village.

In 1864, the third year of the Tongzhi Emperor's reign, the war subsided. Wu, by now 21 years old, reunited with the rest of his family in his hometown. But, to his considerable grief, nine family members had died due to disease, warfare and famine. As a result, he and his father had to depend on one another, making a living through farming. Whenever possible, they would immerse themselves in traditional Chinese literature and the arts. His father, a master of traditional Chinese poetry and seal engraving, taught Wu his skills, fostering in him a profound interest in these disciplines. Empowered by his deep thirst for knowledge, Wu Changshuo had to walk long distances by himself across mountains and harsh environments to borrow books in which he buried himself during his breaks on the farm. On many an evening, he burnt the night oil, assiduously equipping himself with knowledge and, on some occasions, even making copies of borrowed books by hand so that he could read them over and over again. Ever inquisitive, he clarified any confusion that arose by consulting others until he had worked everything out. As a result, he fostered the habit of cherishing and preserving books, something that he continued to do throughout his life. He even endeavoured to make his own books by putting together fragments of texts and binding wherever possible in order to make them available to future generations. Back then, candidates were required to write in the eight-legged essay (八股文) style in order to be eligible for the imperial examinations, the prerequisite for any official career in the Ming and Qing dynasties. But he was far less interested in this essay style than his peers and instead obsessed over exegetical studies (文字训诂之学), inspired by his lasting passion for Chinese calligraphy and seal engraving. He unwillingly took and passed the county-level imperial examination at the age of 22, following continual pressure from the education officers in his county. But preferring to pursue his original aspirations, Wu Changshuo opted not to take the next round of examinations or take up an official post. He married Shi (her surname) at the age of 29 and left his home shortly afterwards, travelling to Huzhou City, Hangzhou City, Suzhou City and Shanghai in his quest to become an apprentice to masters and to make a living. Befriending others on his travels, he met three esteemed antique collectors, Wu Dacheng, Wu Pingzhai and Pan Zhenghe in Suzhou City, where their recognition of Wu gave him a golden opportunity. He came to appreciate the priceless antiques they collected, including cultural relics, inscriptions and epigraphs, along with Chinese calligraphy works and paintings. During this time, he absorbed all the knowledge and practical first-hand experience of the classical arts, refining his practical skills in relevant disciplines as he befriended recognised calligraphers and painters.

At the age of 51, Wu joined the army under the direct leadership of Wu Dacheng during the First Sino-Japanese War (1894–95) (甲午之战). During this time, he visited different regions and incredible landscapes across China, enabling him to nurture his artistic accomplishments in later life.

In 1899, at the age of 56, Wu Changshuo took office as the County Magistrate of Andong (the current day Lianshui County in Jiangsu Province), upon the recommendation of his countryman Ding Baoyuan. Born with a tranquil character 'unrestrained like wild geese who live idly and carefree', as he described himself, he wasn't interested in the political side of things, of pleasing and flattering his superiors, particularly if it was at the cost of the welfare of ordinary people. So, he resolutely resigned one month later. He then fully committed himself to furthering his endeavours in the arts, including poetry, calligraphy, painting and seal engraving. His lifelong pursuit and dedication ultimately enabled him to establish himself as a 'master of exceptional skill' who developed an exclusive school of thought and artistic style.

I learned poem-writing in my thirties and painting in my fifties —Wu Changshuo's Life Aspirations

Wu Changshuo self-deprecatingly portrayed himself as 'a man who learned to write poems in his thirties and to paint in his fifties'. As a matter of fact, he polished his poem-writing techniques at the age of 23 when he became the apprentice of Shi Xuchen, and honed his painting skills at the age of 30 when he apprenticed for his countryman Pan Zhiqi, who is well-known for his masterful craft of plum blossom painting. Some might take such self-evaluation as a manifestation of Wu's aspirations but, in fact, he was strict with himself when acquiring his artistic skills: starting at the age of 30, he dived into a two-decade journey of parallel learning of poetry, calligraphy, painting and seal engraving. Following a scientific, progressive path, he prioritised learning calligraphy, inscription and epigraph engraving, poetry, and classical literature, both theoretically and practically, as a solid foundation for painting later on. The only way to achieve mastery is through a comprehensive study of the subject; this would lead to Wu reaching new heights in the arts.

Calligraphy and painting are known to share the same origin, dating back to the Yuan dynasty during which Chinese painters combined calligraphy with painting. Since the vast majority of them were proficient in the art of calligraphy, the calligraphy-inspired brushstrokes in their paintings added an extra artistic element. Fast forward to the Qing dynasty and the sphere of culture and art began to embrace radical changes following the unearthing of cultural relics in an increasingly large volume. Enthusiastic advocates of calligraphy, including Bao Shenbo and Kang Changsu, facilitated the flourishing of stele inscription studies (碑学), fuelling the painters' interest and respect for seal engraving studies (印学). As a result, calligraphy and painting professionals also specialising in seal engraving blossomed everywhere. This elevated the essence of painting from its trinity with poetry and calligraphy to create a quaternity made up of poetry, calligraphy, painting and seal engraving. Wu Changshuo grew up in this period of major transformation and societal change as well as chaos. It is worth noting that the First Opium War (1840–42) (第一次鸦片战争) broke out four years prior to Wu's birth (1844), after which the Second Opium War (1856–60) (第二次鸦片战争), the Sino-French War (1883–85) (中法战争), the First Sino-Japanese War (1894–95) and a series of wars of aggression took place, causing the Qing dynasty to falter. The incompetent Qing government, mired in corruption, conceded many of its territorial and sovereignty rights and paid indemnities to foreign nations under humiliating terms, resulting in ordinary people falling into dire poverty and causing severe misery.

As the Chinese feudal society became semi-feudal and semi-colonial, its prowess and knowledge of culture, art, science and technology underwent profound changes as a result. In addition, the unearthing of cultural relics triggered the study of epigraphy and exegesis, which to a large extent helped the literature and arts at that time to progress. This turbulent yet vibrant historical backdrop, alongside his family tradition of farming and reading, directly shaped Wu's outlook on life. Witnessing the extravagant lifestyle of the upper ruling classes, who endlessly repressed and extorted the poor, and making it through arduous journeys himself, he was awash with indignance. Meanwhile, as an unrecognised talent, Wu Changshuo felt bewildered in the face of his bleak prospects and longed to communicate how he felt. This propelled his lifelong dedication to the study of literature and the arts. Endeavouring to achieve his best work in order to deliver the most fruitful outcome, he broke down his goal into thoughtfully designed plans and steps and was strict with himself in following them, acquiring the relevant techniques to facilitate his objective.

At the age of 29, he left his newly-married wife and home to become an apprentice to masters in his pertinacious pursuit of his goal. His master in Gujing Jingshe (the academy for the exegesis of the classics) (诂经精舍) in Hangzhou city was Yu Quyuan, a renowned

Confucianist, who taught him mainly poetry, prose and exegetical studies. Later, he became acquainted with Yang Jianshan, a prominent epigrapher in Suzhou City, and made great strides in calligraphy and epigraphy thanks to Yang's meticulous teaching. In addition to Yang, he befriended a number of epigraphers and calligraphers, who all supported and profoundly inspired him. The connection he made with antique collectors Wu Dacheng, Wu Pingzhai and Pan Zhenghe in Suzhou City gave him access to ancient inscriptions, epigraphs, works of calligraphy and original paintings by masters, along with experts who could teach him about these important works of art. The recognition from three esteemed antique collectors, Wu Dacheng, Wu Pingzhai, and Pan Zhenghe in Suzhou City granted him the golden opportunity to appreciate the priceless treasure they had collected, including ancient inscriptions and epigraphs, and original masterpieces of paintings and calligraphy by historical figures. His artistic prowess was considerably elevated through these sources of inspiration. His affection for poetry, and poem recitation in particular, motivated him to frequently exchange poems with prominent poets, enabling him to progress his skills. This versatile man then delved into Chinese painting as well, befriending Ren Bonian and Pu Zuoying, from whom he drew meaningful references and advanced in leaps and bounds. His frequent visits to friends, both old and new, and his tireless pursuit of masters and the mastery of arts, all helped to enrich his knowledge and build upon his progress and accomplishments.

As representative figures of revolutionary Chinese painters, Wu Changshuo, Xu Gu, Pu Zuoying and Ren Bonian co-founded the influential Shanghai Painting School (海上画派).

Seeking rustic charm in calligraphy learning in my thirties —Wu Changshuo's Calligraphy Journey

When working on calligraphy, Wu Changshuo assiduously learned and improved the characters he wrote, aiming to master this art form fully. Since he couldn't afford the rice paper and ink brushes required for calligraphy in his early days of poverty, he would make time at dawn and during breaks on the farm to practice using pens without brushes on the bricks and stones in front of his house, imitating the calligraphy characters whenever possible. He started with regular script (楷书), first imitating the 'Yan' calligraphy style of Yan Zhenqing, also known as Yan Lugong, a celebrated calligrapher, and then turning to the style of Zhong Yao or Zhong You. He also imitated the style of Huang Tingjian (who styled himself as Shangu) as testified by the epitaph he wrote for his friend Pu Hua. After establishing a firm foundation in calligraphy, he advanced with the running (行书) and cursive (草书) scripts. He imitated Wang Duo's style first before integrating those of Ou Yangxiu and Mi Fu for the running script, forging a refreshing style of a robust, fluid and grand nature. As for the cursive script, he imitated *The Manual of Calligraphy* (书谱) and *Shi Qi Letters* (十七帖), as well as original pieces by other leading Chinese calligraphers.

Following the end of the reign of Jiaqing and Daoguang Emperors, epitaph relics from the Han dynasty and the Southern and Northern dynasties were unearthed in large volumes. These were valuable references for scholars dedicated to the classics and historiography and, more importantly, they triggered a new era of development in the sphere of calligraphy. Stele inscription studies evolved and even replaced the existing 'tie rubbing' in calligraphy (帖学). Some bold innovators endeavoured to introduce new styles and paths, challenging the dominance of the works of Wang Xizhi and Wang Xianzhi, two sages of calligraphy. Such artful breakthroughs evolved into new and refreshing styles and would go on to influence the mindset of Wu Changshuo both directly and indirectly as he himself refused to be restrained by convention.

Wu's imitations of the Stone Drum inscriptions (石鼓文) from the Warring States period were never pure copies of each brushstroke. Instead, he carefully studied inscriptions in depth found on the standard weighing apparatus from the Qin dynasty, the inscribed stone tablets at Mount Langya and Mount Yi, and a variety of other styles. He 'enriched his artistic visionary world day by day' through thoughtful internalisation and by injecting his own understanding into those imitations.

He spent his entire life figuring out the essence of 'rustic charm' in the art of calligraphy. More significantly, he 'internalised' new knowledge, transferring it to his own artistic endeavours. So how did he succeed in truly absorbing ancient knowledge without blindly following it? His answer is to accept change: 'nowadays, people admire the ancient artworks, but they rarely approach our contemporary arts'. He adds, 'I am the subject while the ancient people are my objects'. By ceaselessly breathing new life into the 'rustic charm', he sought a balance in the evolution of ancient artistic traditions becoming new contemporary trends.

His imitation of the Stone Drum inscriptions present the Chinese characters with an inspiring, natural flavour, rustic shapes, and fluid yet robust strokes and brushmarks, establishing himself as the exclusive creator of the 'harmony between ancient and contemporary styles of calligraphy'. His brushstrokes in inscriptions such as these became firmer and more natural as he grew older, as is evident in his works of cursive script and running script, as well as in his paintings. His portrayal of grapes, for example, was condensed into concise cursive script strokes of the grapevine through years of practice and learning. When fuelled by an urge to practise calligraphy, he composed highly cursive script (狂草) using seal script (篆书) and clerical script (隶书) styles, shaping exhilarating, expressive brushstrokes on rice paper. In other examples, his drawings of plum blossom clearly show his passion as 'unstoppable like roaring lakes and sea', in which the 'indistinguishable' fusion of plum blossom and seal script is testament to his painting techniques having absorbed inspiration from calligraphy in all its grandeur and vigour.

A mastery of the essences of poetry, calligraphy and painting matters deeply to me —Wu Changshuo's Painting Excellency

Based on his mastery of epigraphy and his internalisation of the structure of ancient and contemporary Chinese characters, Wu Changshuo blended calligraphy and poetic feeling with painting, undoubtedly shaping extraordinary artistic pieces. He was quoted as saying: 'I am not a painting master, but I am proficient with painting theories.' It is clear that his so-called 'painting theories' reference the ultimate essences distilled from his lifelong, industrious artistic practices. His incisive outlook on aesthetics has been comprehensively expressed in his numerous notes, correspondence, and his legacy.

His 'painting theories' can be summarised into four concise concepts: capture the essence; master the foundation; reveal the originality; and express the negative and the positive.

(1) Capture the essence: it is important to base an artwork on the outward resemblance (形似) of the subject, but one should also strive to capture the deeper, essential qualities or 'spiritual resemblance' (神似). This means going beyond the surface appearance and expressing the inner essence or emotion of what is being depicted, an intricacy that requires years of practice and an accumulation of knowledge.

(2) Master the foundation: integrity is inseparable from quality, both of which should be developed in equal measures to excel at any type of work, particularly in the case of art practitioners. Achieving a solid foundation of knowledge and prowess in multiple disciplines related to literature and the arts is essential for achieving originality and creativity.

(3) Reveal the originality: while innovation and originality are important in a work of art, it is just as essential to go beyond the achievements of previous artists. However, one should not be tempted to take shortcuts by using creativity as a justification – all artworks should adhere to established principles and methods, showing a respect for the foundational techniques of the past.

(4) Express the negative and the positive: the world is full of joy and honour, but also injustice and turmoil; all are equally poignant topics. By expressing both positive and negative feelings in poems and paintings, one can breathe new life into a piece of work.

As well as adding expression to his subject matter through calligraphy strokes, Wu was very detail-oriented. He paid attention to every aspect of his craft, such as outlining (钩筋), stamen painting (点蕊), wiping (擦皴) and dotting (点苔). As is evident in his work, harmony and consistency are achieved through light, thick, rich or simple brushstrokes. The font and amount of inscriptions added have been carefully thought out: more space would not necessarily mean more inscriptions, and vice versa. The same is true for the position, size, number, and the red-and-white layout of the carved seal. Moreover, he achieved the perfect marriage of patterns, enhancing the subject through his thoughtful contrast and colour choice. Flowers, including orchids and chrysanthemums, are commonly contrasted with stones to highlight their pureness and nobility. Other pairings of peony and narcissus, red rose with plantain, and impatiens with loquat ensured beauty through harmonious contrasts.

Wu's paintings and his calligraphy craftsmanship are by far the most noteworthy of his artistic legacy. Facilitating these achievements, though, are his poetry and prose, which in turn support his pursuit of seal engraving, which, coming full circle, enhances the expressiveness of his calligraphy and painting.

Feed the art arena with groundbreaking innovations.
Bring about radical transformations, just as countless great artists have done before.

Lofty integrity is the prerequisite for any artist wishing to achieve artistic merit. As remarked by Cheng Yuan, 'Language expresses the creators' inner world while calligraphy reflects their underlying outlook, which is more or less related to their integrity. Those who aim high opt for exquisite styles while unrestrained souls demonstrate their ambitious spirit through their artistic expression. If an ordinary person has a demotic and uninteresting character, then it will be fully exposed in his or her works.' Thus, for the ordinary person, their individual character, sentiment, lifestyle, and mental outlook are all inextricably linked to moral integrity and artistic and cultural literacy.

Forever a patriot of his mother country, Wu Changshuo joined the army at the age of 51 under the direct leadership of Wu Dacheng and headed for the northern regions to fight the enemy during the First Sino-Japanese War. In spite of the treacherous circumstances, he never declined nor hesitated.

His love of Chinese cultural relics remained unwavering. To buy back the Han San Lao Stele (a stele inscribed with the names and death dates of San Lao and his families in the Han Dynasty, 汉三老碑), a priceless national treasure stolen and sold to foreign merchants, he and other members of the Seal Engravers' Society of Xiling (西泠印社) spread the word to everyone they knew. Wu diligently painted around-the-clock and sold his work to raise the funds. Ultimately, they collected 8,000 yuan (an astronomical price at that time) and redeemed this national treasure. A stone chamber was specially designed by the Seal Engravers' Society of Xiling for its safekeeping. Their good intentions and patriotism have since been widely recognised by Chinese nationals and the world beyond.

Despite making a name for himself in his seventies, Wu Changshuo maintained his plain and frugal lifestyle, helping poor relatives and friends in the countryside on countless occasions. He practised what he preached by teaching his children and grandchildren to be helpful, studious, frugal, and to live contentedly.

Upon being selected as the first director of the Seal Engravers' Society of Xiling, Wu composed the following lines: 'Doesn't seal engraving have an origin? People read voraciously to accumulate knowledge, despite the ups and downs of life, and some of them established the Zhejiang School of Engraving. I feel humbled to have been selected as the director of this society as I am just a simple farmer from a village who can merely identify the inscriptions and epigraphs.'

His heartfelt modesty and sincerity are manifest in his simple self-evaluation as 'just a simple farmer from a village'.

He respected each of his students, adapting his teaching methods according to each one's ability and requirements, and having great expectations for them all. As a result, they forged close, caring teacher–student relationships. One example is his brilliant disciple Chen Shi; wholeheartedly grateful for Wu Changshuo's guidance, recognition and understanding, he named his room 'Rancang' (meaning 'influenced by Cang', an alias of Wu). Similarly, another disciple Zhao Shinong showed his deep admiration for Wu Changshuo by naming his cottage 'Baifoulu' (meaning 'bow to Foulu', another alias of Wu).

In 1919, ravaging floods hit five provinces – Henan Province, Hebei Province, Anhui Province, Zhejiang Province and Jiangsu Province. Dismayed by the misery of the flood-stricken population, Wu Changshuo did his utmost, day and night, to raise flood-relief funds, expressing his feelings through his poetry as well as his actions.

His integrity gave weight to the importance of his painting. Back then, in the late 19th century between the late Qing dynasty and the 1911 Revolution (辛亥革命), the arts sphere was a dynamic one and welcomed innumerable bourgeoning talents of different specialties. Influential calligraphers Bao Anwu and Wu Rangzhi were among those who made a name for themselves. In poetry, Chen Sanli and Chen Yan established themselves as representatives of the Fujian and Jiangxi Poetry School (闽赣派), endeavouring to continue in the style of Song poetry. In seal engraving, the eight specialists of the Seal Engravers' Society of Xiling (西泠八家) were renowned figures, along with Zhao Zhiqian. And painting masters Zhang Zixiang, Hu Gongshou, Ren Weichang, Ren Fuchang and Ren Bonian all emerged one after another. It is testament to Wu Changshuo's eminence that he stood out from such intense competition, overcoming many challenges and achieving such accomplishments, thus developing and improving his exclusive school of thought. His success was certainly not the result of pure luck or coincidence; rather, it was all due to his extraordinary knowledge and skills, his confidence to 'feed the art arena with groundbreaking innovations', his resilience to 'transcend traditional techniques', his aspiration to 'compose artworks that voice one's own thoughts rather than mere imitations', and the ultimate purpose of 'bringing about radical transformations, just as countless great artists have done before'. As the proverb goes, where there's a will, there's a way. His rich artistic legacy is widely recognised and respected across China and the world beyond. In my eyes, the evaluation of his accomplishments as being unprecedented remains true, as time has proved!

Seeking Excellency: Wu Changshuo's Painting, Calligraphy and Seal Cutting

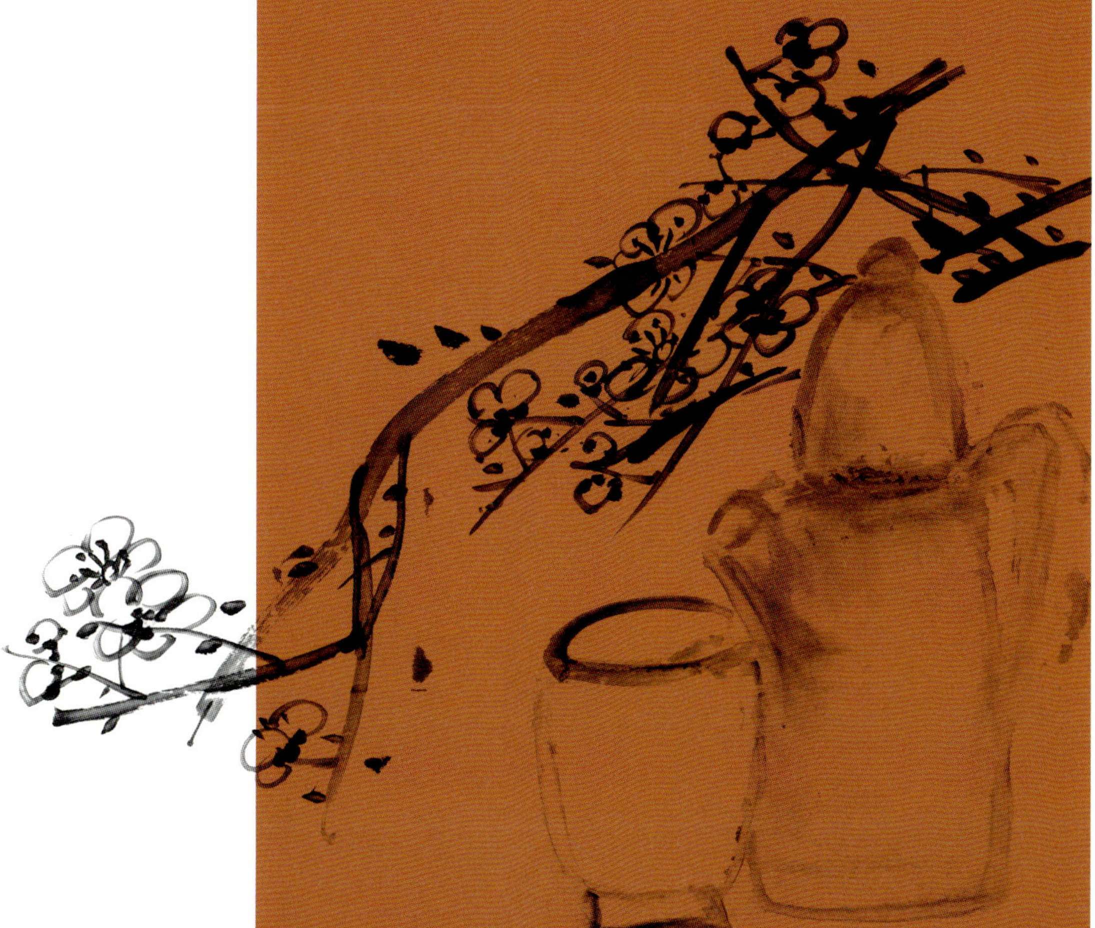

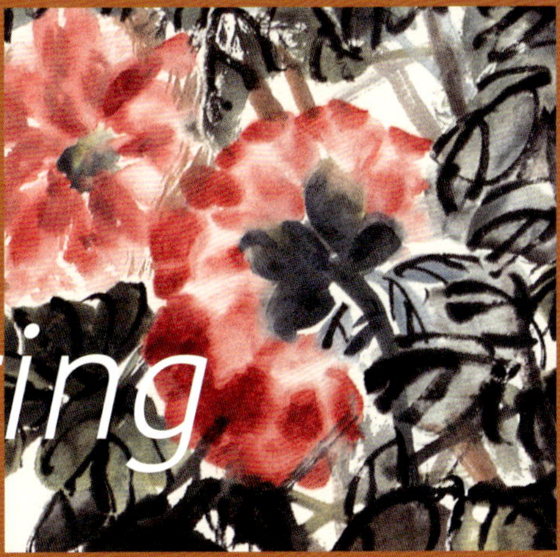

Spring

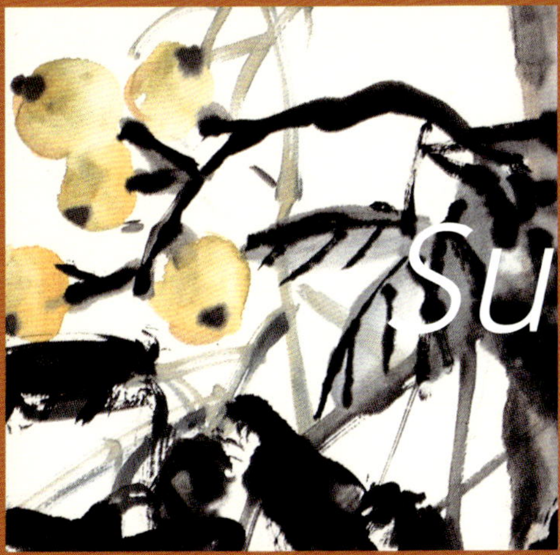

Summer

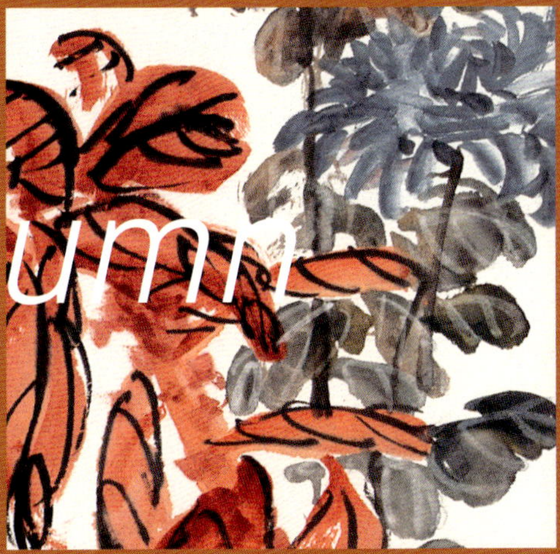

Autumn

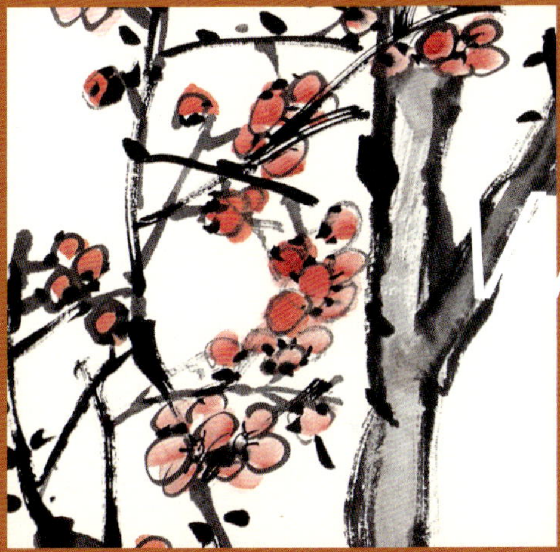

Winter

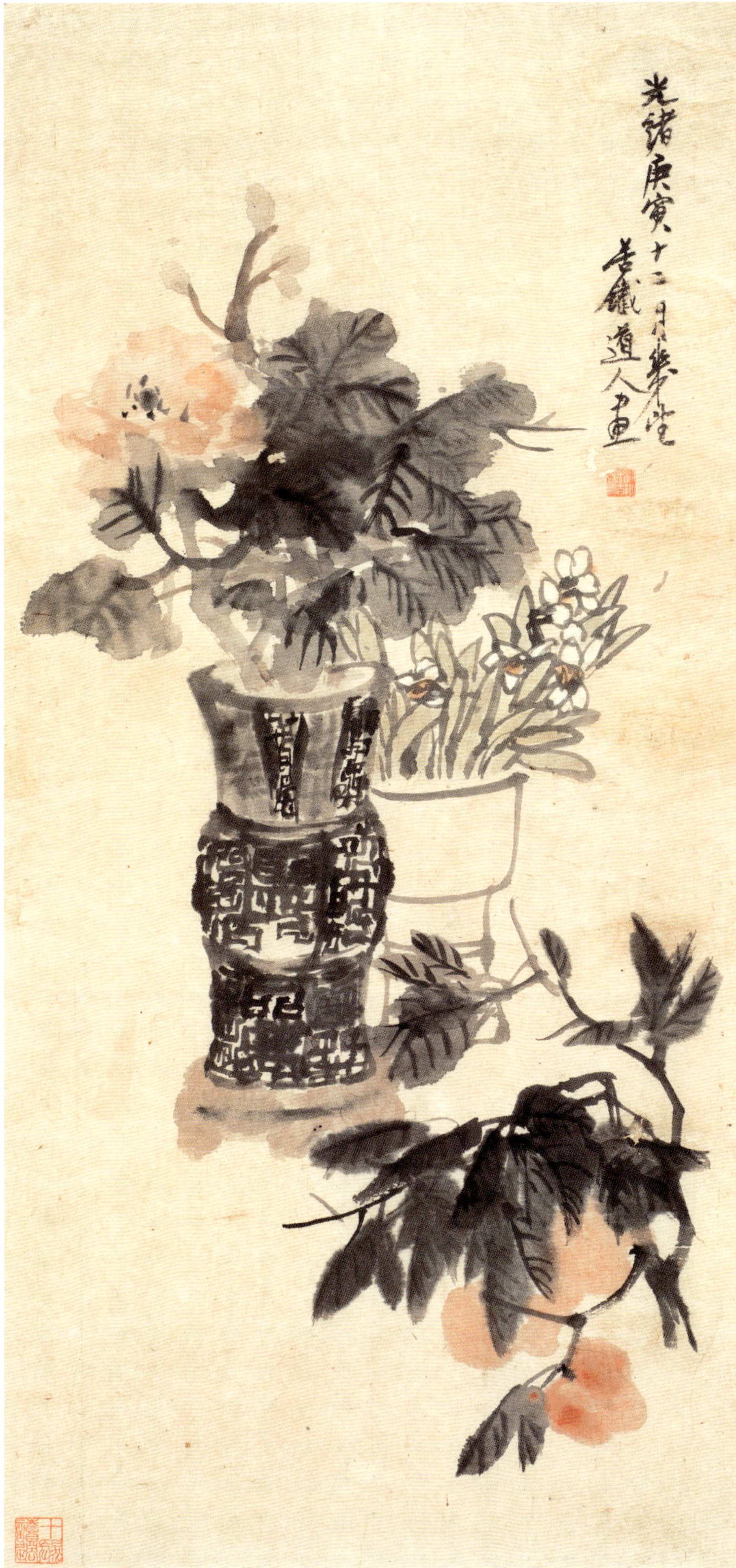

Wu Changshuo
Life in the New Year handscroll
Ink and colours on paper
Height 92cm, length 42cm
1890

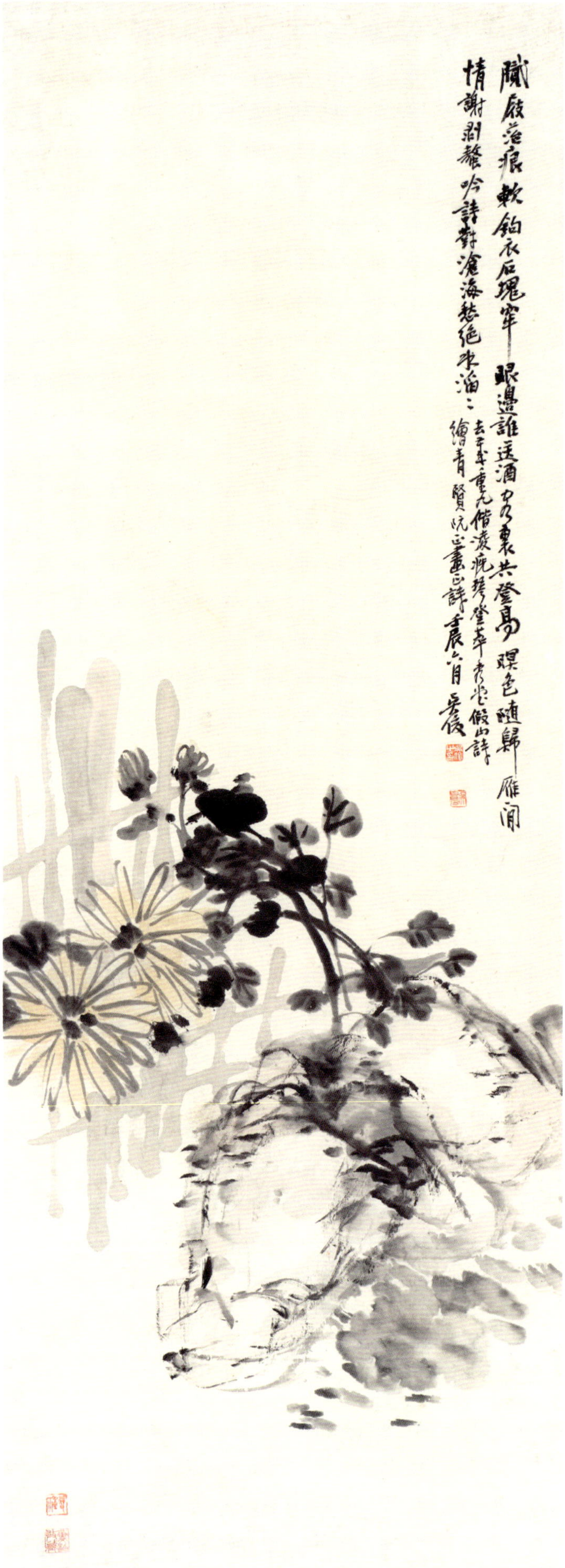

Wu Changshuo
Chrysanthemum handscroll
Ink and colours on paper
Height 130cm, length 47cm
1892

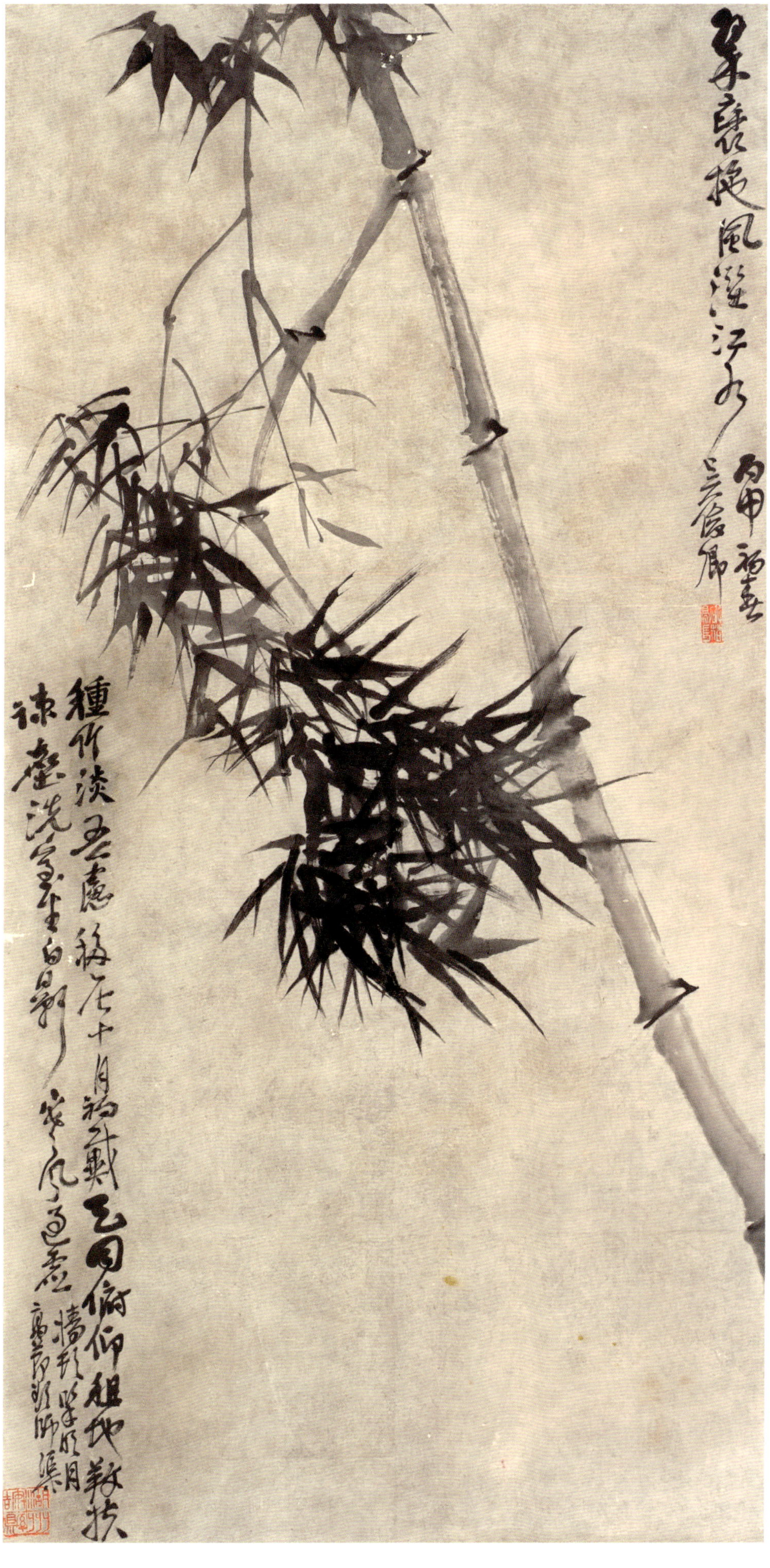

Wu Changshuo
Bamboo
Ink on rice paper
Height 133cm, length 66cm
1896

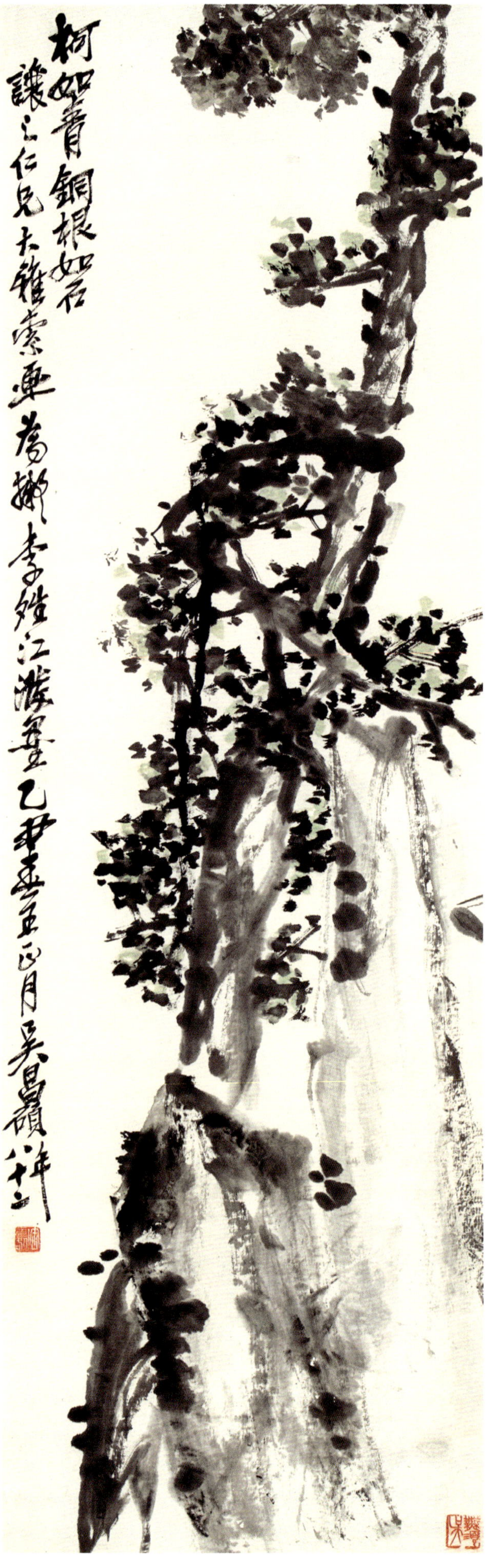

Wu Changshuo
Cypress handscroll
Ink and colours on paper
Height 111cm, length 34cm
1925

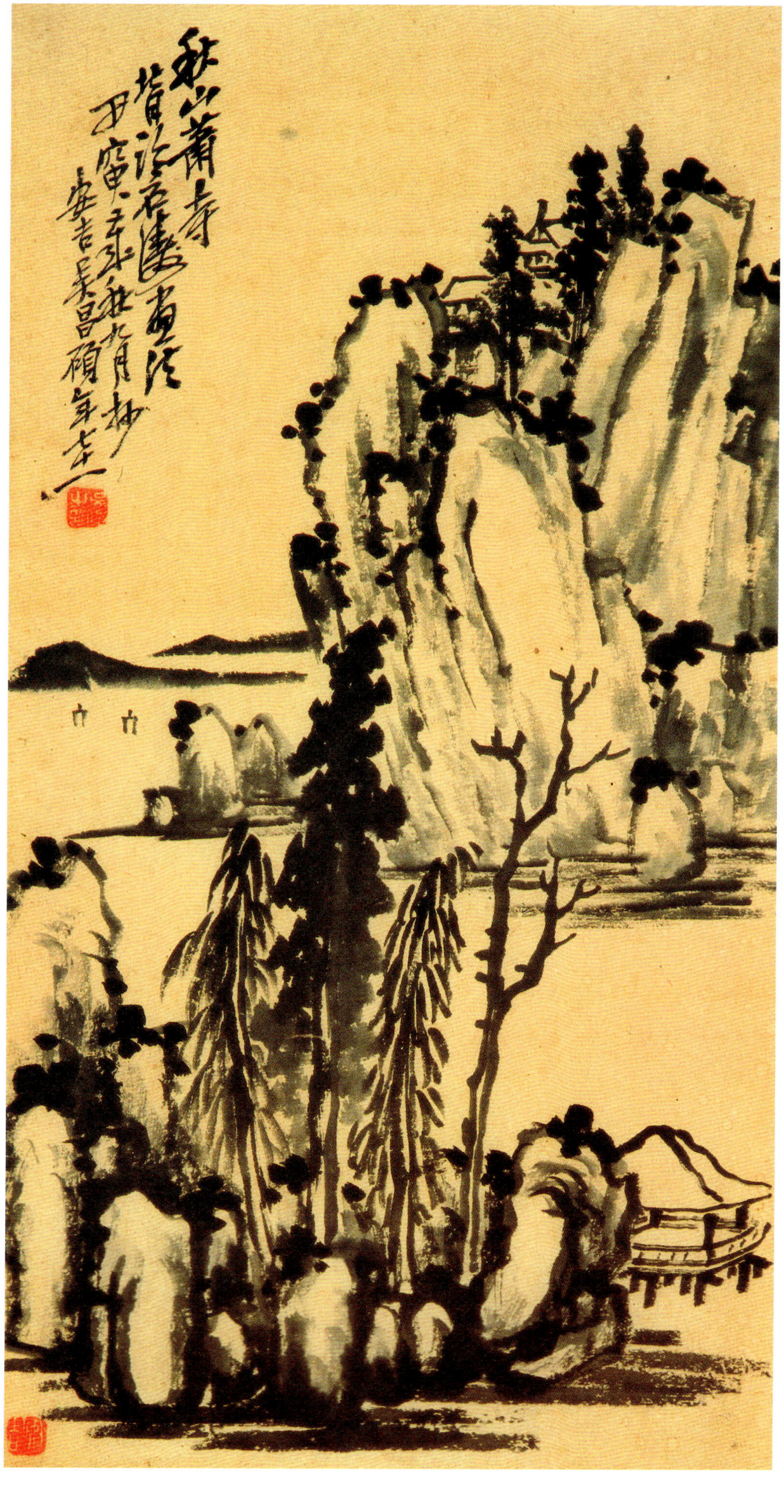

Wu Changshuo
Autumn Mountain and Temple handscroll
Ink and colours on paper
Height 56cm, length 29cm
1914

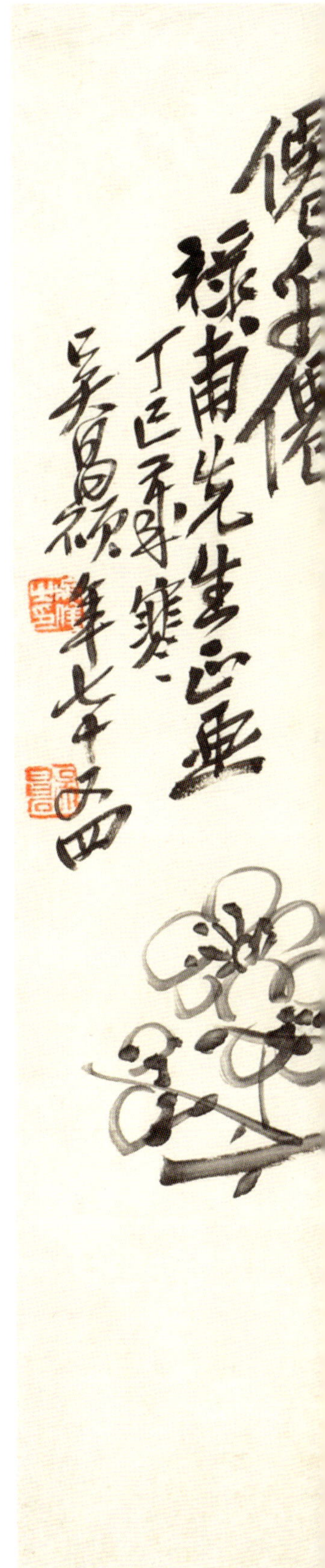

Wu Changshuo
Spring Plum Blossom handscroll
Ink and colours on paper
Height 41cm, length 44cm
1917

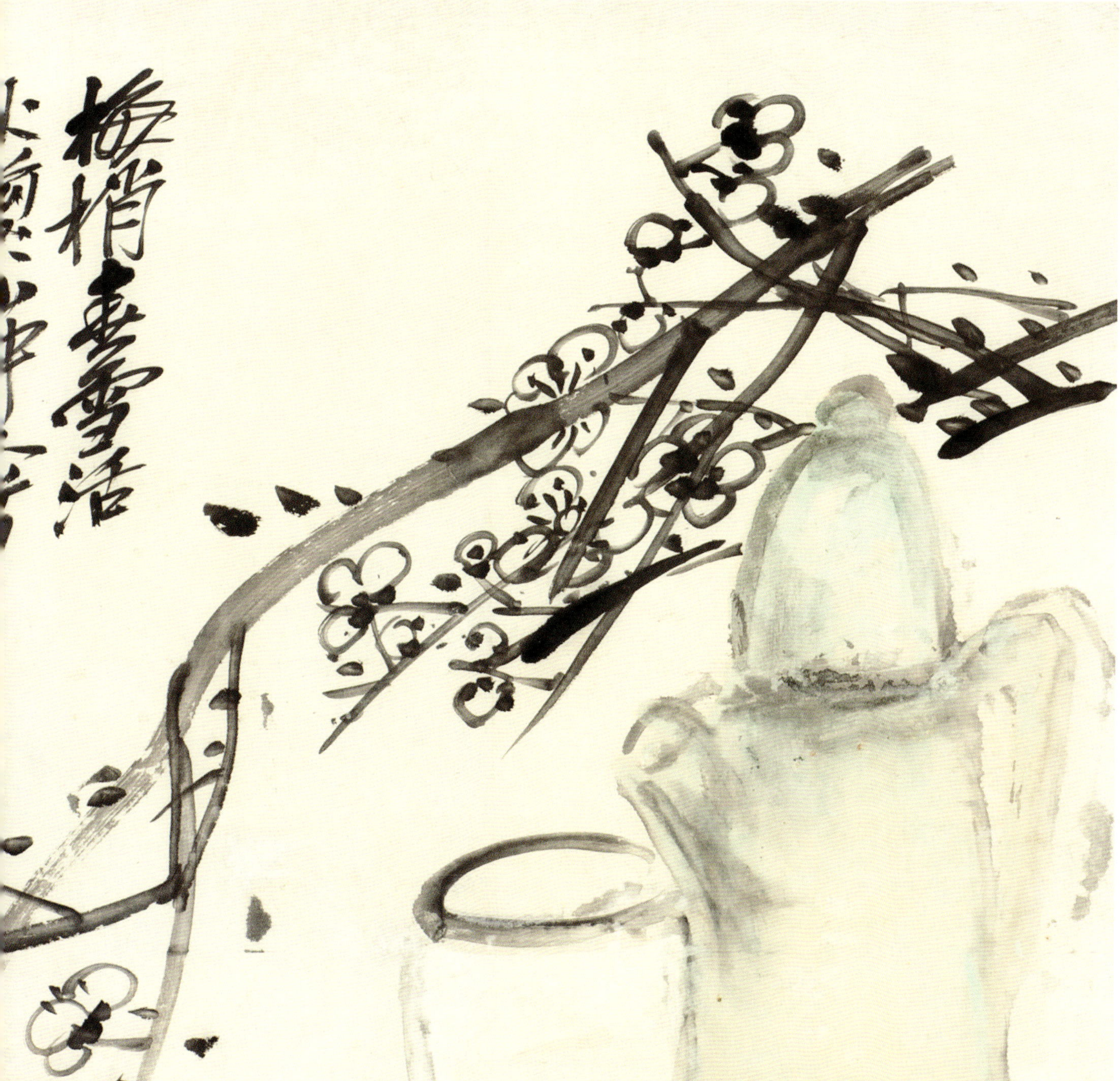
梅梢春雪活

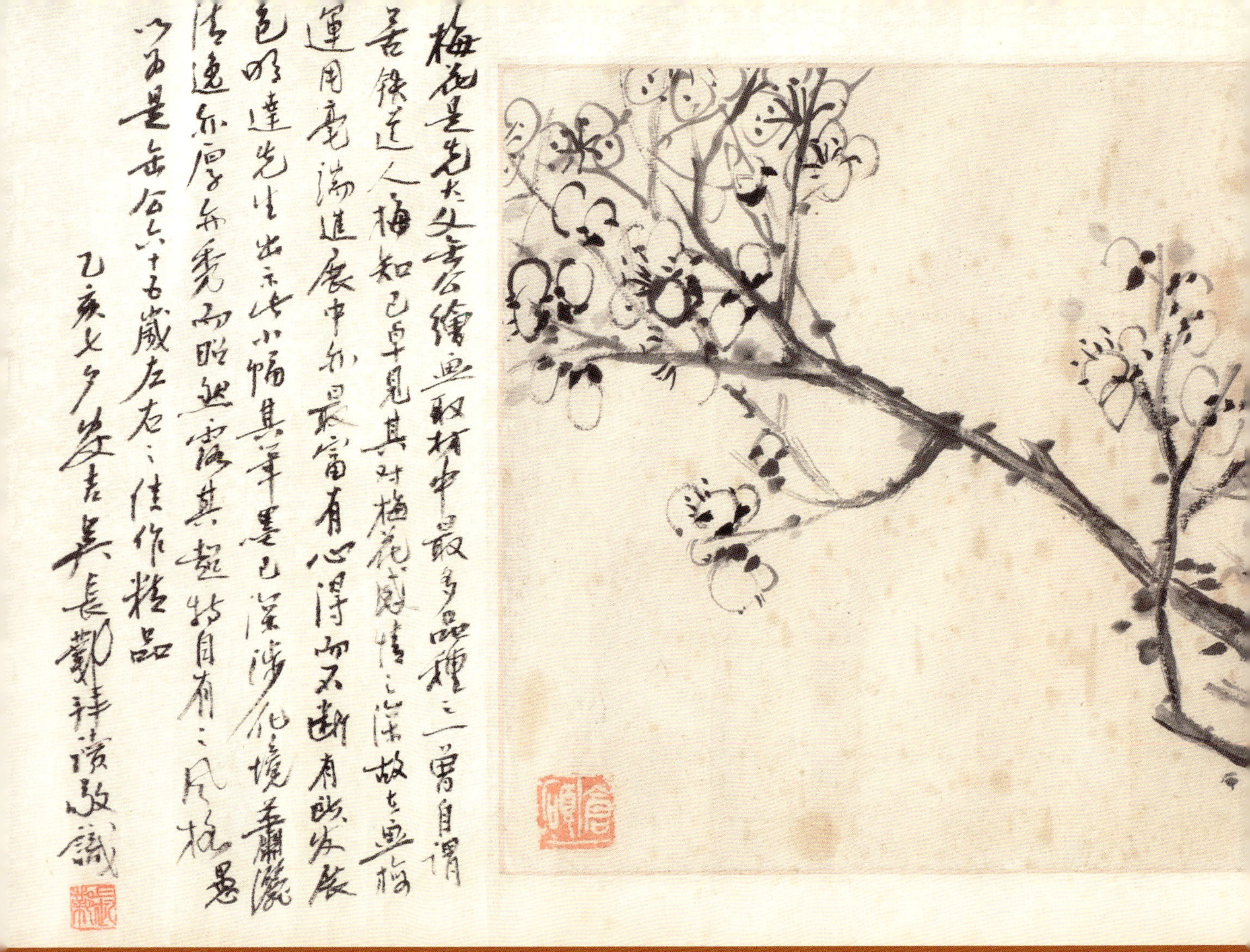
梅花是先大父缶公繪畫取材中最多品種之一嘗自謂
苦鐵道人梅知己早見其對梅花感情之深故其畫梅
運用毫端進展中亦最富有心得而不斷有所發展
邑明達先生出示此小幅其筆墨已深涉化境蕭灑
清逸亦厚亦秀而昭然露其超特自有之風格是
以為是缶公六十五歲左右之佳作精品
乙亥七夕孫吉 吳長鄴拜讀敬識

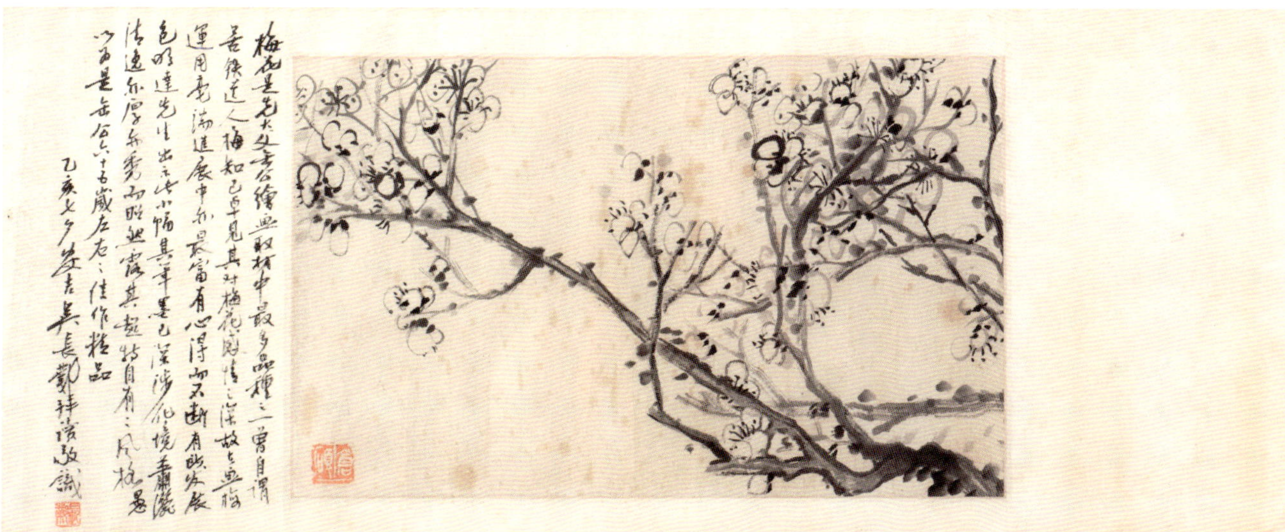

Painted by Wu Changshuo c.1908
Inscribed by Wu Changye 1995
Plum Blossom
Ink and colours on paper
Height 23cm, length 37cm

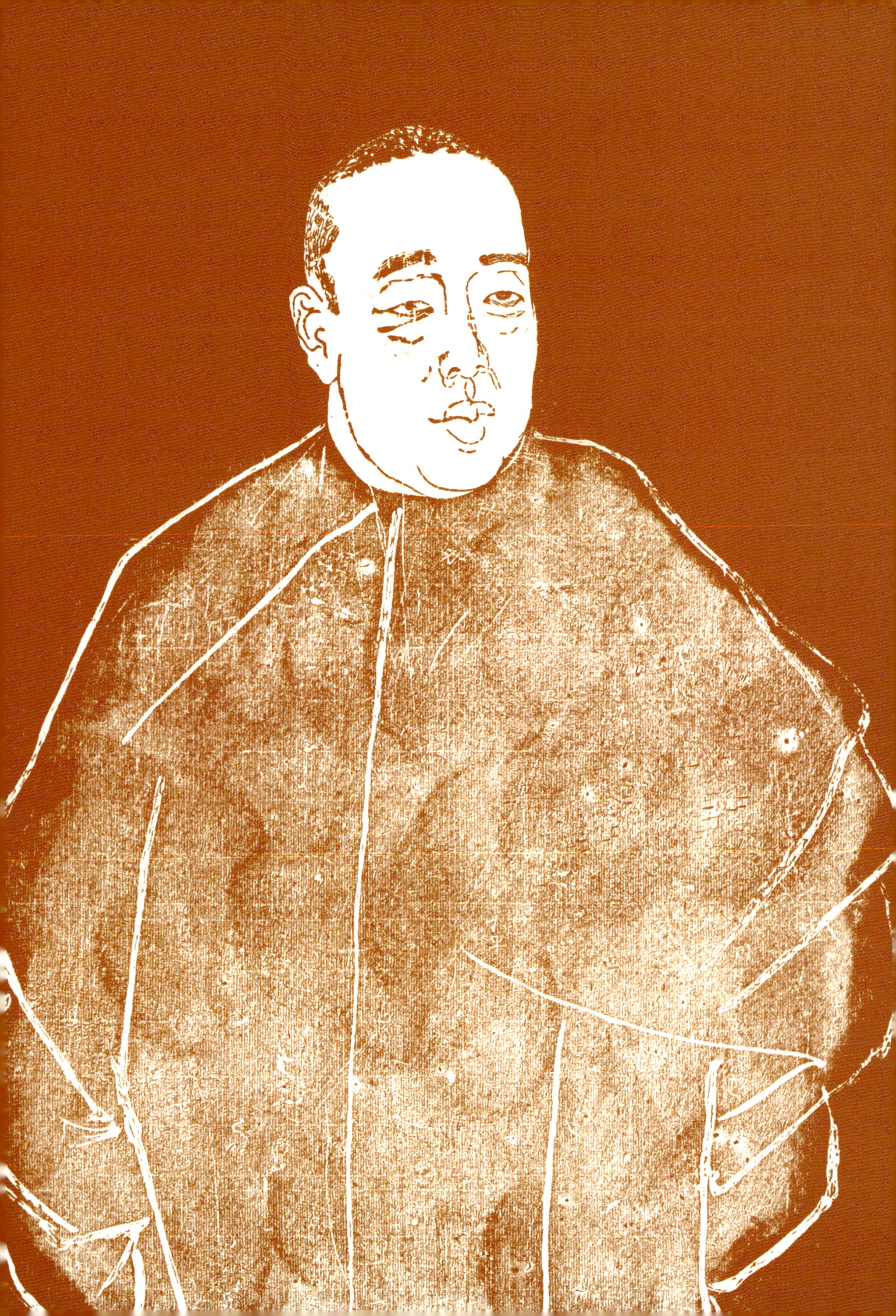

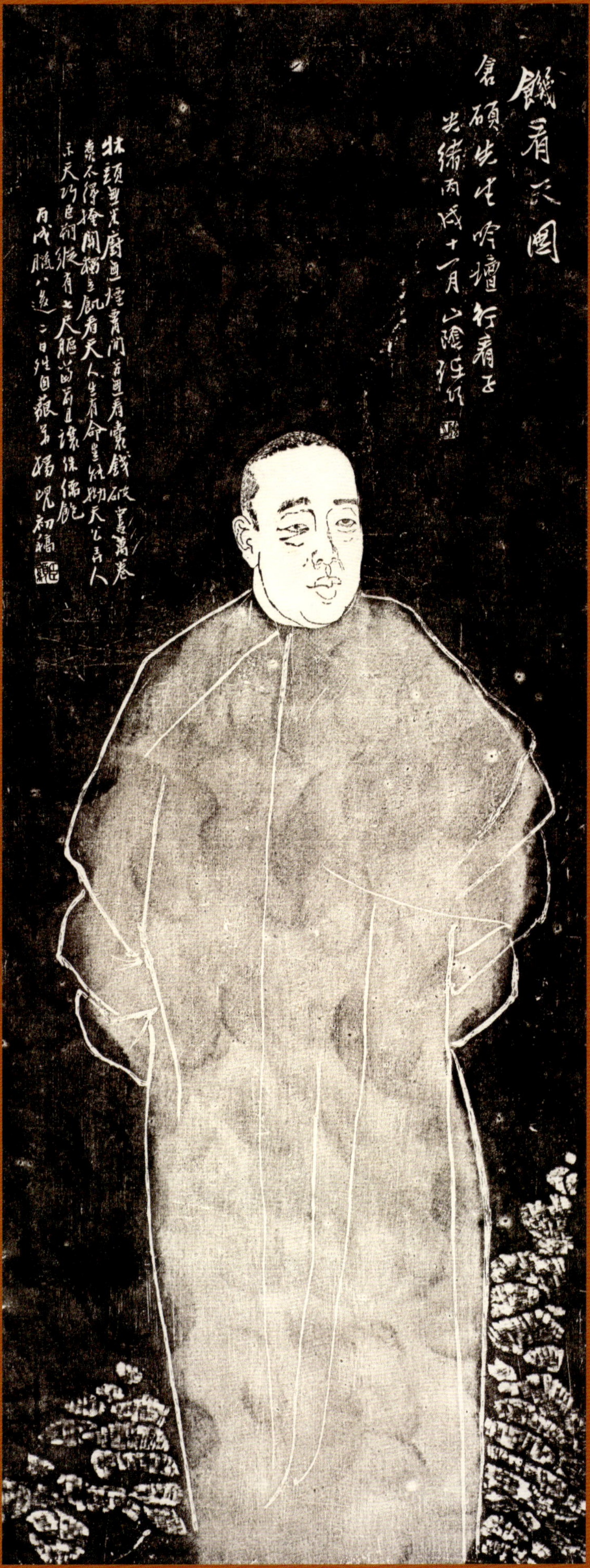

Wu Changshuo
Wu Changshuo Wistfully Looking at the Sky
Inscriptions by Ren Bonian and Yang Xian
Rubbing of the original painting, ink on paper
Height 110cm, length 42cm
1886

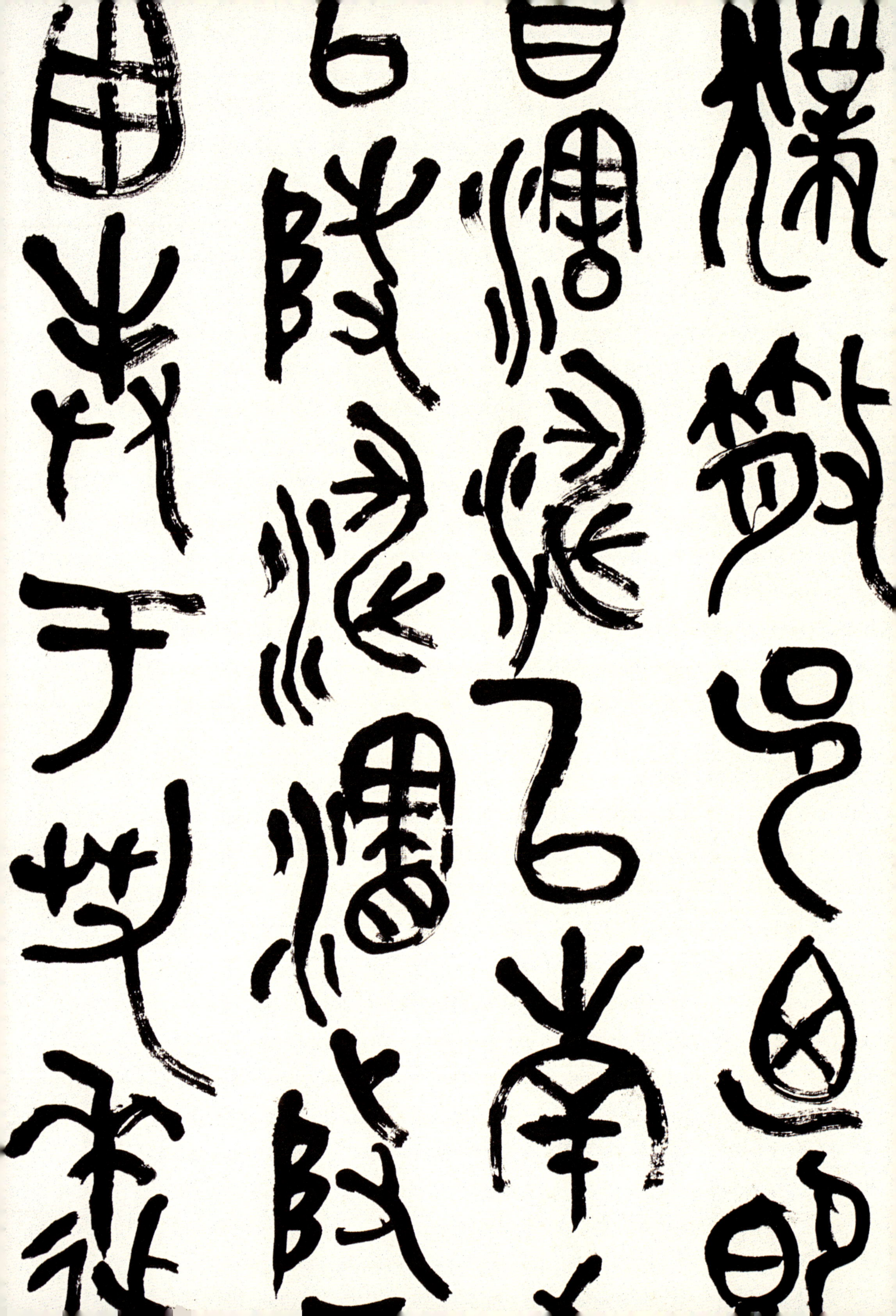

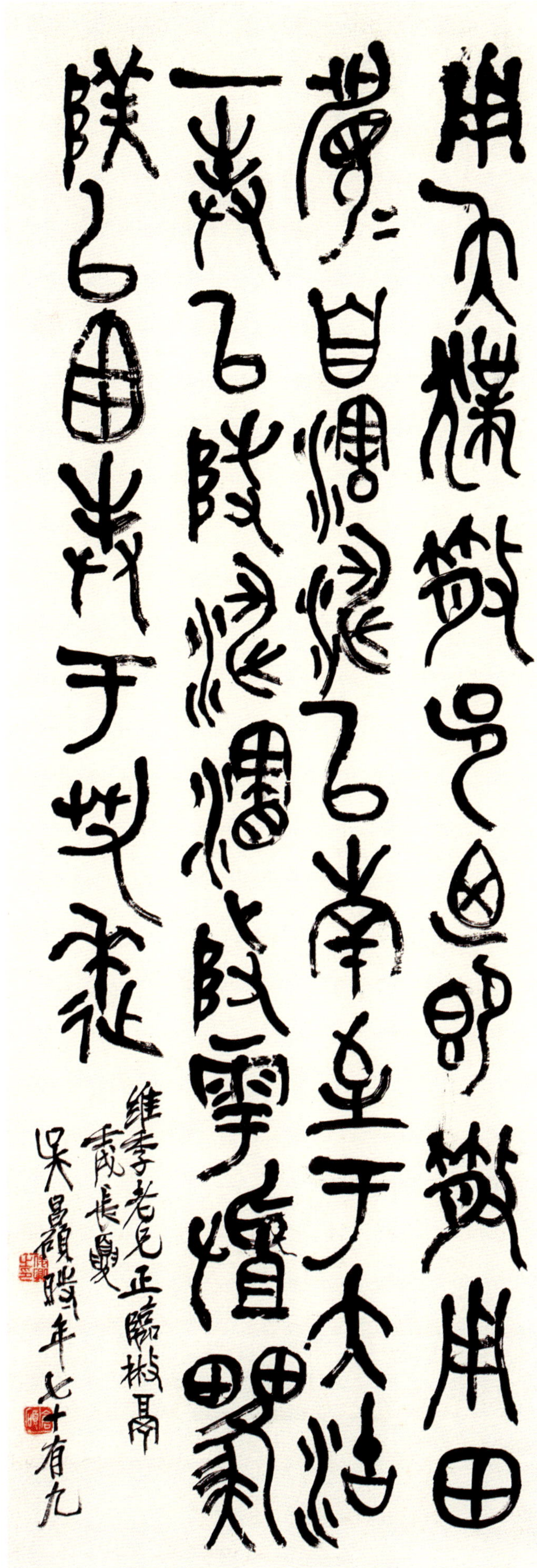

Wu Changshuo
Seal script handscroll (imitation of the San family plate)
Ink on paper
Height 118cm, length 40cm
1922

Wu Changshuo

Seal script handscroll (imitation of the San family plate, excerpt from)
Ink on paper
Height 109cm, length 57cm
1922

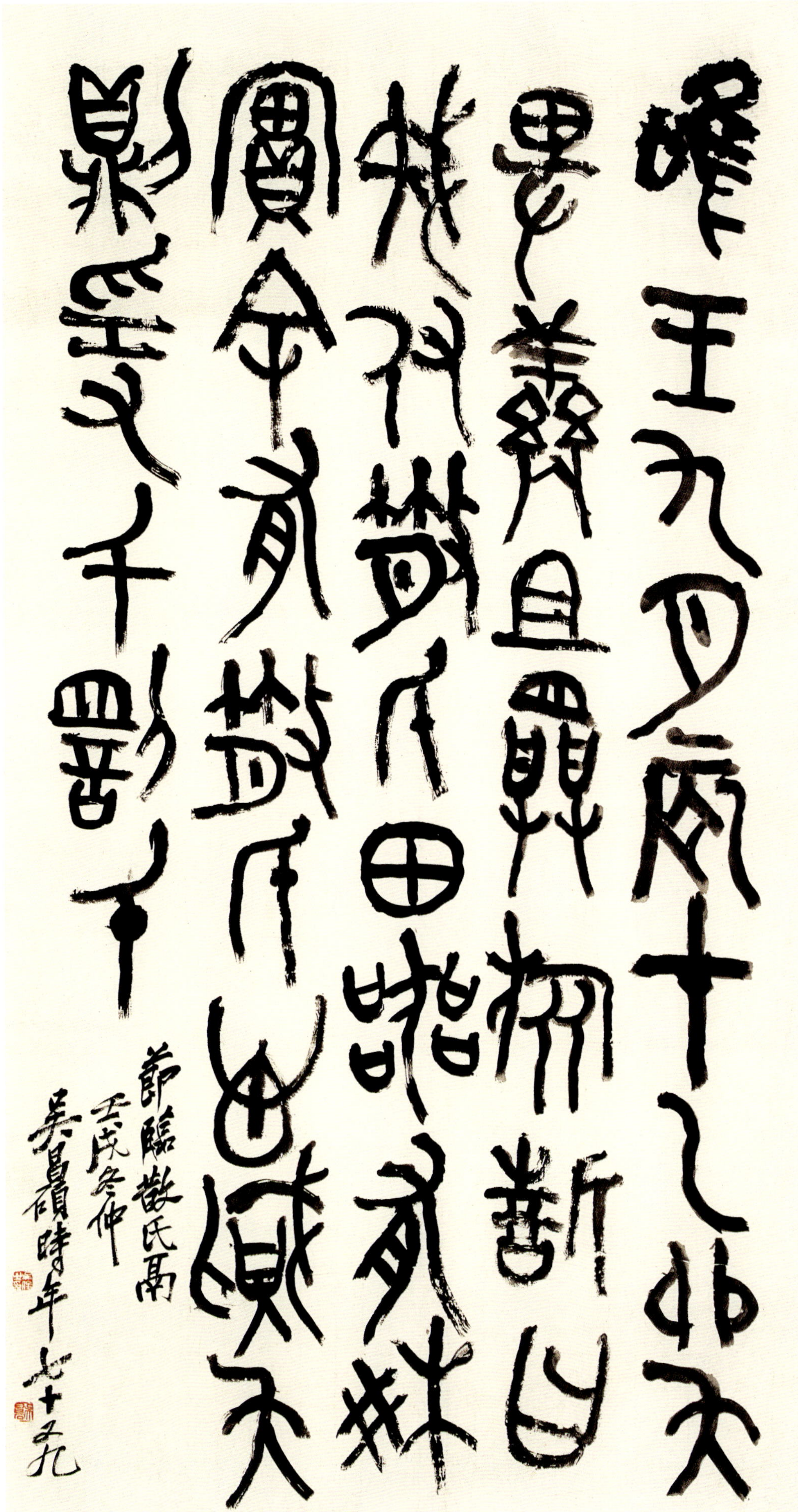
節臨散氏盤
壬戌冬仲
吳昌碩時年七十又九

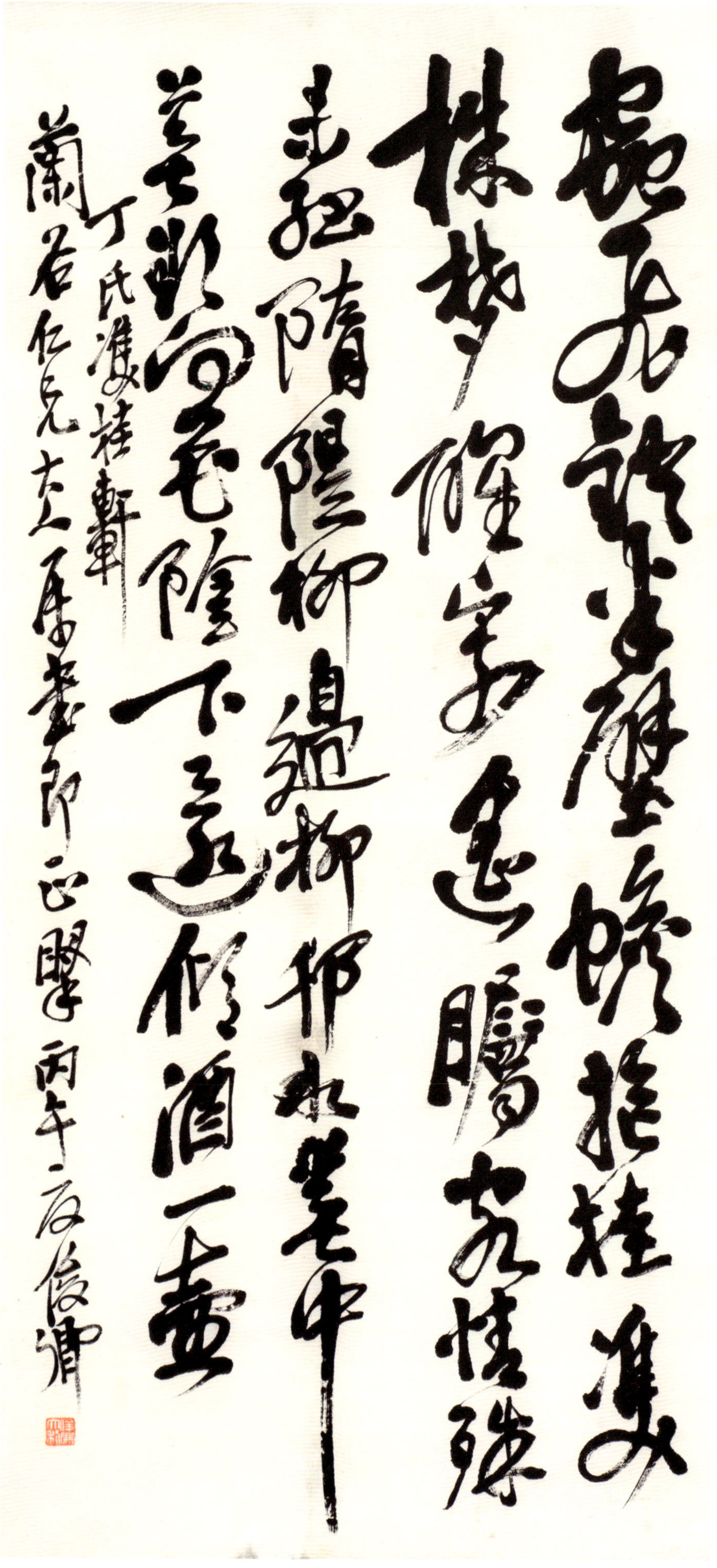

Wu Changshuo
Running script handscroll
Ink on paper
Height 106cm, length 50cm
1906

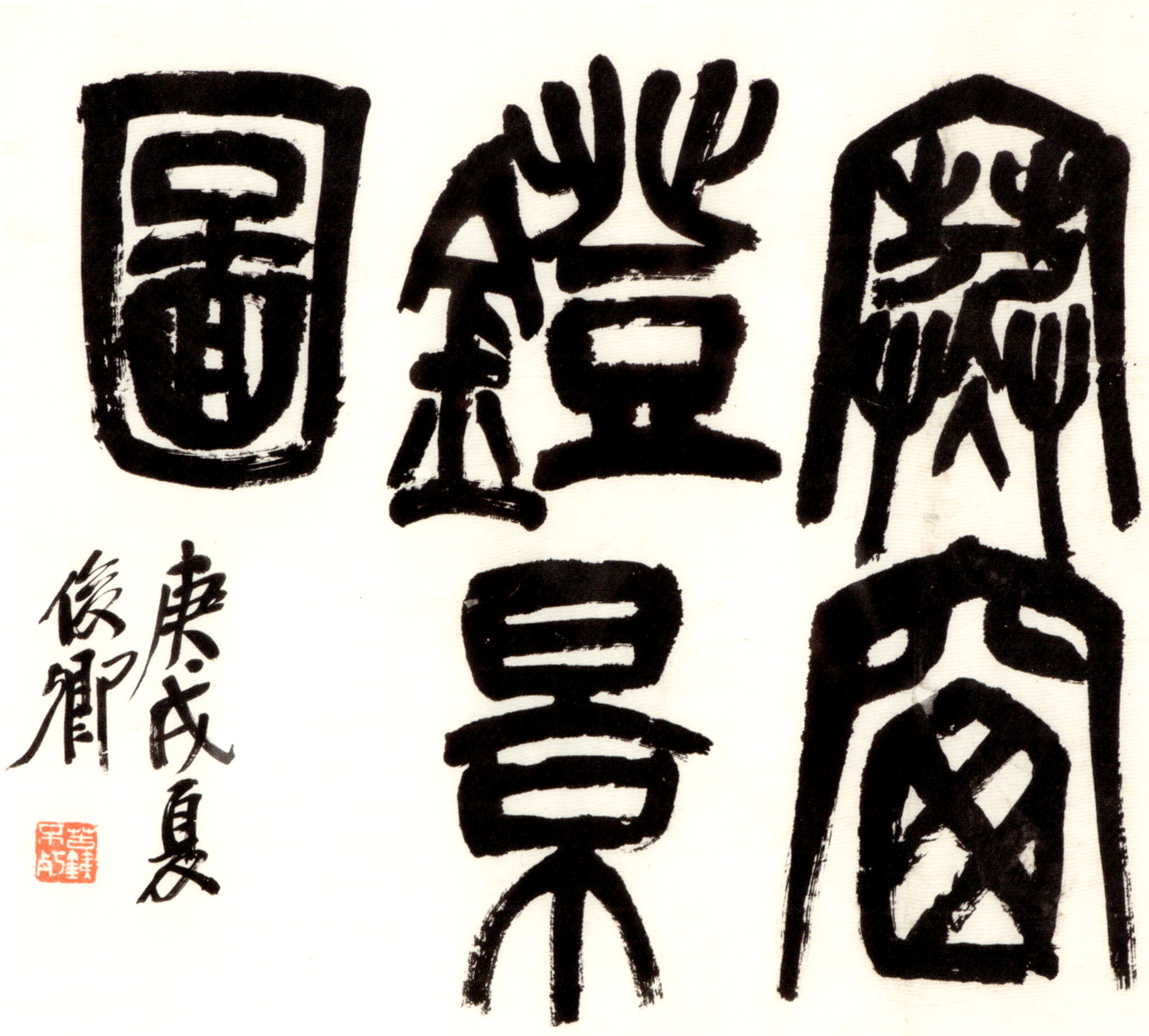

Wu Changshuo
Calligraphy work
Ink on paper
Height 31.5cm, length 29cm
1910

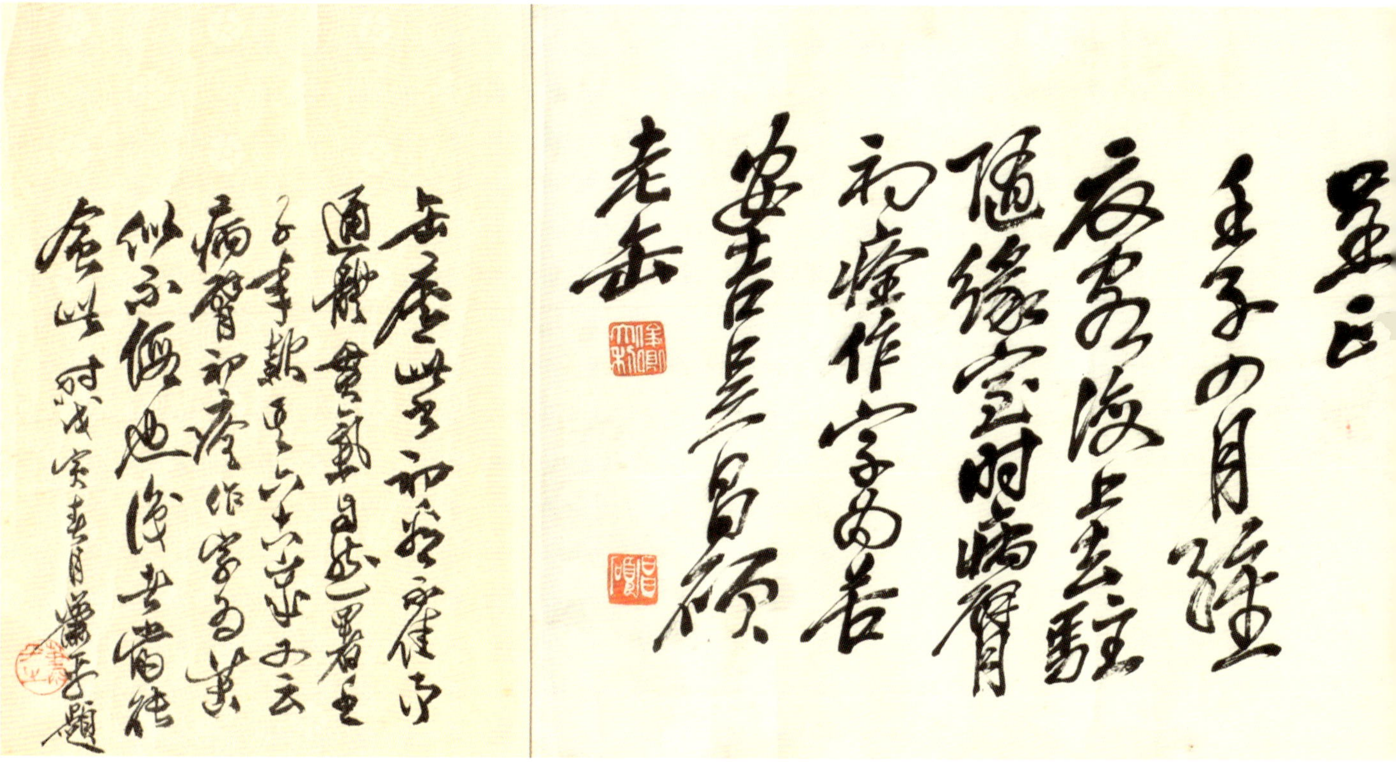

Painted by Wu Changshuo 1912
Inscribed by Xiao Ping 1998
Trees in the Pavilion calligraphy scroll
Ink on paper
Height 80cm, length 26cm

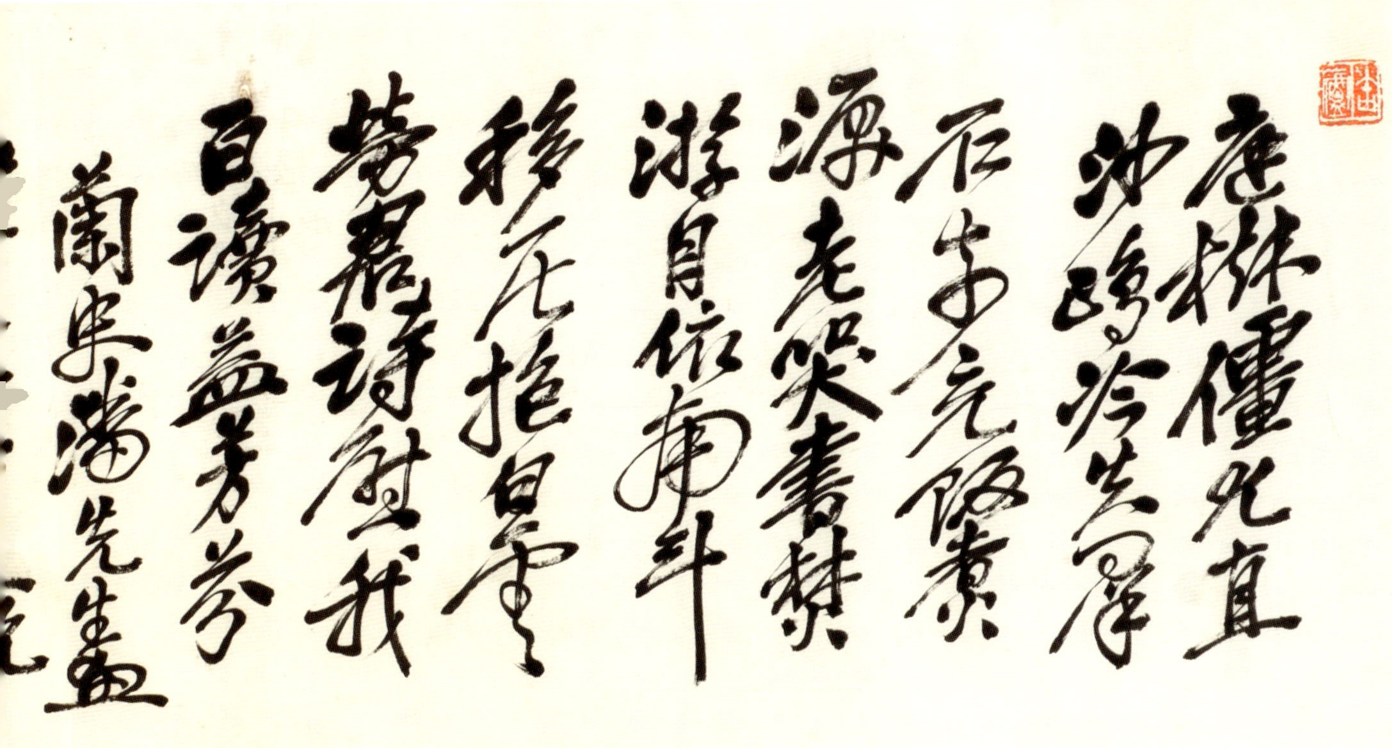

Wu Changshuo

Calligraphy work (manuscript of the poem written for and sent to Sun Deqian)
Ink on paper
Height 20cm, length 78cm
c.1923

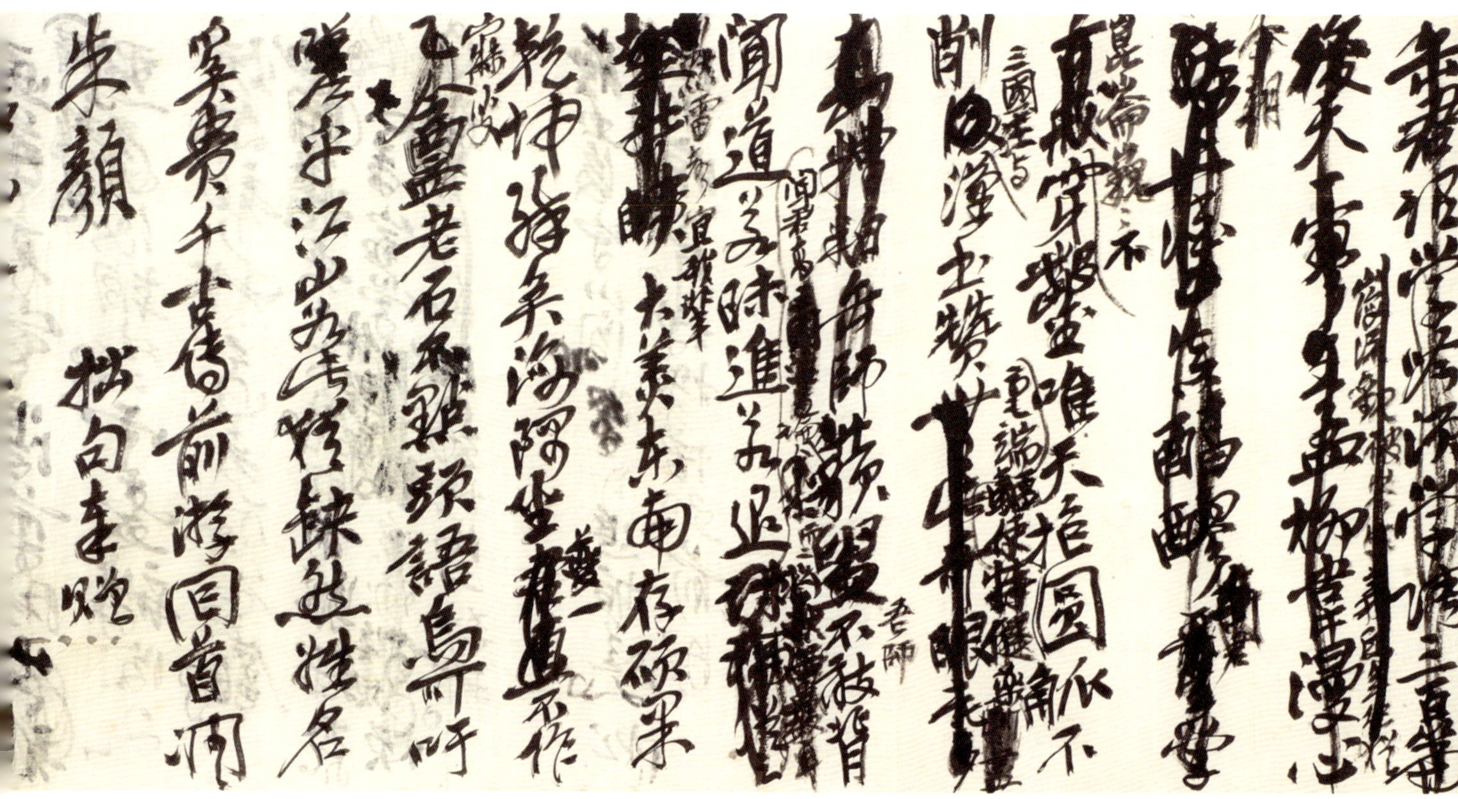

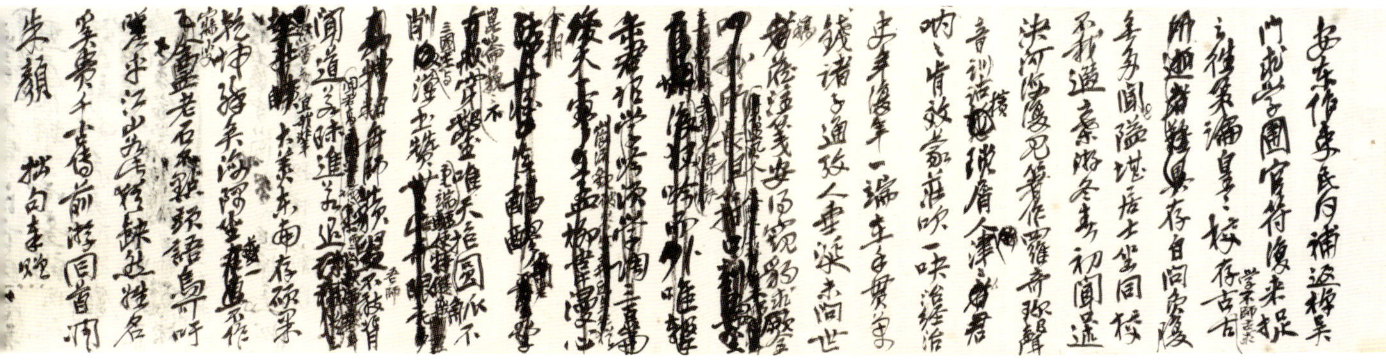

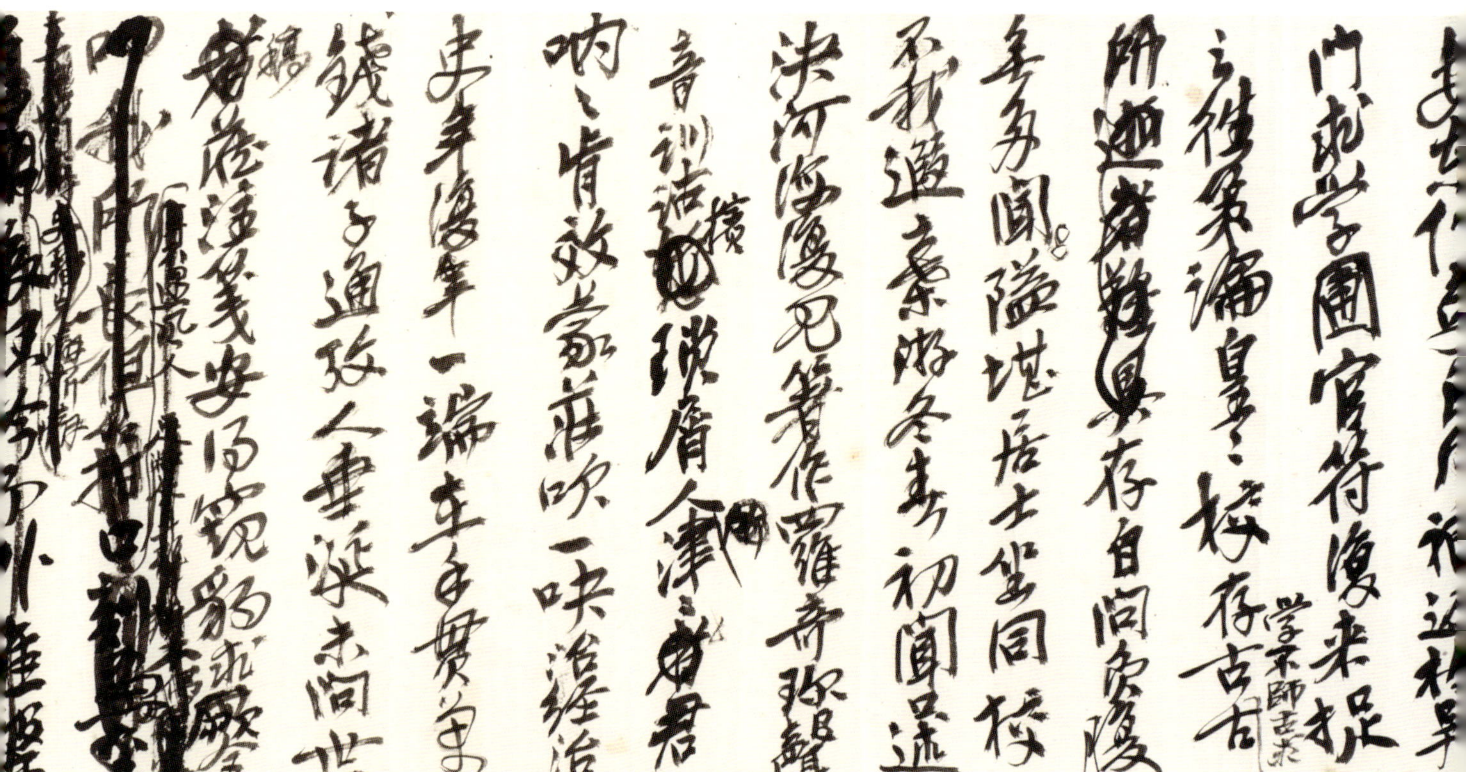

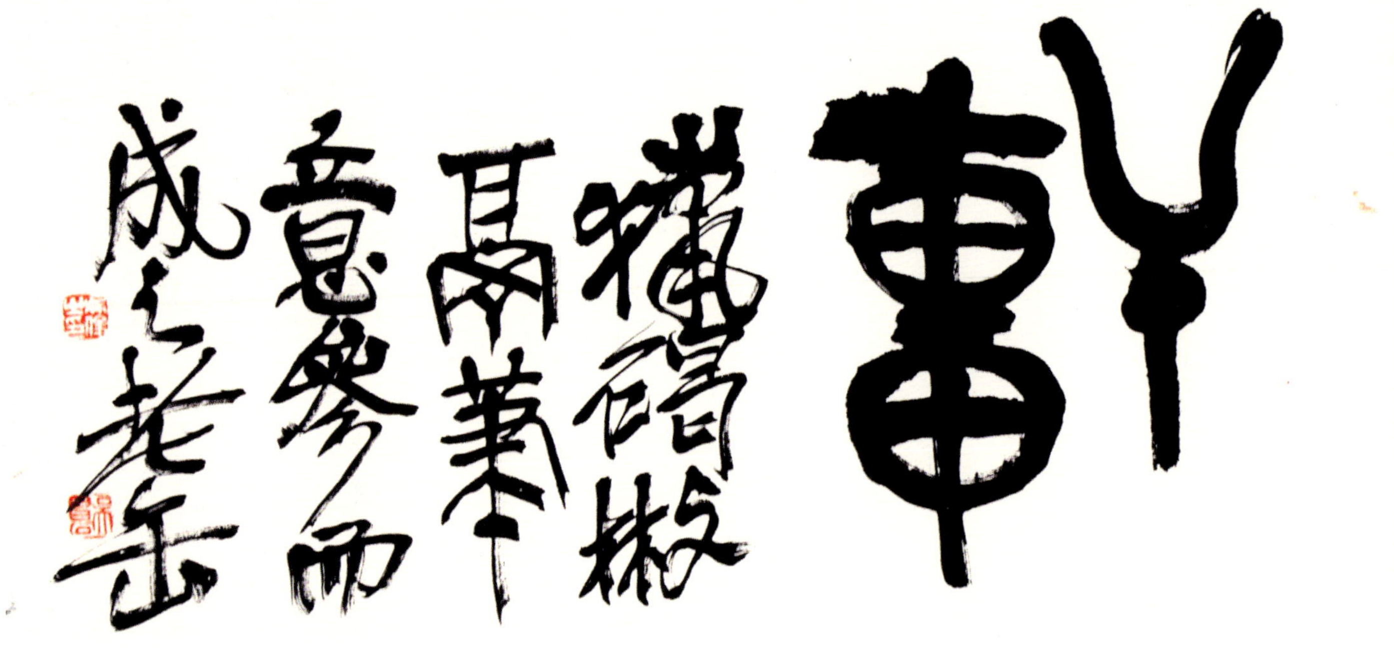

Wu Changshuo
Bell-cauldron script of *Xi Shuang Xuan* (西爽軒)
Ink on paper
Height 19cm, length 87cm
Date unknown

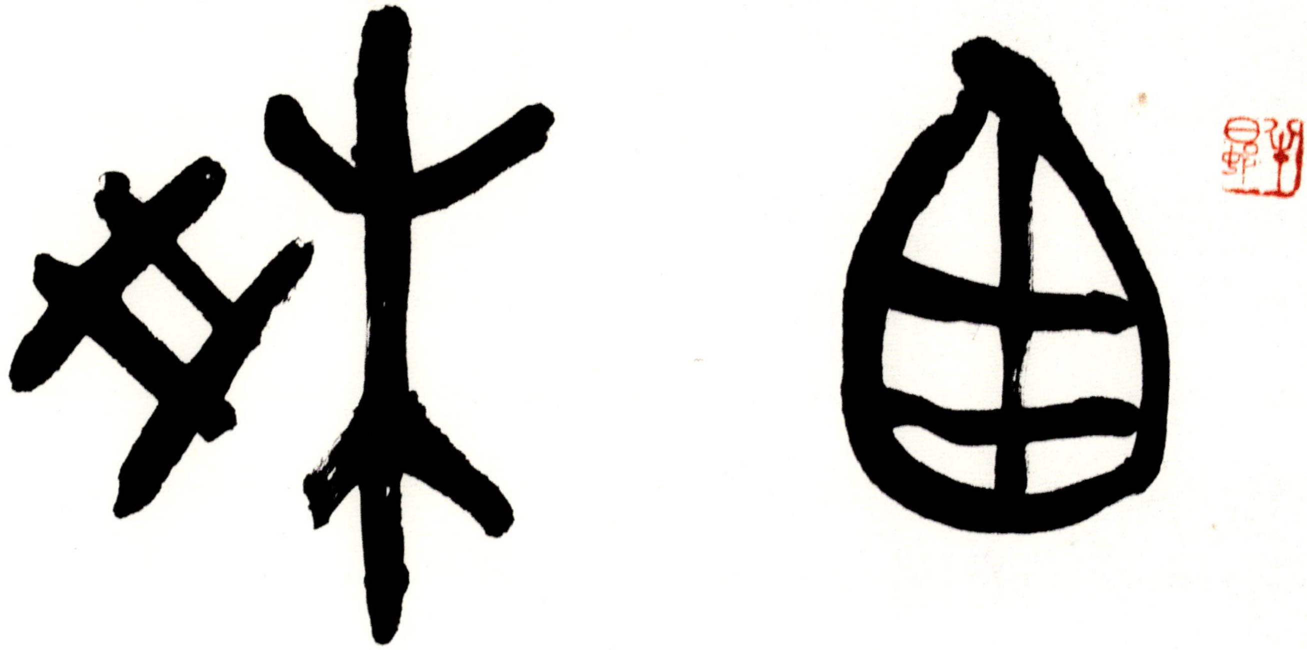

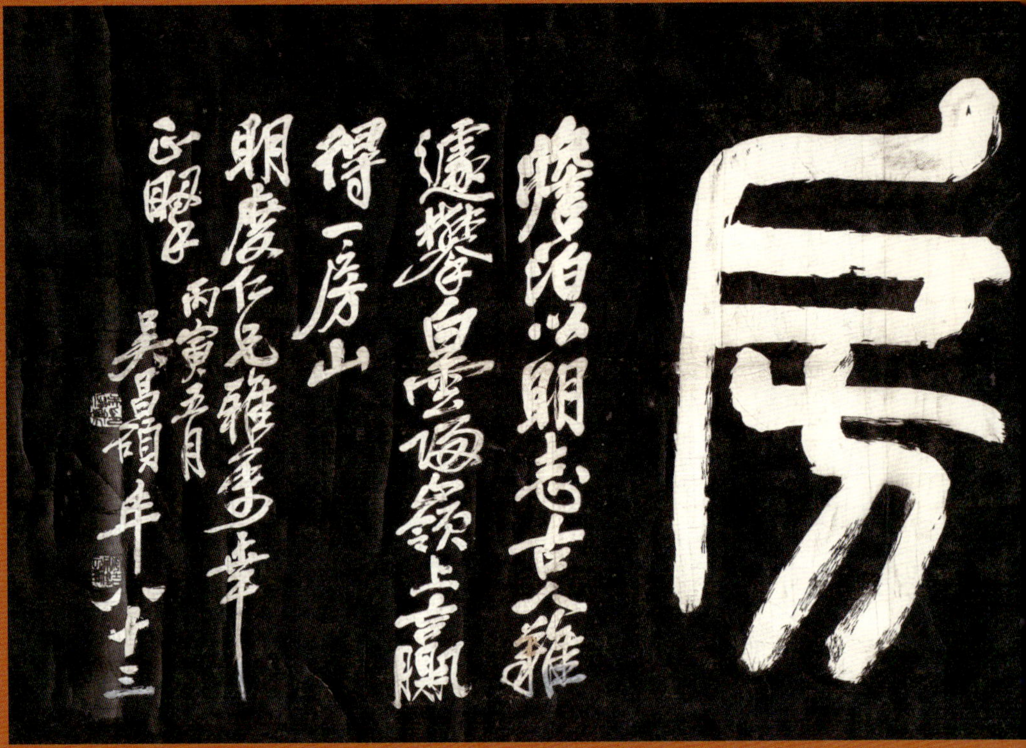

Wu Changshuo
Danbo Garden
Rubbing of the original work, ink on paper
Height 64cm, length 142cm
1926

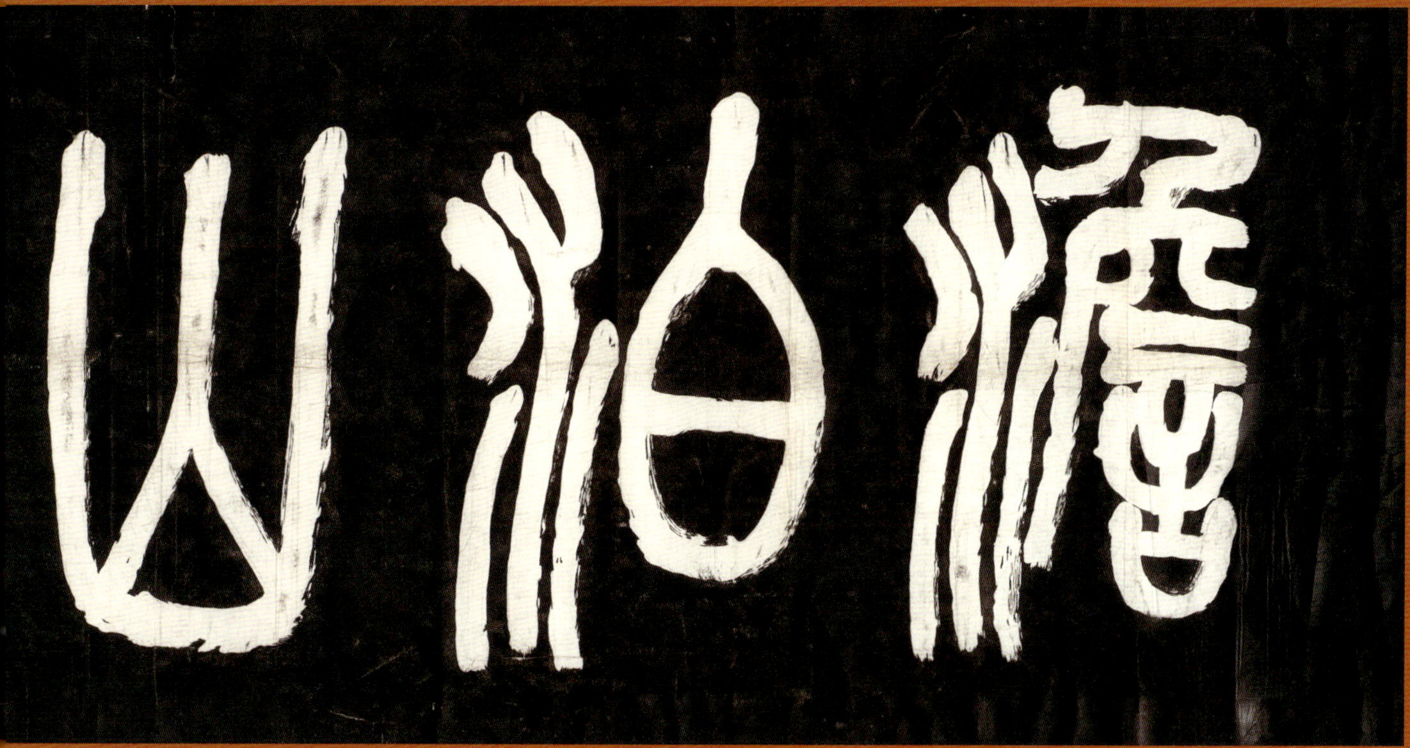

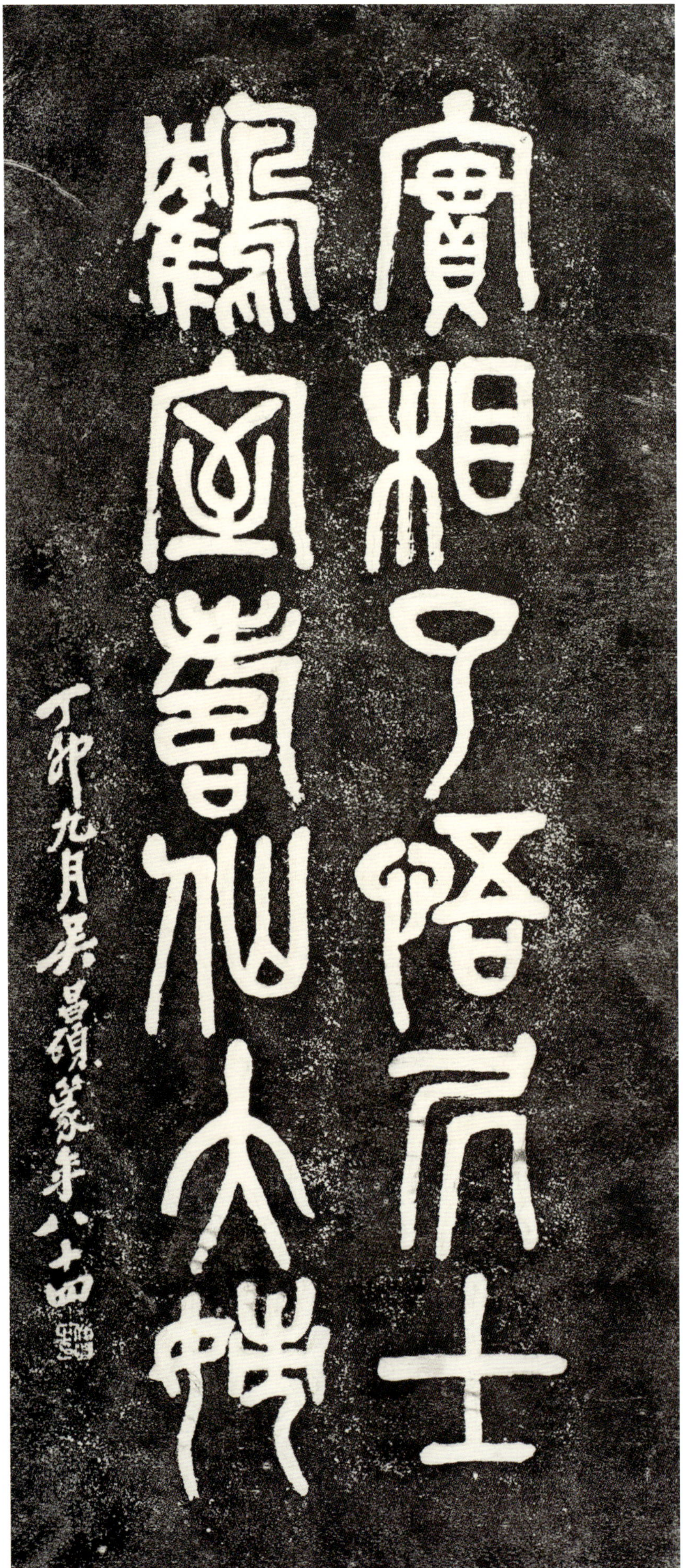

Wu Changshuo
Stone Drum inscriptions
Rubbing created in Japan, ink on paper
Height 92cm, length 40cm
1927

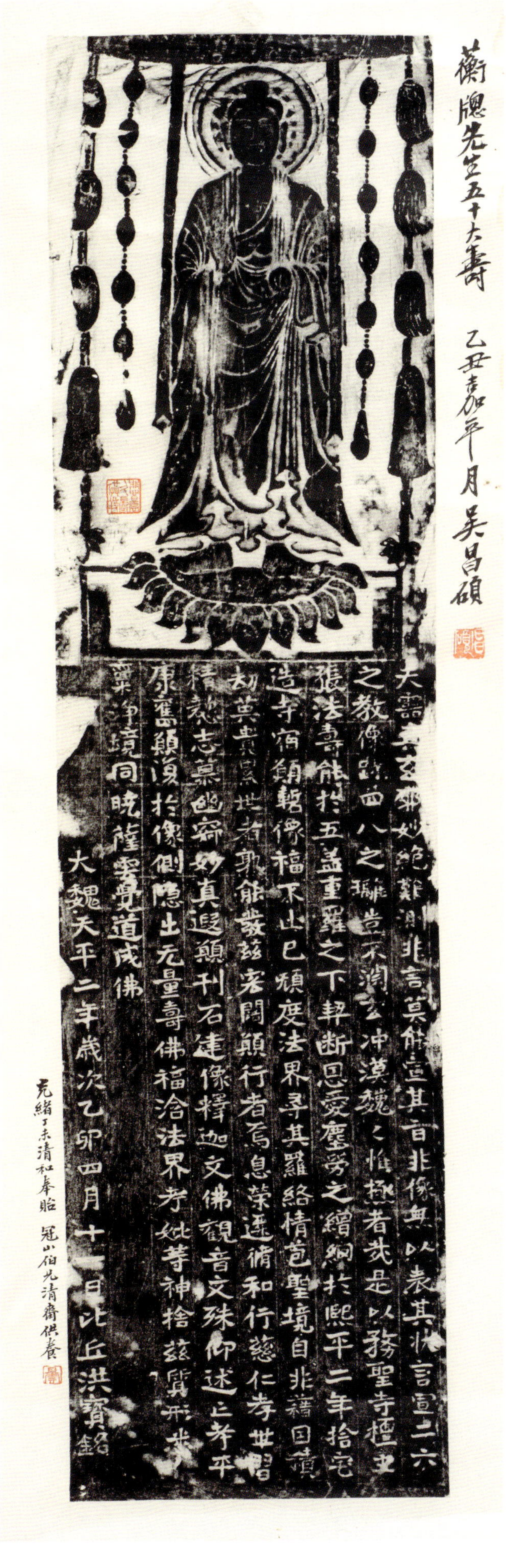

Wu Changshuo
Inscribed rubbing of a statue from the era of Tianping in the Eastern Wei dynasty
Ink on paper
Height 81cm, length 21cm
1925

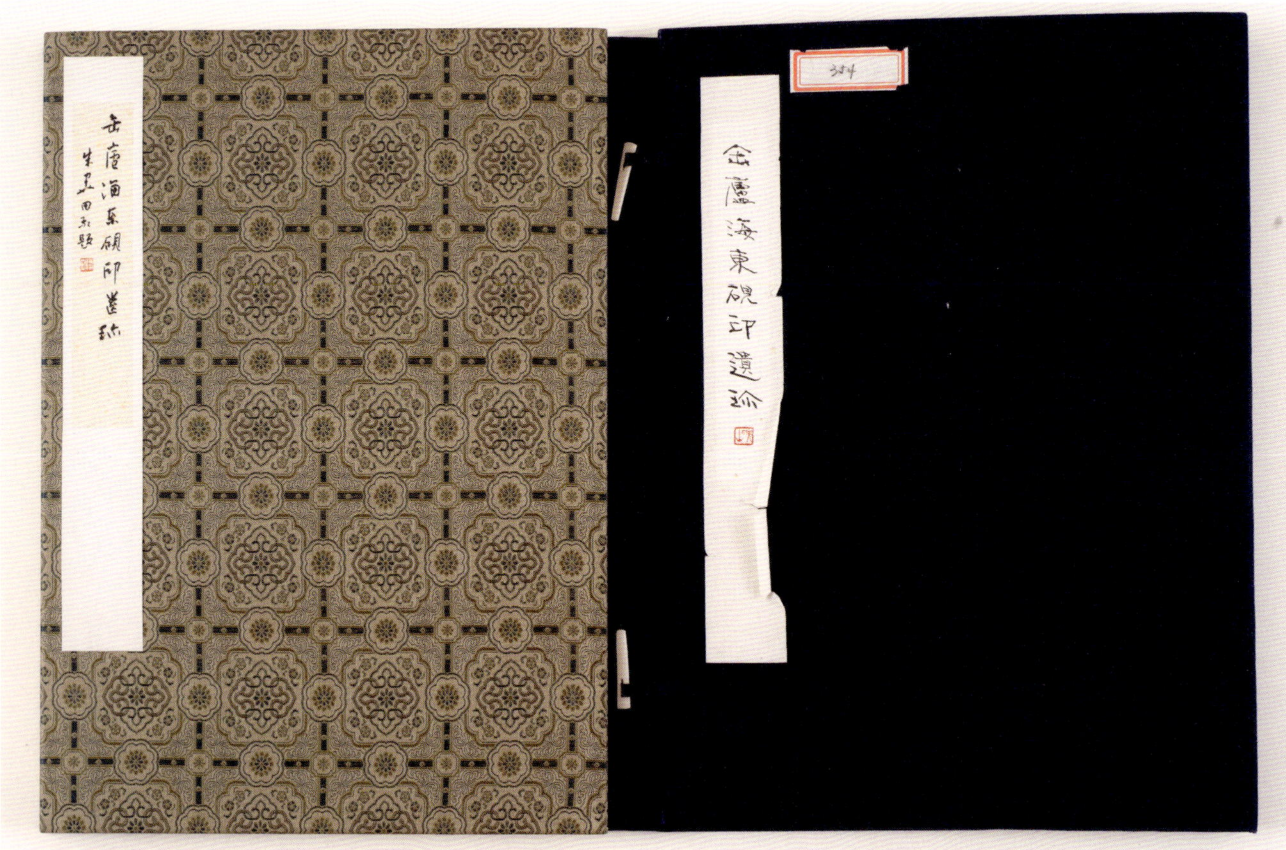

Wu Changshuo
Album of selected inkstones and seal engravings
Date unknown

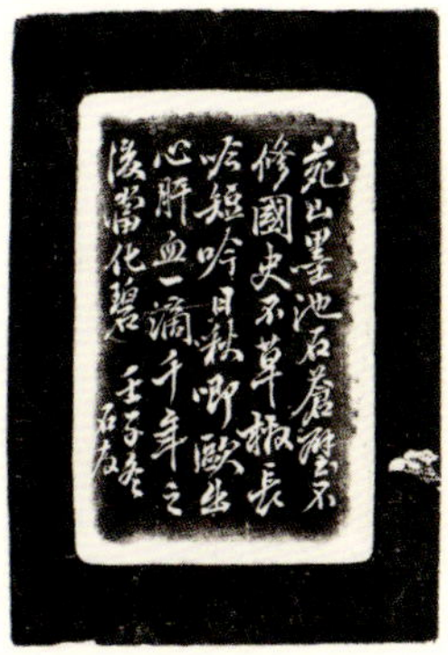

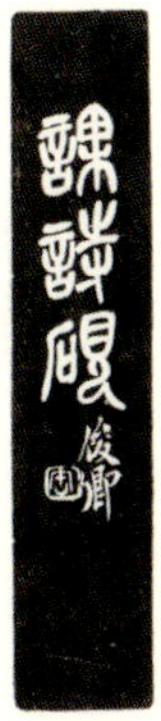

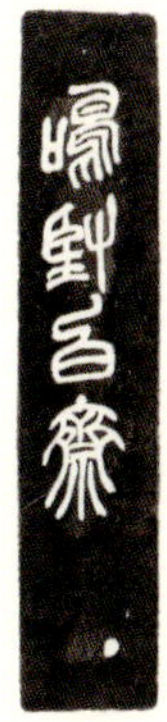

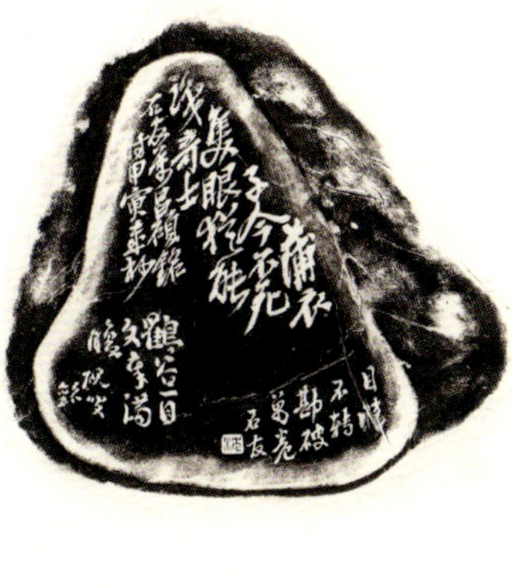

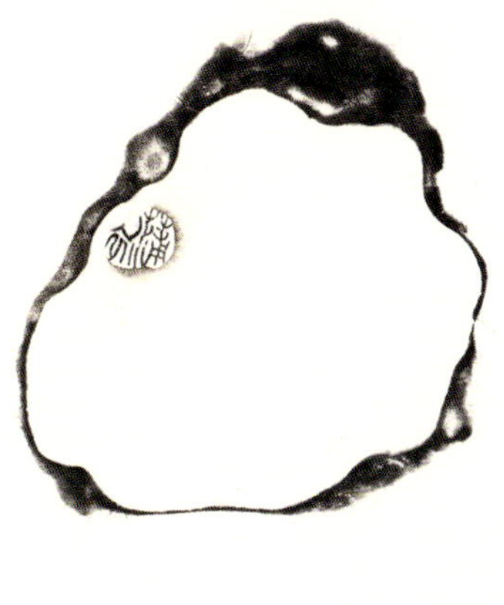

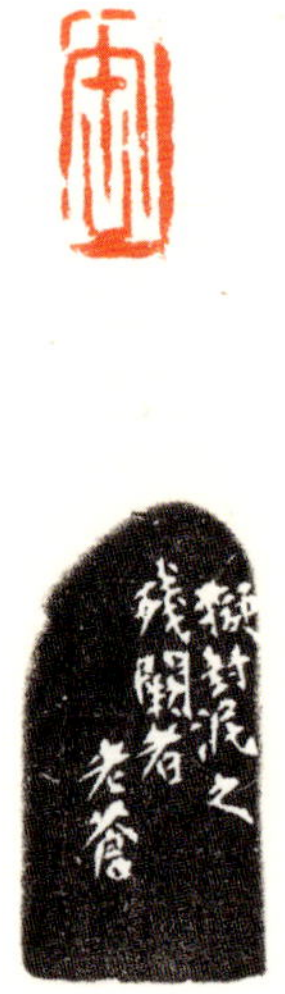

擬封泥之
殘闕者
老蒼

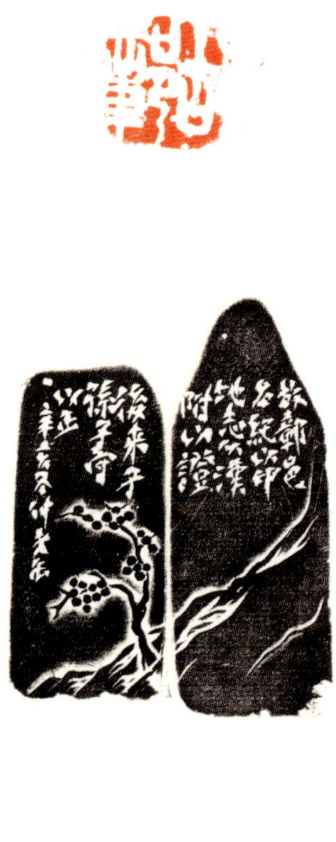

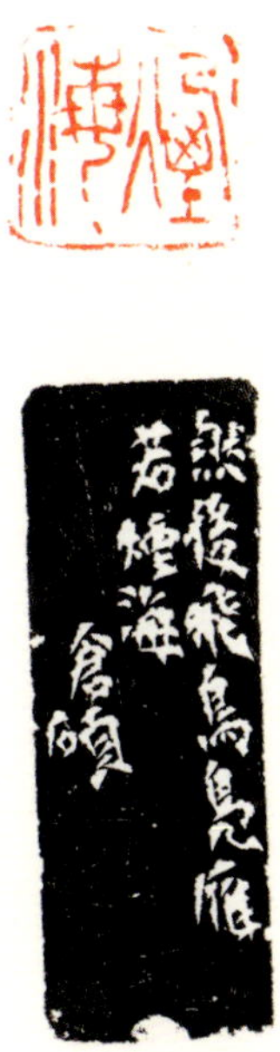

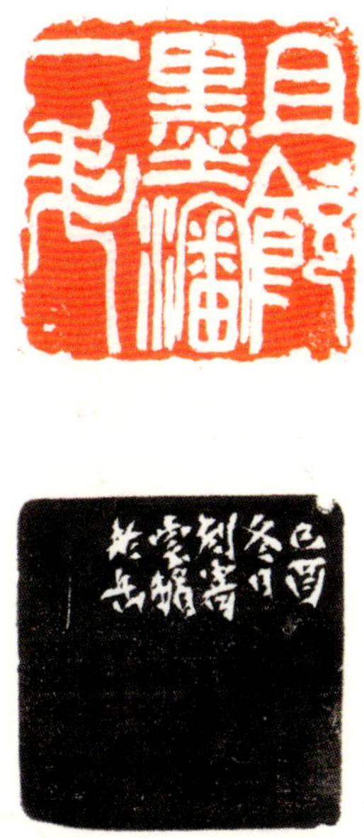

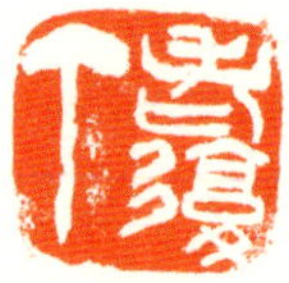

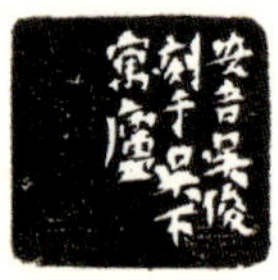
安吉吴俊
刻于吴下
寓庐

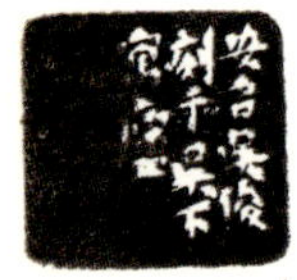
安吉吴俊
刻于吴下
寓庐

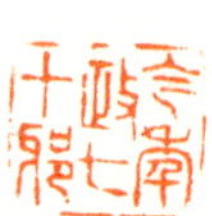

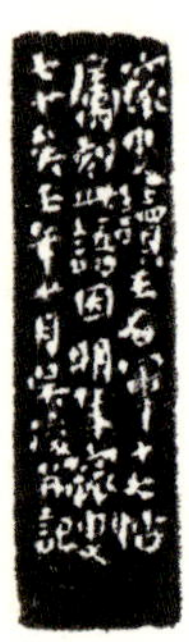

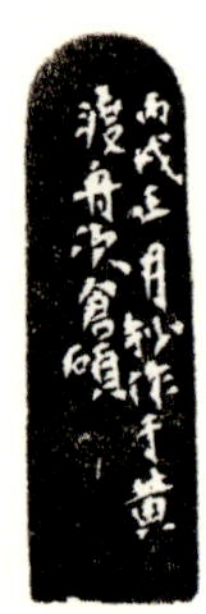

Transcending Borders: The Artistic Exchange Between Wu Changshuo and Kansai Artists

Wu Yue

This year marks the 180th anniversary of the birth of Wu Changshuo, master of arts. Since the beginning of this year, four major museums in Japan – Tokyo National Museum, Asakura Museum of Sculpture, Taito City Calligraphy Museum and Hyogo Prefectural Museum of Art – have held special exhibitions on Wu Changshuo and his work, in commemoration of the 180th anniversary of his birth. In celebration of the 50th anniversary of the friendship between Shanghai and Osaka, and in honour of what would have been Wu Changshuo's 180th birthday, I have written this article with enthusiastic support from the Shanghai People's Association for Friendship with Foreign Countries (SPAFFC). I extend my heartfelt thanks to friends from all walks of life in China and Japan for their long-standing and passionate support.

Wu Changshuo (1844–1927) was a master of Chinese calligraphy, painting, poetry and seal engraving, and a trailblazer in a modern Chinese art that embodied the legacy of ancient Chinese artistic traditions. His dedication to teaching cultivated a generation of exceptional artists in both China and Japan, ushering in a new era in the Chinese art scene. Although Wu never visited Japan in his lifetime, his art had a significant impact on modern Japanese calligraphy and painting.

Friendship and Mentorship Forged in Poetry, Calligraphy and Seals

Wu Changshuo's rigorous academic achievements in epigraphy and calligraphy, along with his extensive knowledge of art, significantly influenced Japanese art circles. In March 1891, the esteemed Japanese calligrapher Kusakabe Meikaku (日下部鸣鹤) sojourned in China to meet this great master. Inspired by their interaction, Kusakabe penned a series of poems titled 'Miscellaneous Poems on Travelling in Eastern Wu', capturing his delight. One verse reads: 'The name of the Sage of Calligraphy spreads across the sea; brushwork flows on paper like clouds and mists, shaming even the works of gods. After travelling thousands of miles to seek the ancient traditions across millennia, here in Eastern Wu holds the essence of the brush.' By likening Wu to Zhang Xu, the revered 'Sage of Cursive Calligraphy', Kusakabe was expressing his profound admiration. Wu, in turn, held Kusakabe's work in high regard. In a poem to Kusakabe, he wrote: 'The calligraphy of the Youjun is studied and imitated by many followers.'

Through exchanges of poetry and calligraphy, their friendship was formed, and Kusakabe Meikaku became Wu's first Japanese poet friend.

Kawai Senro (河井仙郎), a Kyoto native, had his early calligraphy training under the tutelage of Kusakabe Meikaku. His artistic path took a decisive turn when he encountered Wu Changshou's work through his mentor. Captivated by Wu's mastery, Kawai dedicated himself to rigorous practice and in 1897, seeking guidance, he courageously sent his own works to Wu, whom he had never met. Upon receiving Kawai's letter and works, Wu provided meticulous critiques and a lengthy, encouraging letter. The letter was not only filled with heartfelt advice and praise but also included one of his own carved seals as a token of support. This unexpected kindness from Wu deeply moved Kawai. Inspired by Wu's mentorship, he continued his diligent practice. In the winter of 1900, accompanied by Tanaka Keitaro (田中庆太郎), owner of Bunkyudo (文求堂), Kawai travelled to Shanghai. Through introductions from Luo Zhenyu and Wang Kangnian, Kawai finally met Wu Changshuo in person and studied under his guidance. With Wu's mentorship, Kawai honed his skills in seal carving and calligraphy, achieving remarkable proficiency. In 1904, the Xiling Seal Art Society was established in Hangzhou City, with Wu Changshuo nominated as its first director following a unanimous vote by members. Kawai Senro, recognised for his dedication and talent, became one of the first Japanese members of the society.

In 1912, Wu Changshuo settled in Shanghai, making his home in Jiqingli on Shanxi North Road in the Zhabei district (a former district of Shanghai, now part of the Jing'an district). His residence quickly became a revered destination for Japanese artists. Among the many visitors from Japan, particularly from the Kansai region, there were notable figures such as Hashimoto Kansetsu (桥本关雪), Tomioka Tessai (富岡铁斋), Kojima Torajiro (儿島虎次郎), Mizuno Sobai (水野疏梅), Shiraishi Rokusaburo (白石鹿叟), Asakura Fumio (朝仓文夫) and Shibata Rokuji (柴田六次).

Hashimoto Kansetsu (1883–1945) was a celebrated Japanese painter and a towering presence in the Kansai art field during the Taisho (大正) and Showa (昭和) eras. Beginning in 1914, Hashimoto visited China over 30 times, forging deep connections with Chinese artists such as Wu Changshuo, Wang Zhen, Huang Binhong and Qian Shoutie. In 1926, Qian Shoutie travelled to Japan, bringing with him Wu's calligraphy of the Chinese 'dragon' and 'tiger' characters as a gift. Hashimoto was so captivated by these pieces that he had them engraved on his chessboard, keeping them in a place where he could admire them daily. Hashimoto's profound admiration for Wu's work is immortalised in his extensive collection, now displayed at the Hashimoto Kansetsu Memorial House in Kyoto.

Born in Kyoto, Tomioka Tessai was a renowned literati painter during Japan's Meiji (明治) and Taisho periods. In 1917, Tessai, who greatly admired Wu Changshuo's art, respectfully requested a seal from him. The two men became friends with Wu holding Tessai, eight years his senior, in high regard. Knowing that Tessai shared a birthday with the esteemed Chinese poet Su Dongpo, he crafted three special seals for him: 'Born on the Same Day as Su Dongpo', 'Tomioka's Hundred Refinements', and 'Tessai Waishi' (his pen name). Tessai cherished these seals and used them prominently on his artworks in his later years. This exchange of artistic seals and calligraphy works built a bridge of friendship and mutual respect between these great masters from China and Japan.

Building on the artistic exchange between Wu Changshuo and these Japanese artists, from 19–23 February 1922, the art department of the Takashimaya Gofukuten (高岛屋吴服店) in Osaka, Japan (the predecessor of Takashimaya department store), held the first 'Wu Changshuo New Works Exhibition' at its Edobori main store (江户堀本店). The department's director Tanikami Ryusuke (谷上隆介) edited and published the collection Ink Play of Fouweng , which included 42 paintings and 6 calligraphy works from the exhibition. The cover was inscribed and the preface was written by Nagao Kou (长尾甲), with an inscription by Tomioka Tessai that read, 'Developing new ideas, clearing away old conventions', and Wu himself inscribed it with, 'Reading a painting is like reading Chinese cursive script'.

On 28 June 1952, artists from the Kansai region gathered in Kyoto for a symposium on Wu Changshuo's artworks. Renowned scholars such as Nagahiro Toshio (长广敏雄) presented academic discussions on the impact of Wu Changshuo's poetry, calligraphy, painting and seal engraving on Japan.

A Special Bond with Waseda University: An Extraordinary Exhibition

From 11–13 June 1927, the 'Wu Changshuo and Wang Yiting Joint Calligraphy and Painting Exhibition' was held at the Asahi Shimbun (朝日新闻) headquarters in Osaka, organised by Waseda University. The story between Wu Changshuo and Waseda University dates back to 1926, when the 83-year-old master received a letter from Takata Sanae, the president of Waseda University, requesting Wu's major works in calligraphy and painting for the newly established art department at the university. Despite his advanced age and frail health, Wu, who had been avoiding social activities and struggling with arm pain, spent several months creating 30 calligraphy pieces and 30 paintings for the university. Similarly, Wang Yiting produced an equal number of works. Together, the two masters generously donated a total of 120 pieces to Waseda University.

The university, deeply appreciative of the contributions of these two Chinese art giants, spent over a year preparing an exhibition, which they successfully hosted at the Asahi Shimbun headquarters in Osaka. University president Takata Sanae wrote the preface, praising the generosity of the Chinese masters and expressing his heartfelt gratitude. This cross-national support for art education by Chinese art masters has become a celebrated chapter in the history of cultural and educational exchanges between China and Japan.

In 2018, I made my first visit to Waseda University, where I was warmly welcomed by university officials. During the visit, they reiterated their profound gratitude for the invaluable support Wu Changshuo and Wang Yiting had extended to Waseda's art education.

Continuing the Legacy: The Flourishing of Wu Changshuo's Art in the Modern Era

The era of reform and the Open Door Policy in China has provided a gateway for the flourishing and development of Wu Changshuo's art. With ink that nourishes the soul and seals that forge connections, this period marked a new chapter in the cross-cultural appreciation of Wu's work. In April 1985, with the support of the SPAFFC, Wang Geyi, a disciple of Wu Changshuo and the director of the Shanghai Chinese Painting Academy, was invited to Osaka by Bai Joteki, president of the Japan Calligraphers Association, to give lectures and hold an exhibition.

To celebrate Wang's 88th birthday, Bai organised the 'Wang Geyi Calligraphy and Seal Carving Exhibition' in Kyoto, showcasing over 50 pieces of Wang's work from his collection. Captivated by Wang's exceptional calligraphy and seal engraving, Bai expressed a deep desire to become his disciple, a request Wang gladly welcomed. This marked the beginning of Wu Changshuo's artistic legacy flourishing in Osaka for a third generation. Local artists have actively commemorated Wu Changshuo's artworks through various artistic exchanges, celebrating his birthday, death anniversary, and friendships with Japanese peers. These activities have included exhibitions, lectures and symposiums. Notable events held in Kobe, Sakai, Kyoto and Toyota, such as the 'Wu and His Four Generations' exhibition and the 'Wu Changshuo and His Disciples' exhibition, have further enriched the vibrant cultural dialogue between China and Japan.

On 12 September 1995, the Wu Changshuo Art Museum was inaugurated in Pudong, Shanghai. Bai, accompanied by nearly 100 disciples, visited Shanghai to celebrate the occasion, further deepening the cultural exchange between Shanghai and Osaka and strengthening the friendship among Wu Changshuo's disciples and followers in both countries.

Entering a new era, efforts have been made to promote traditional culture and showcase the Haipai cultural heritage, fostering mutual understanding and connection between our two peoples.

In recent years, a series of exhibitions have been organised in collaboration with the Japanese Seal Engravers Association, including the 'Wu Changshuo's Calligraphy and Painting Exhibition' at the Kyoto City Kyocera Museum of Art, the 'Wu Changshuo & Kojima Torajiro Art Exhibition' in Takahashi City Nariwa Museum of Art in 2014, and the exhibition that showcased the works of two masters' descendants: the 'Kojima Kaitaro & Wu Yue Art Exhibition' in Kasaoka city in 2015. In 2016, to celebrate the 60th anniversary of the founding of SPAFFC, the exhibition 'In the Footsteps of Masters: Honouring Wu Changshuo and Kojima Torajiro' was held in the Wu Changshuo Art Museum. Also in 2019, the exhibition 'Eternal Master Wu Changshuo and His Artistic Heirs: Five Generations of Excellence' was held in Osaka. Through continued exchange, Wu's artistic legacy supports and nurtures the deepening cultural connection between China and Japan.

Commemorating the 175th Anniversary of the Great Master – Eternal Master and His Artistic Heirs: Five Generations of Excellence held in Wolu Museum of Art in Osaka in January 2019

Since 2020, the global spread of COVID-19 has disrupted many facets of life, yet the artistic exchange and mutual support between Chinese and Kansai region artists have thrived undeterred. Virtual academic dialogues and the sharing of research on Wu Changshuo's art have not only persisted but deepened, fostering a genuine connection.

This year commemorates the 50th anniversary of the sister-city bond between Shanghai and Osaka and the 180th birthday of Wu Changshuo. In celebration of these milestones, Wu's artistic heirs in both China and Japan are exchanging art pieces, conveying messages of friendship, and revelling in the joy of creation. Across Osaka, Kobe, Kyoto and Okayama, cultural events are unfolding to honour Wu Changshuo's legacy, blossoming from the seeds of friendship sown by Wu and his Japanese contemporaries.

Wu Changshuo's calligraphy piece '道德文章', meaning 'morals and literature', dedicated to Waseda University, exemplifies his philosophy of imparting principles through literature and teaching art through virtue. Japanese artists have drawn deeply from Wu's mastery and the cultural confidence of Chinese artists, marked by diligent exploration and innovation. Despite geographical distances and shared adversities, the effort to uphold and pass down the pioneering spirit of Sino-Japanese artists endures, widening the pathways of cultural exchange between these two nations.

Atmosphere Shapes Artistic Tastes

Wu Chao

Born in the Jiachen Year (the 41st year of the 60-year cyclical Chinese calendar) (甲辰), Wu Changshuo engraved a red seal called 'Xiong Jia Chen' as a declaration of the year he turned 60. Another Jiachen Year falls in 2024, which means that two Jiazi (first year of the 60-year cyclical Chinese calendar) years (甲子) have passed since then. Commemorative events for the 180th anniversary of Wu Changshuo's birth were first unveiled by Asakura Museum of Sculpture in Tokyo, Japan, on 16 December 2023, as a prelude to the spring of 2024. As we ushered in the Chinese New Year of the Dragon and the gentle breeze of spring, the themed exhibitions of Wu Changshuo's artworks took place in succession at Tokyo National Museum, Taito City Calligraphy Museum, Kensinn Calligraphy Group, and Hyogo Prefectural Museum of Art, respectively. The exhibition was themed 'Wu Changshuo's Artistic World' (also exhibiting the artworks of Shanghai-styled and influential figures from the Xiling Engraver Society) and was held over a period of months in both the Kanto and Kensei regions of Japan, a nation to the east of China. Each exhibition took place in two stages to fully present each exhibit. The whole panoply of exhibits, particularly influential artworks preceding Wu and his successors, served to show the wellspring of his artistic endeavours, as well as lay out the timeline of how his art was shaped throughout his life and how it was inherited following his death.

He started out from the Zhangwu Village in Anji County at the age of 26, and spent his entire life regularly visiting new friends and learning from masters. In the Qin and Han dynasties, there were many pioneering craftsmen who made inscriptions and epigraphs on bronzeware and stone, whom Wu profoundly respected but never communicated with, and predecessors in his era whom Wu didn't have the chance to meet. He succeeded in internalising the calligraphy styles of Deng Shiru, Wu Rangzhi, Zhao Zhiqian, Yang Yisun and He Shaoji in his works, which was partially the result of his industriousness. More importantly, his lifelong network of friends and masters, all highly accomplished, must take credit for introducing Wu to such brilliant works. Weng Tonghe, Yu Quyuan, Yang Jianshan, Wu Pingzhai, Wu Dacheng, and many more well-known figures alike, all selflessly helped and endorsed Wu Changshuo at a time when he was merely an impoverished young man. They offered to take him to appreciate their priceless collections, guided him with patience, and even gave him personal collections as gifts. Ren Bonian, a well-known figure in Shanghai, frequently engaged in all-night discussions with Wu Changshuo so that they might refine one another's artistic expertise, and he travelled to Suzhou City several times to paint portraits of Wu Changshuo. His works from this time include *Portrait of Wu Changshuo enjoying the shade under the plantains* (蕉荫纳凉图) and *Portrait of Wu Changshuo as a poor official* (酸寒尉像) and are currently kept by the Zhejiang Art Museum as a grade-one art collection.

His colleagues, Gao Yong, Jin Jie, Ling Xia, Pu Hua and Li Ruiqing are all prominent scholars and artists. As we appreciate the works from his network of friends and masters, every piece stands out as belonging to its creator and can be intuitively identified from the artists' distinctive, candid styles. There is no vulgarity, hatred or confusion, as seen in the works of some of today's so-called art masters. It is thus to be noted that at that time, people from all walks of life, be it officials of high rank, merchants, or ordinary people, all had respect for traditional Chinese culture and handwriting. As the old saying goes, people with similar interests and ideas tend to associate with one another, and that's true for Wu Changshuo. His connections comprised like-minded masters and friends who together created a meaningful atmosphere to hone foundational skills and advance in poetry, calligraphy, painting and seal engraving simultaneously.

Wu Changshuo's old-school reverence for knowledge and tradition was part of the DNA of his artistic endeavours, and it is through this, coupled with years of hard work, that he succeeded in becoming a legendary master of arts. Even in his late age, Wu remained dedicated to respecting inherited traditions when educating his students and disciples, which nourished them and younger generations, giving them the knowledge and skills to develop and, ultimately, cultivate their own exceptional schools of thought. As a knowledgeable man with a solid foundation in both theory and practice, he delivered a group of talented individuals who excelled at various disciplines; he shaped their individual characters, earning widespread recognition and respect in the process. Above all, his friends and masters forged a powerful network of mutual inspiration that profoundly contributed to his art career, proving to current generations that atmosphere shapes artistic tastes as well.

Wu Changshuo and His Friends

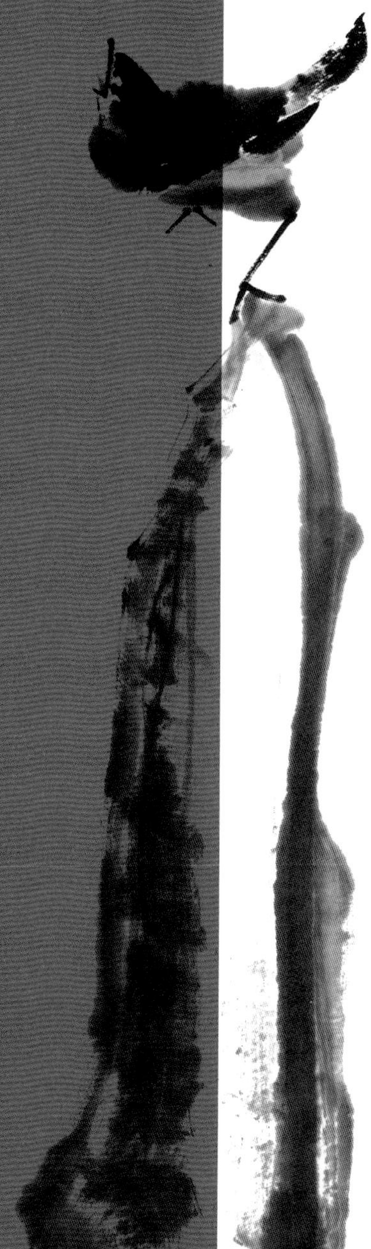

Yu Quyuan (1821–1907)
Calligraphic couplet (five Chinese characters on each piece of rice paper)
Countless pines make spring evergreen,
Bamboos refresh summer with coolness
Ink on paper
Height 100cm, length 20cm
Date unknown

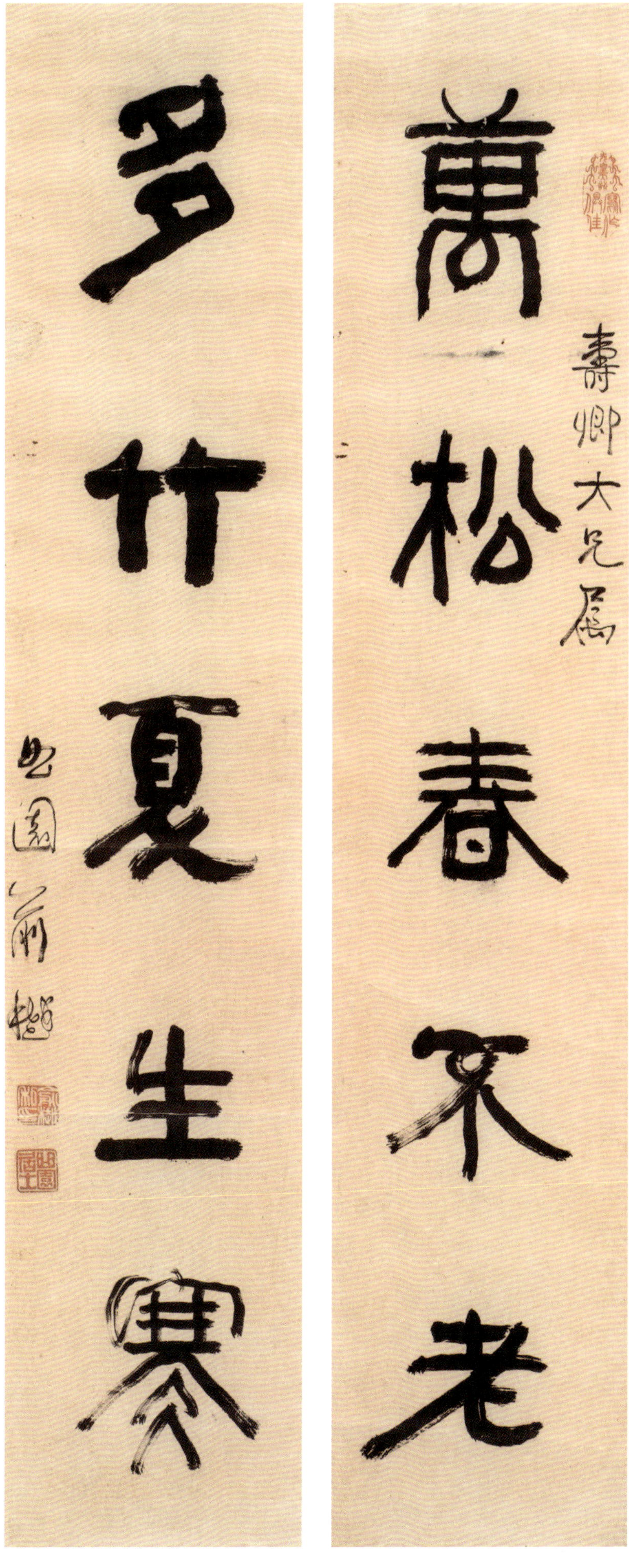
萬松春不老
壽卿大兄屬
多竹夏生寒

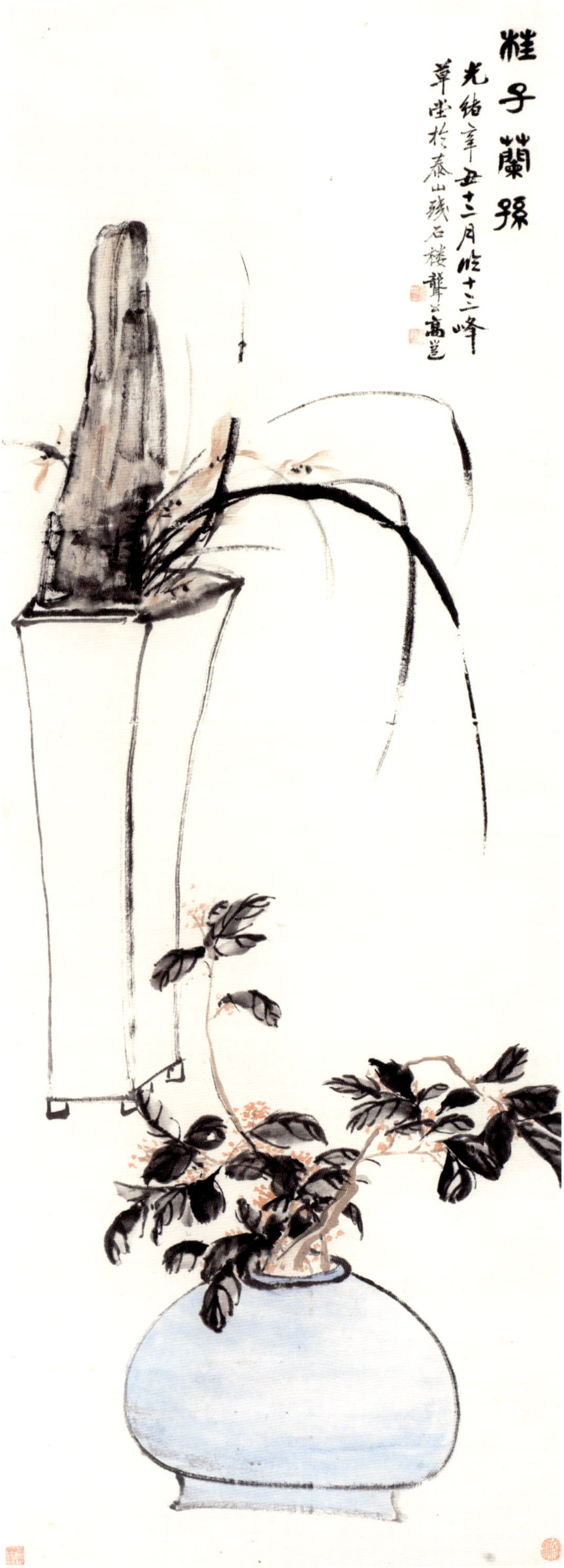

Gao Yong (1850–1921)
Flourishing Orchids and Osmanthus
handscroll (symbolising children)
Ink and colours on paper
Height 132cm, length 46cm
1901

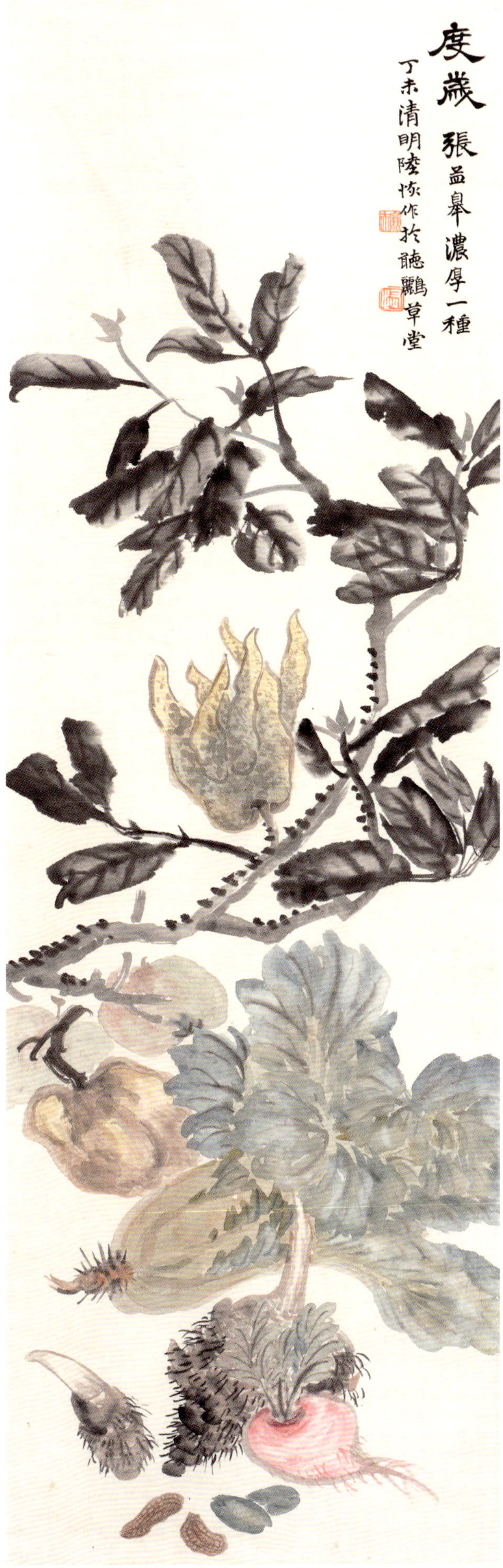

Lu Hui (1851–1920)
Bergamot handscroll
Ink and colours on paper
Height 98cm, length 31cm
1907

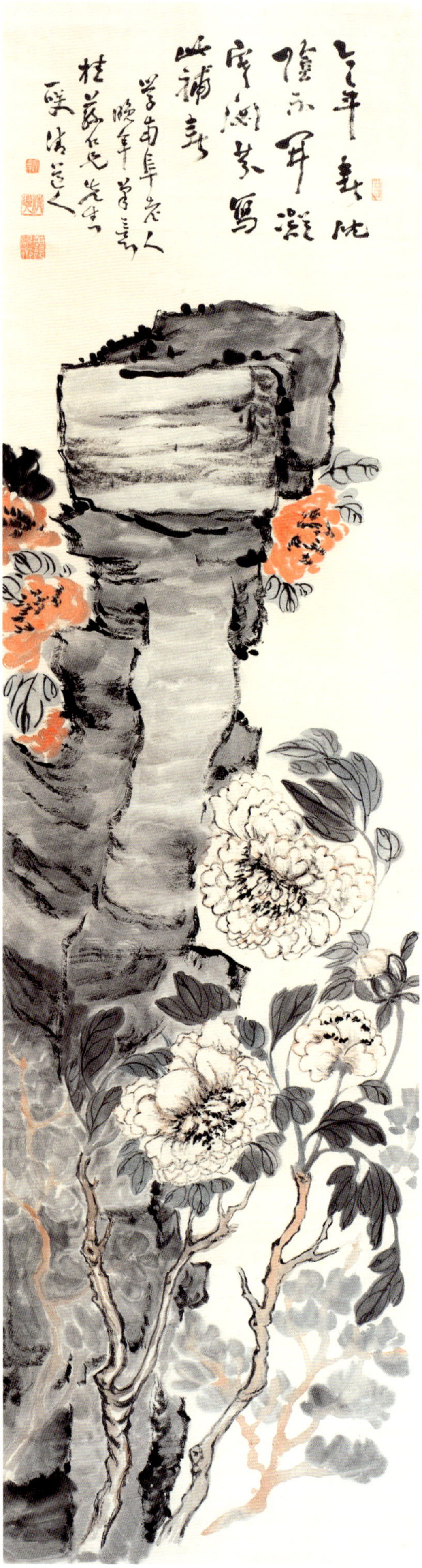

Li Ruiqing (1867–1920)
Peony and Giant Stone handscroll
Ink and colours on paper
Height 178cm, length 46cm
Date unknown

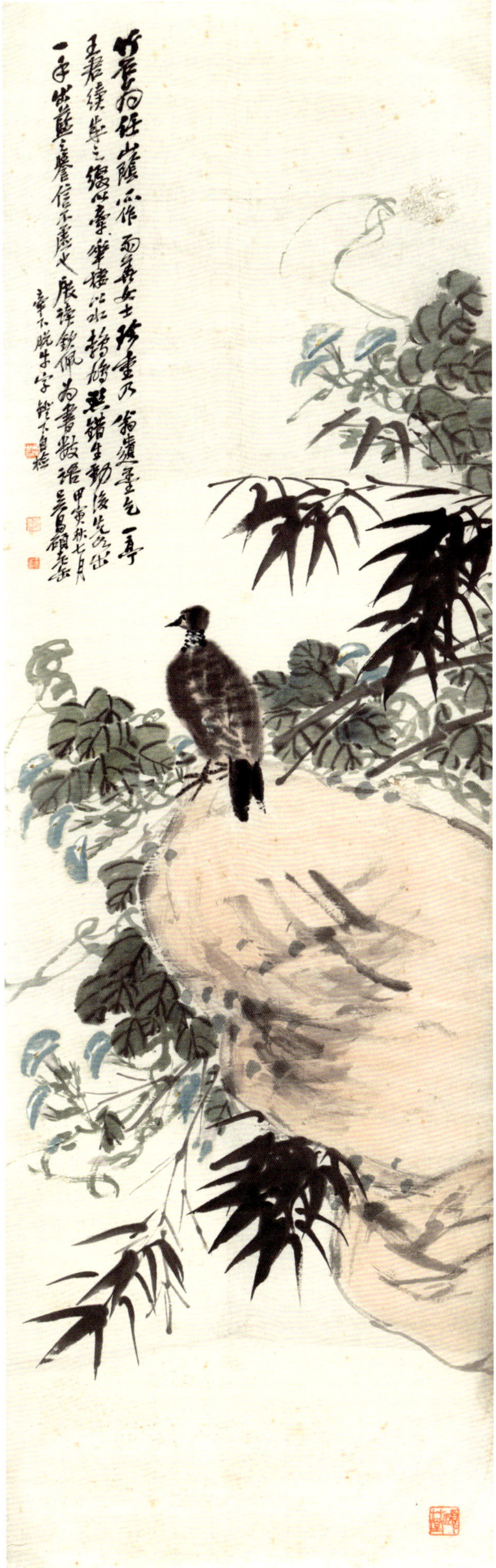

Wu Changshuo, Ren Bonian (1840–96) and Wang Yiting (1867–1938)
Flower and Bird handscroll
Ink and colours on paper
Height 157cm, length 49cm
1914

Wang Yiting (1867–1938)
Chrysanthemum handscroll
Ink and colours on paper
Height 146cm, length 79cm
1917

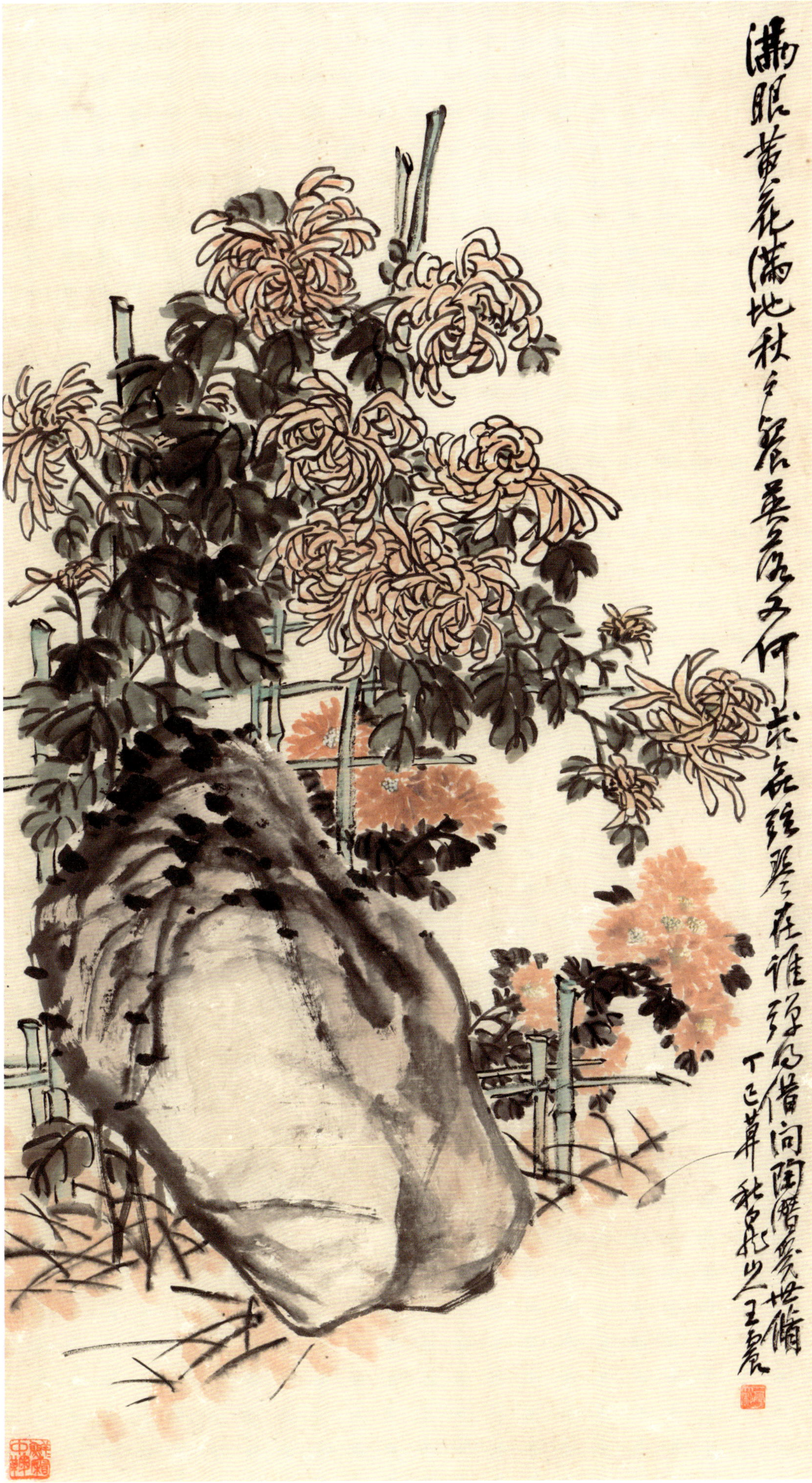

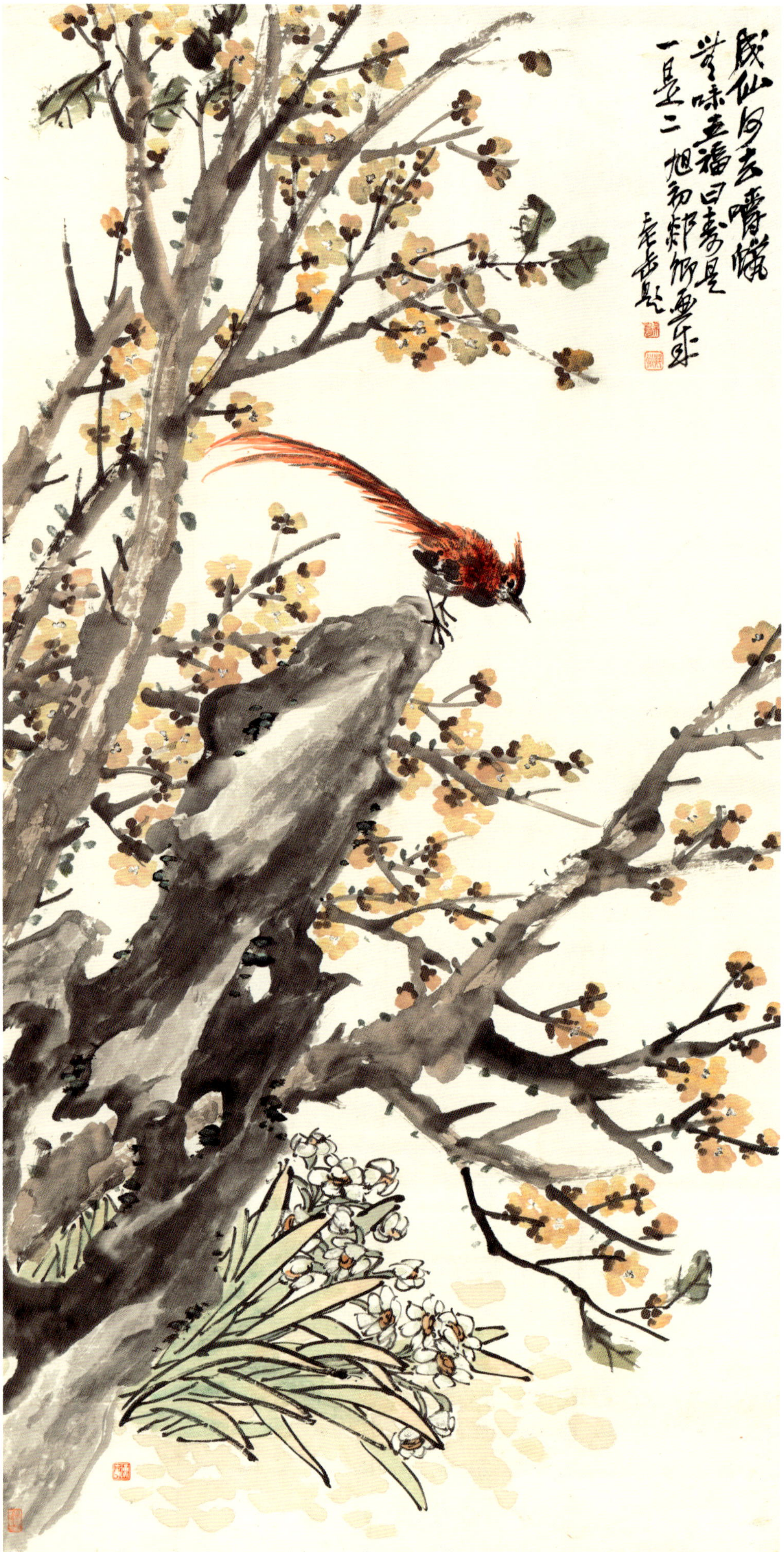

Painted by Huang Shanshou (1855–1919)
and Hu Tanqing (1865–after 1942)
Inscribed by Wu Changshuo
Plum Blossom handscroll
Ink and colours on paper
Height 130cm, length 68cm
Date unknown

Painted by Liu Yu'an (unknown–1926)
Inscribed by Wu Changshuo
Sunrise handscroll
Ink and colours on paper
Height 131cm, length 66cm
1922

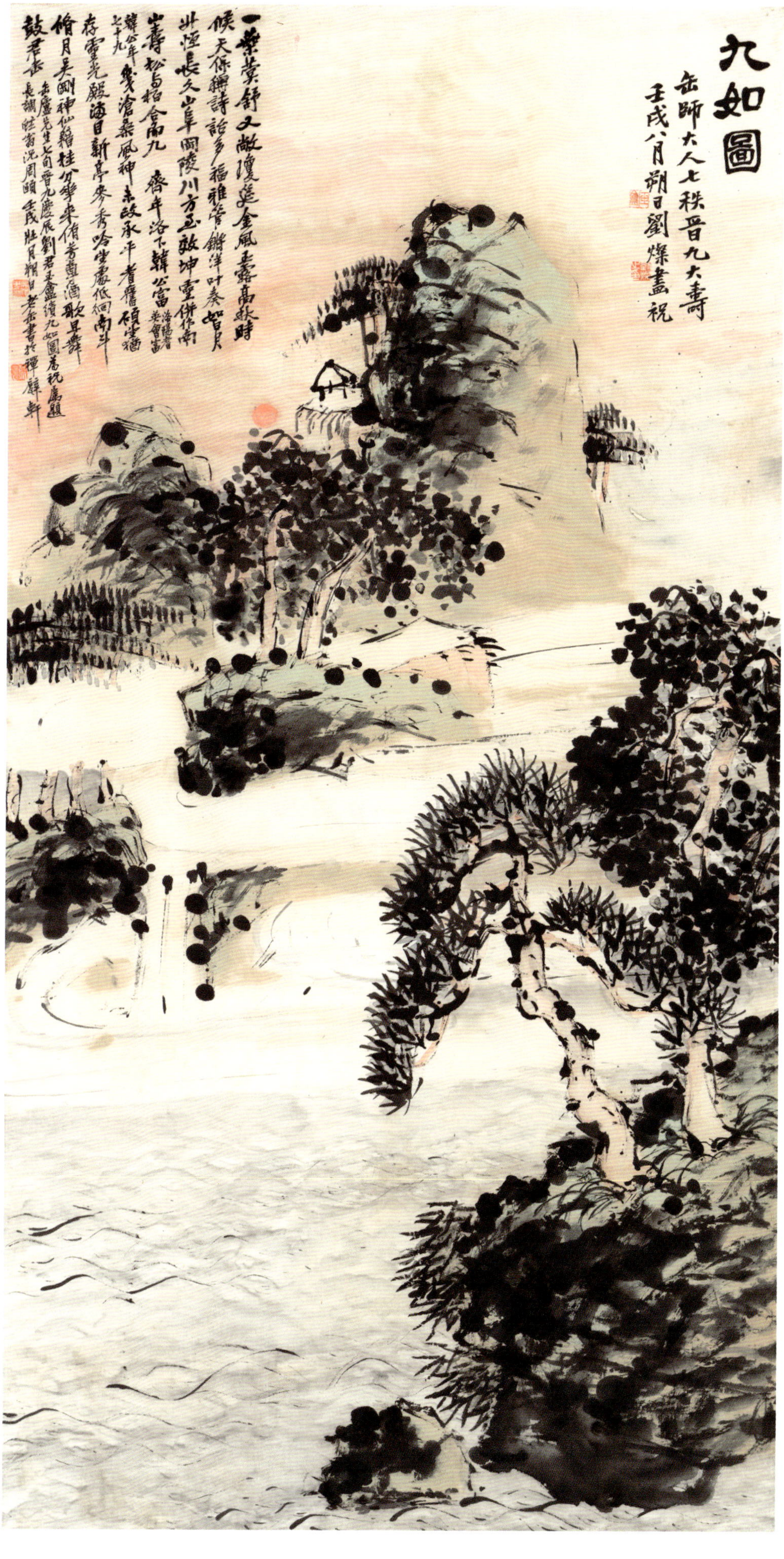
九如圖
岳師大人七秩晉九大壽
壬戌八月朔日劉爍畫祝

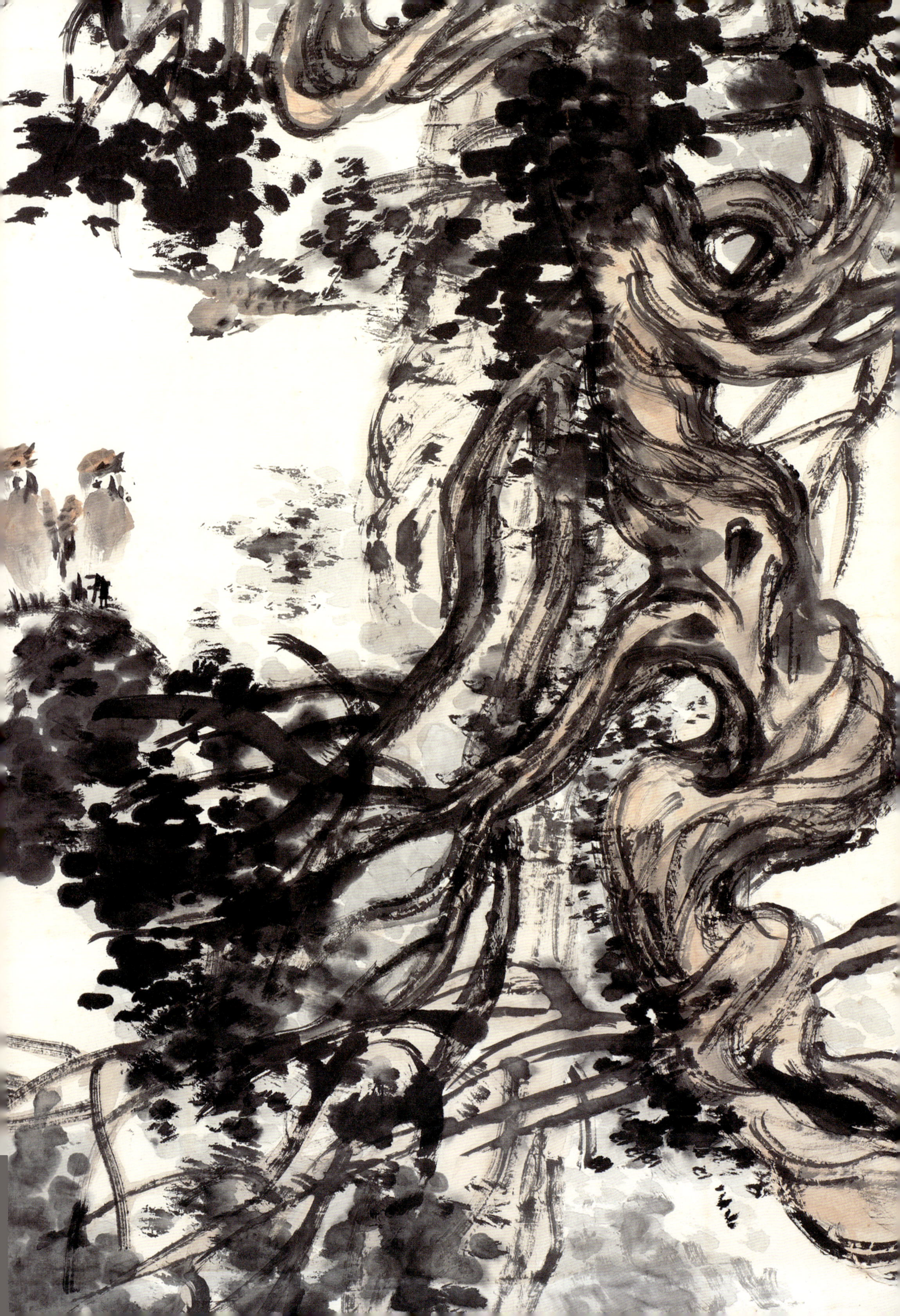

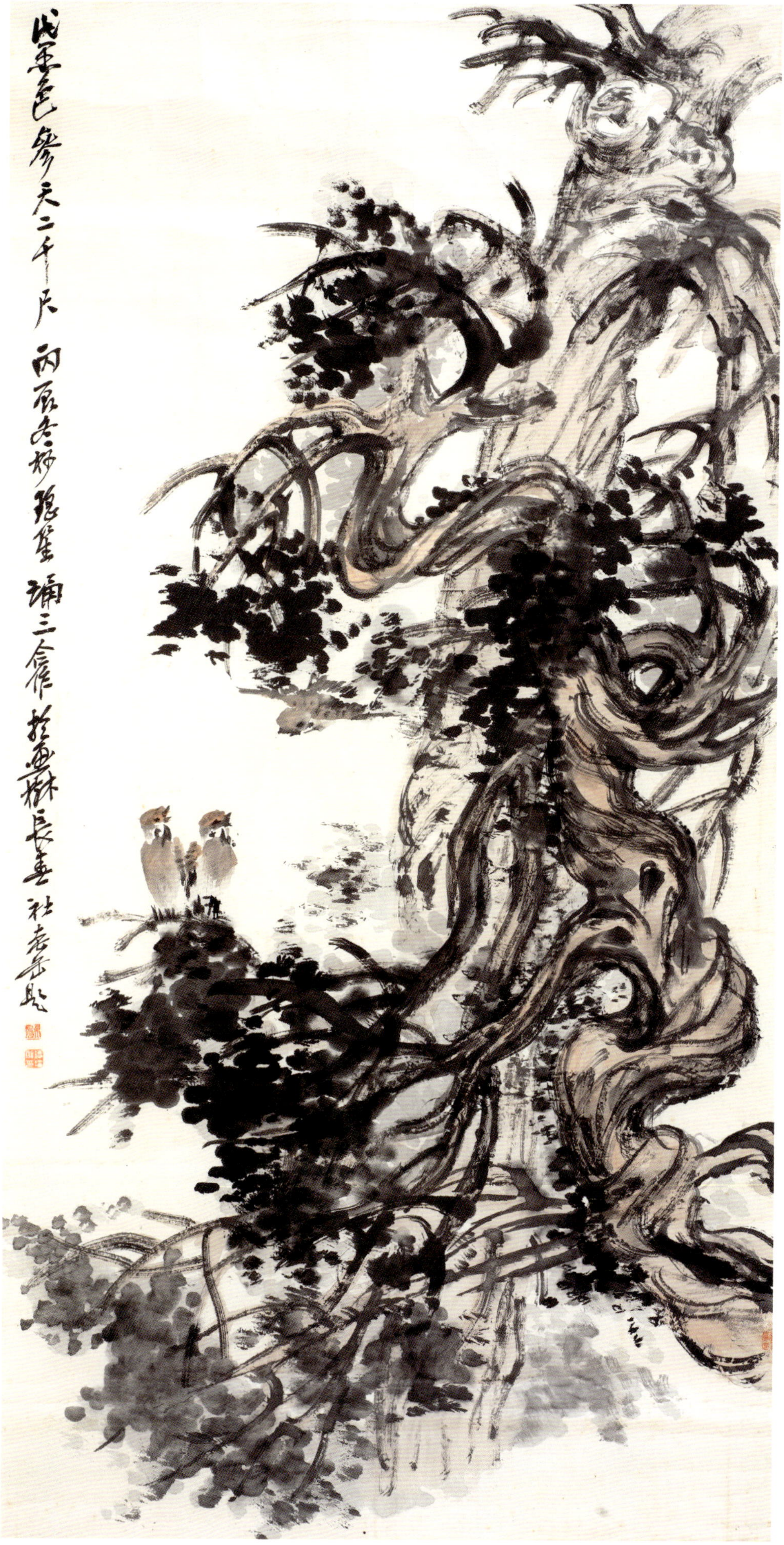

Painted by Cheng Yaosheng (1869–1936) **and Yan Songsan** (1885–1926)
Inscribed by Wu Changshuo
Sparrows on Cypress handscroll
Ink and colours on paper
Height 138.5cm, length 69cm
1916

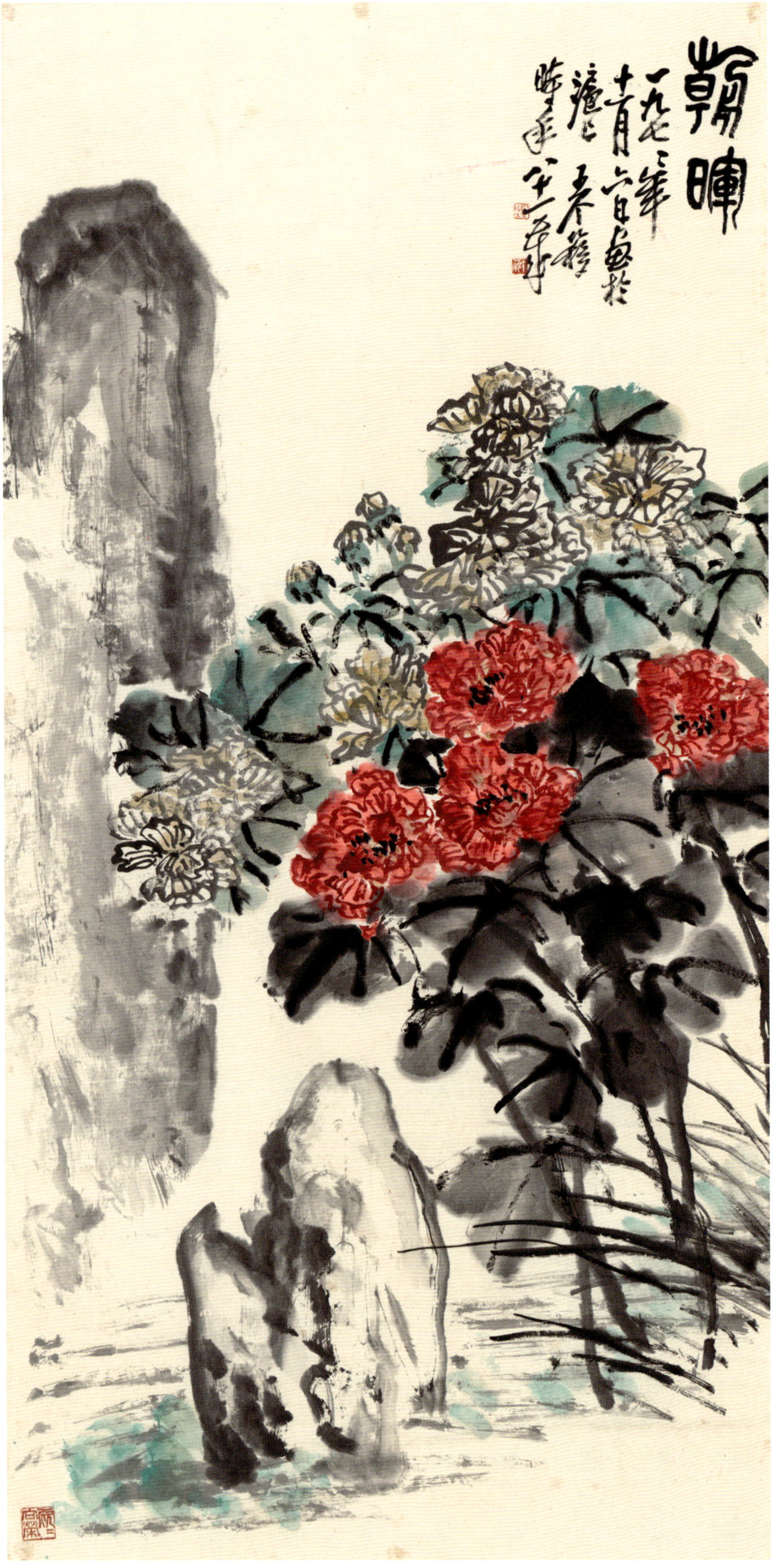

Wang Geyi (1897–1988)
Autumn Hibiscus handscroll
Ink and colours on paper
Height 139cm, length 69cm
1977

Wang Geyi
Red Plum handscroll (large)
Ink and colours on paper
Height 88cm, length 67cm
1983

我有幸參加抗美援朝這一偉大戰爭，初期打運動戰，戰鬥頻繁，物質生活極端艱苦，看不到一份祖國的報紙雜志和畫報。一九五一年進行夏秋季攻勢，由運動戰轉入陣地防禦，在三八線上建立了地下長城（即坑道工事）進行積極防禦，陣綫穩定，但戰鬥更加激烈。據統計敵人每日出動飛機二千五百多架次進行狂轟濫炸，上甘嶺戰役時，敵機在三點七平方公里面積的陣地上一天投彈五百餘枚約二百噸，並傾瀉炮彈二百九十萬發，把山頭削矮一公尺多。後來戰綫穩定，能看到祖國送來的報紙雜志畫報，一年多沒有看到了，所以極爲興奮鼓舞。

在這戰鬥頻繁艱苦卓絕的情況下，精神力量更爲重要。我在三八綫上梨木洞師指揮所坑道內看到畫報上刊載王个簃同志一幅紅梅，上題〝衝風鬥霜放紅花〞。一下就把我吸引住了，我把它剪裁下來，掛在坑道的墻壁上，日夜相伴，反覆看，仔細想，好似有一種魅力縈繞腦際，給我留下深刻印象。從此我愛上了國畫。美術不僅給人精神享受，更重要的是鼓舞鬥志，是一種無形的巨大力量。從一九五一年秋到一九五二年冬季，在這一年多的陣地守備戰中，進行數十次反擊戰，取得了很大的勝利。戰前我欣賞了〝紅梅〞，戰後又反覆觀看，意味更深長，增強了鬥志。敵人衝上來，我們又反擊過去，鞏固了陣地，取得了勝利，的確放出了鮮艷的紅花。

我轉業上海後，參觀了國畫展，看到王个簃同志許多作品。一九七七年我拜訪了他，談起抗美援朝看到《紅梅》時我的心情，他也興致勃勃，談吐瀟灑幽默。他說一个美術家應該把美術作爲武器去鼓舞人民的鬥志。他熱愛社會主義，熱愛黨，關心政治，值得我們學習。我衷心祝他健康長壽。

原載一九八一年《朵雲》第一期，程國璠《紅梅》

一九八三年七月 橫岸承名世書

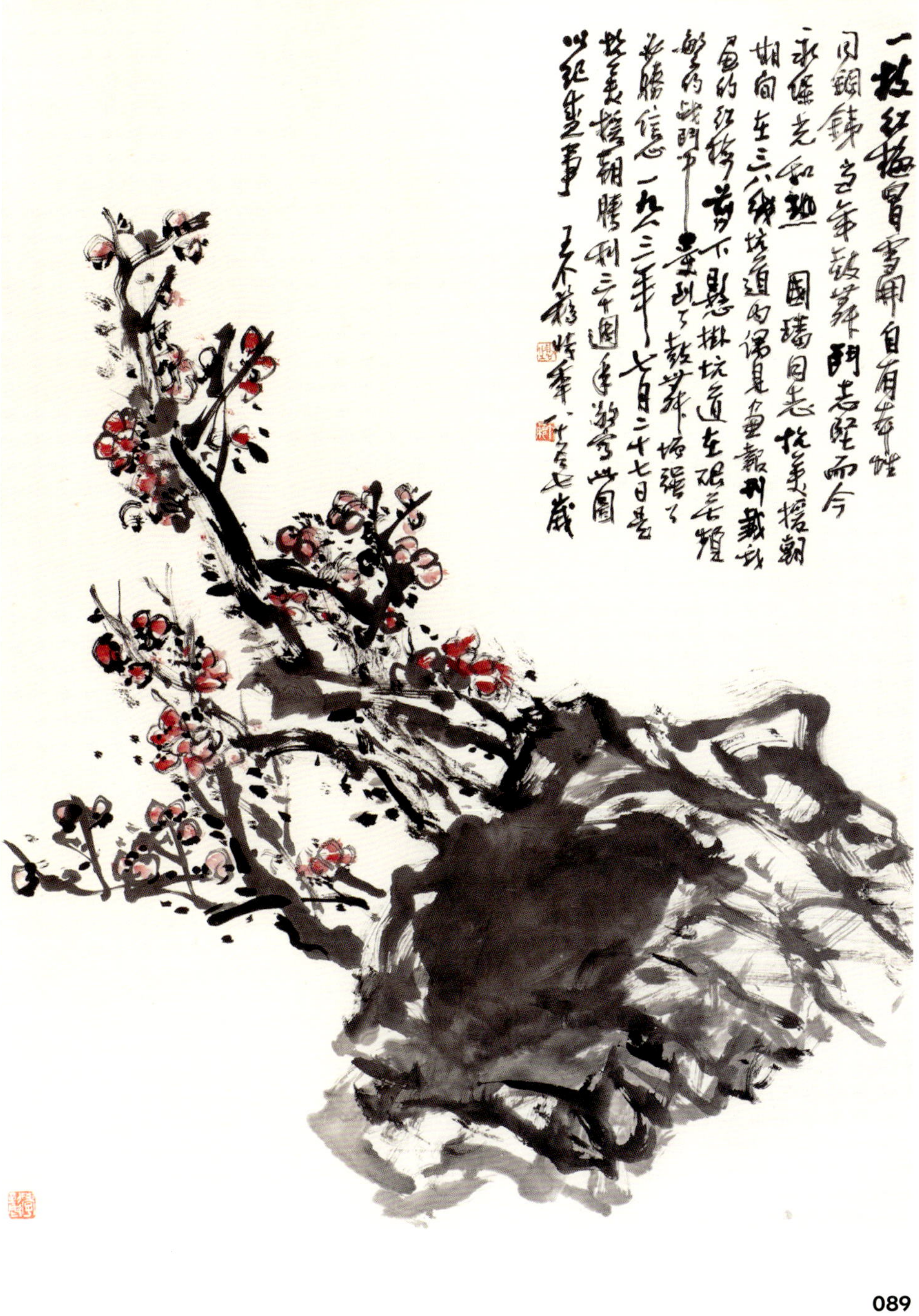

Pu Hua (1832–1911)
Lotus handscroll
ink and colours on paper
Height 132cm, length 80cm
1908

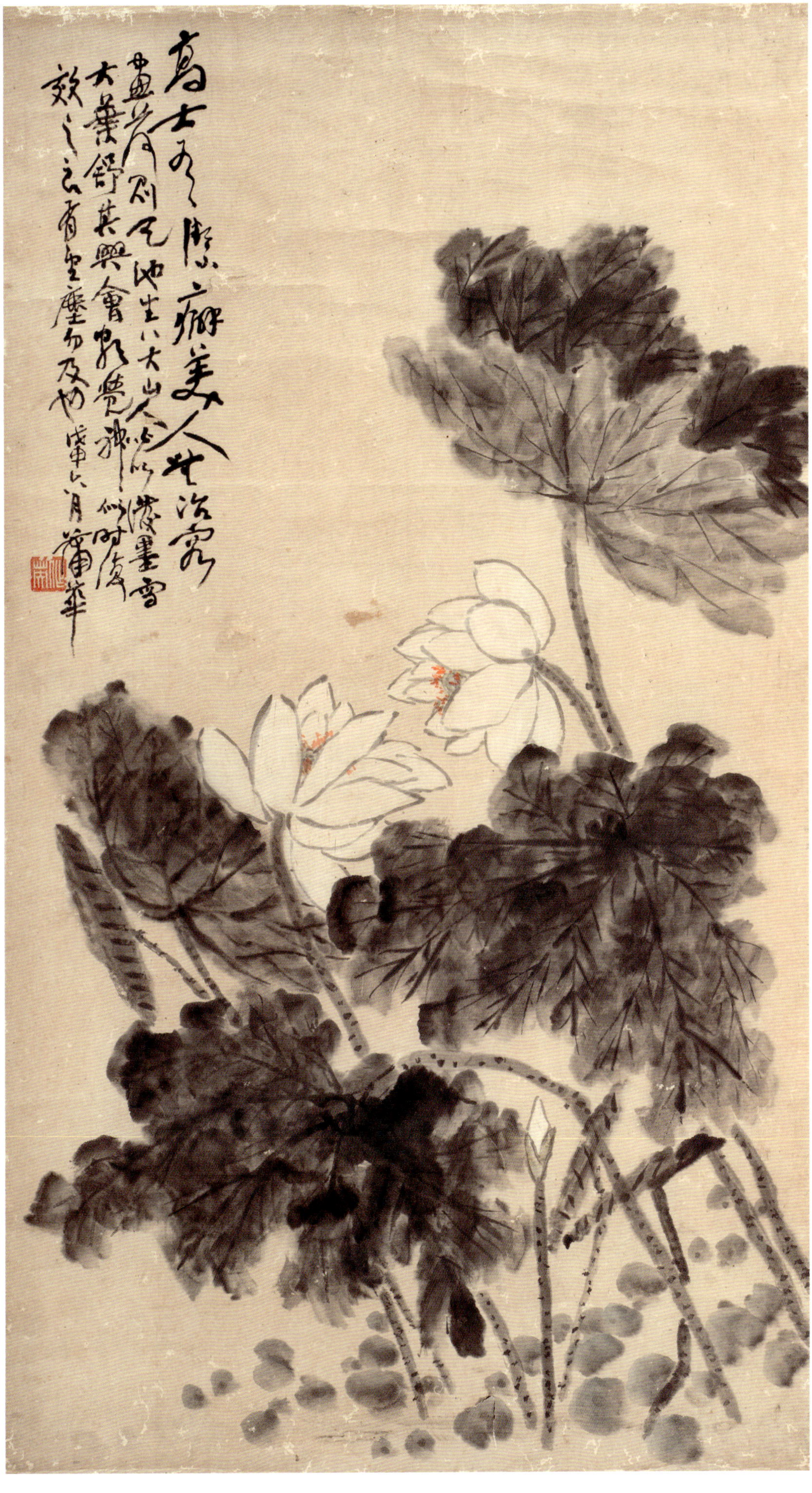

Wu Changshuo
Calligraphy work (epitaph for Pu Hua)
Ink on rice paper
Height 57cm, length 57cm
c. 1911

蒲君墓志銘

海虞沈汝瑾撰　安吉吳俊卿書並篆蓋　趙石刻

浙西山水區士多以才藝聞四方而蒲君獨落拓不得志以窮死君諱華字作英秀水人其先無攷性簡易無所不可善畫及草書尤喜畫竹諱老不蓄鬚自匿其年常以五十對寓滬上旁近有伎館伎多從學者友拉之出從圍觀嘖嘖曰某臨池某墓畫毋贗歟課讀之如嚴師少爲諸生無資貢成均遇三年試一題作二三篇不耐楷錄聽代者分與之

Qi Baishi (1864–1957)
Lichee and Dragonfly handscroll
Ink and colours on paper
Height 80cm, length 33cm
1947

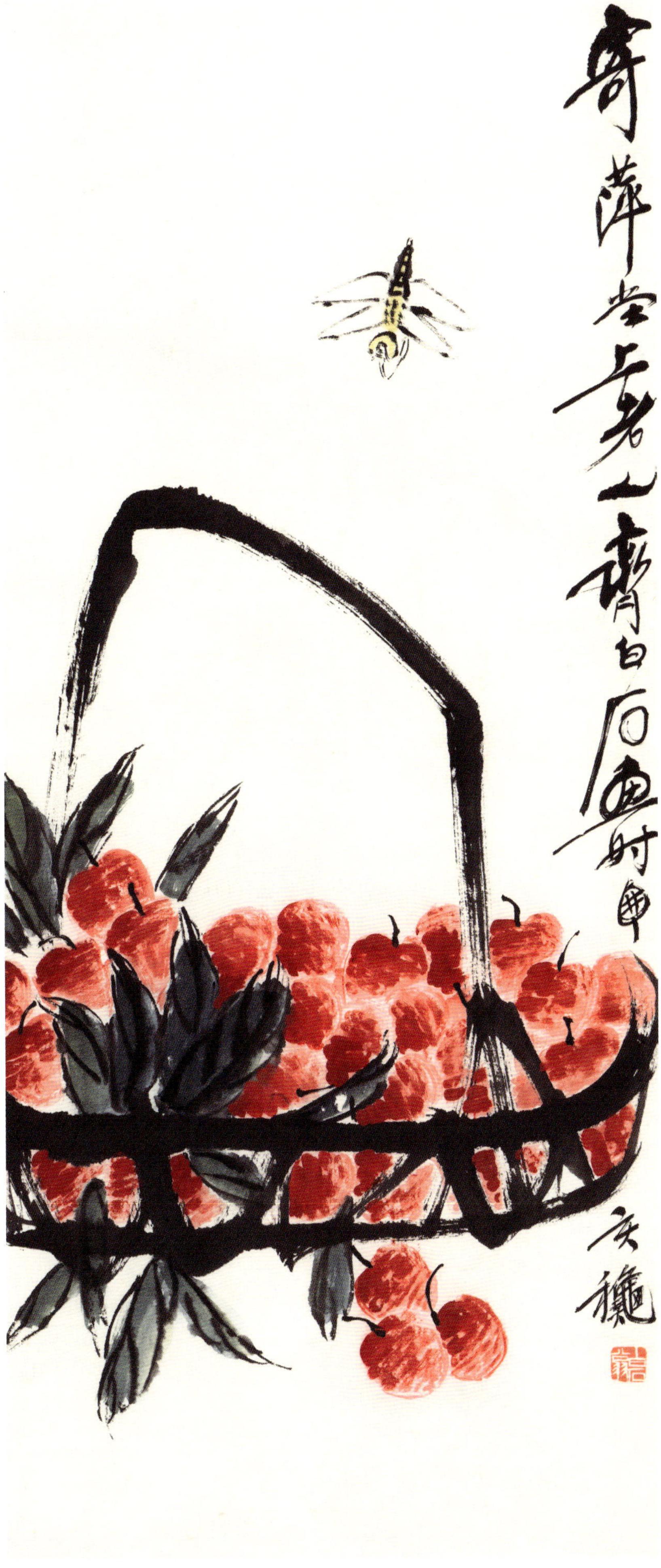

Chen Shizeng (1876–1923)
Camellia and Plum Blossom handscroll
Ink and colours on paper
Height 68cm, length 34cm
Date unknown

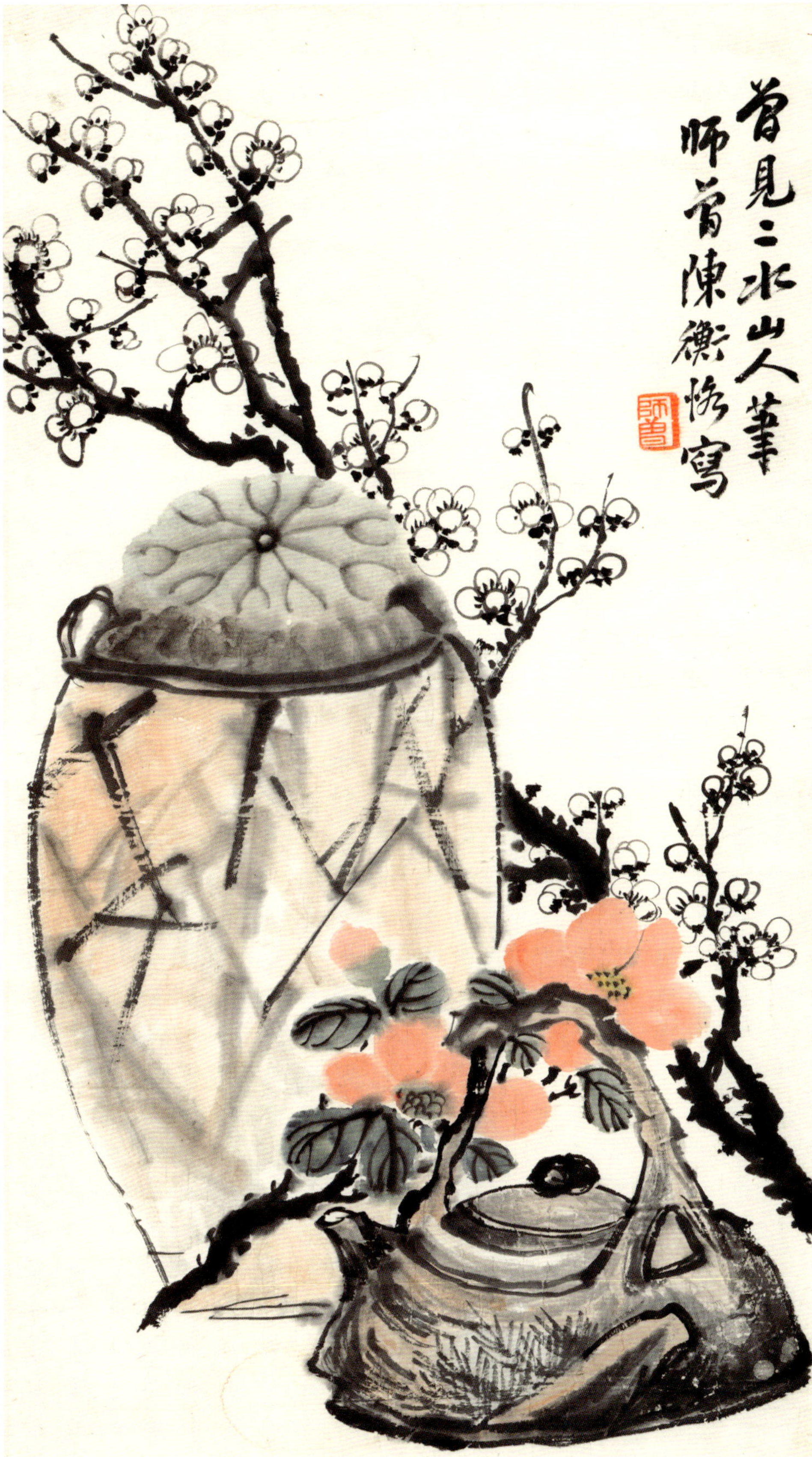
曾見二水山人筆
师曾陳衡恪寫

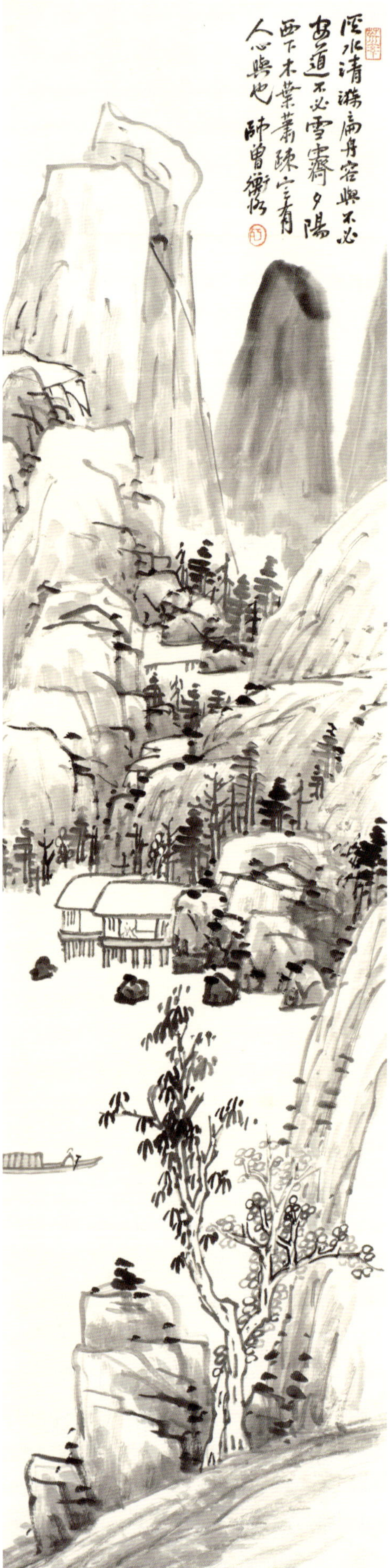
溪水清漣扁舟容與不必
安道不必雪霽夕陽
西下木葉蕭疏亦有
人心興也
師曾衡恪

Chen Shizeng
Landscape handscroll
Ink and colours on paper
Height 135cm, length 33cm
Date unknown

Zhao Guni (1879–1933)
Calligraphy handscroll (two separate works)
Ink on paper
Height 26cm, length 34cm (top);
height 31cm, length 34cm (bottom)
1930

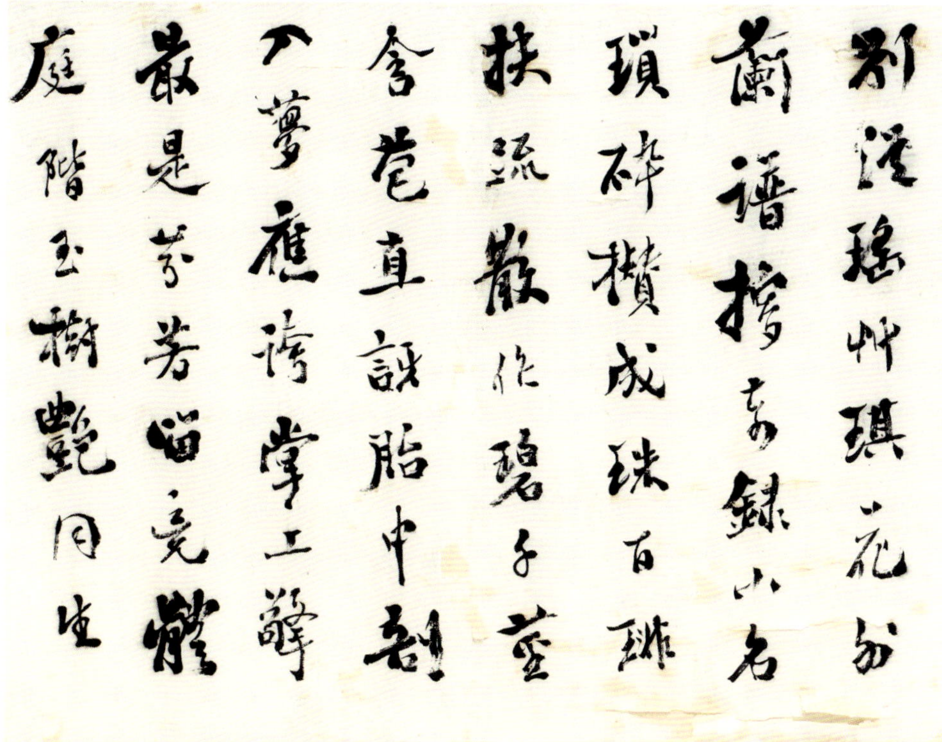

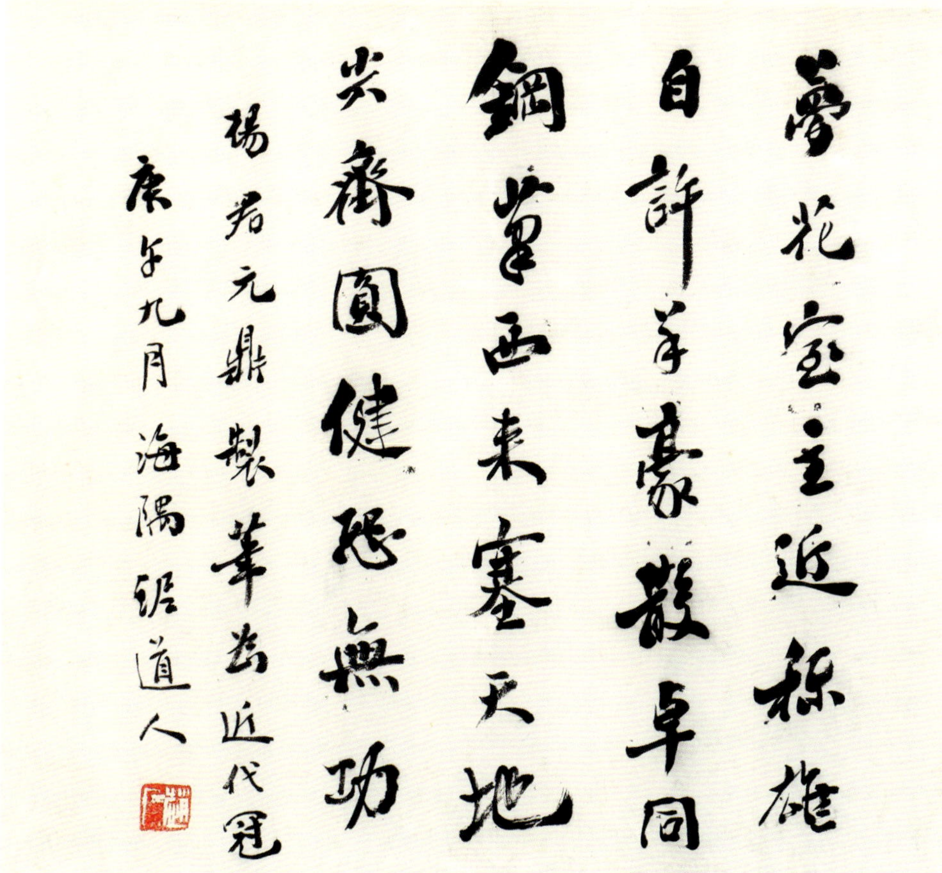
夢花室主近稱雄
自許筆豪散卓同
鋼筆西來塞天地
尖鋒圓健總無功

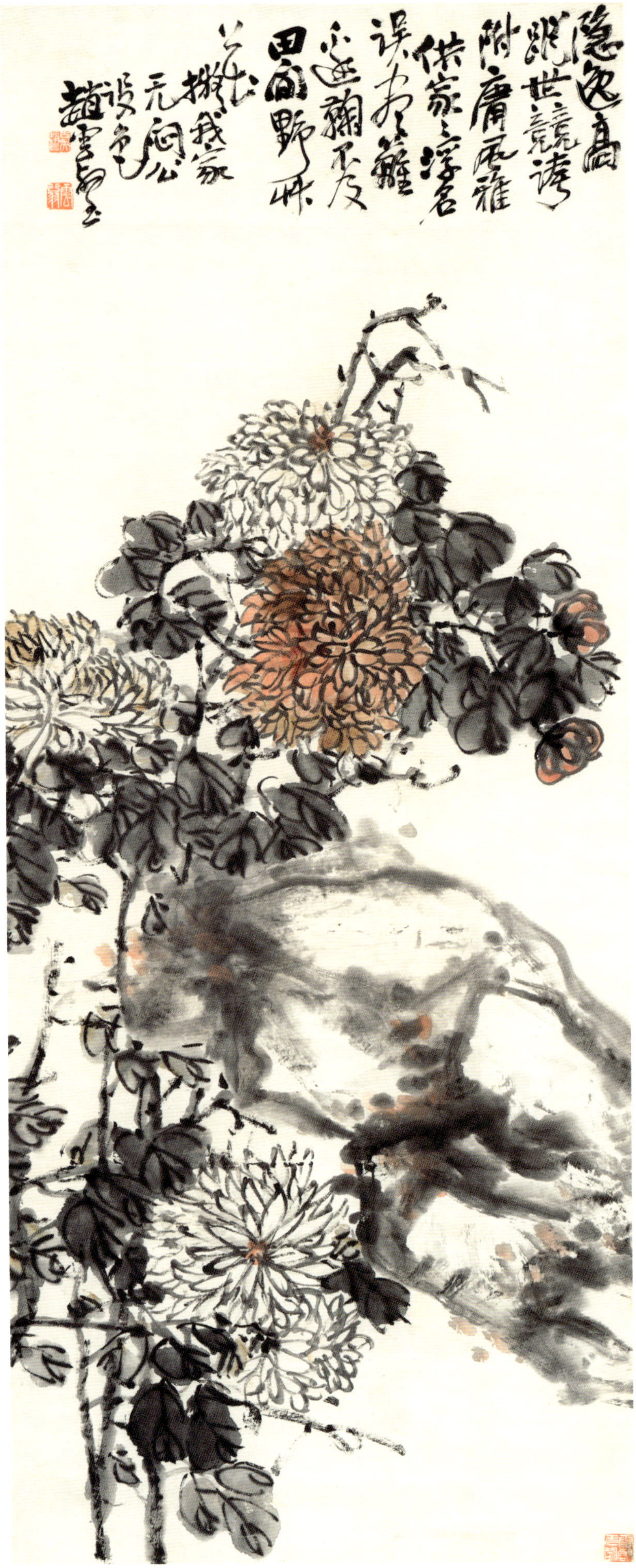

Zhao Yunhe (1874–1955)
Autumn Chrysanthemum handscroll
Ink and colours on paper
Height 119cm, length 47cm
Date unknown

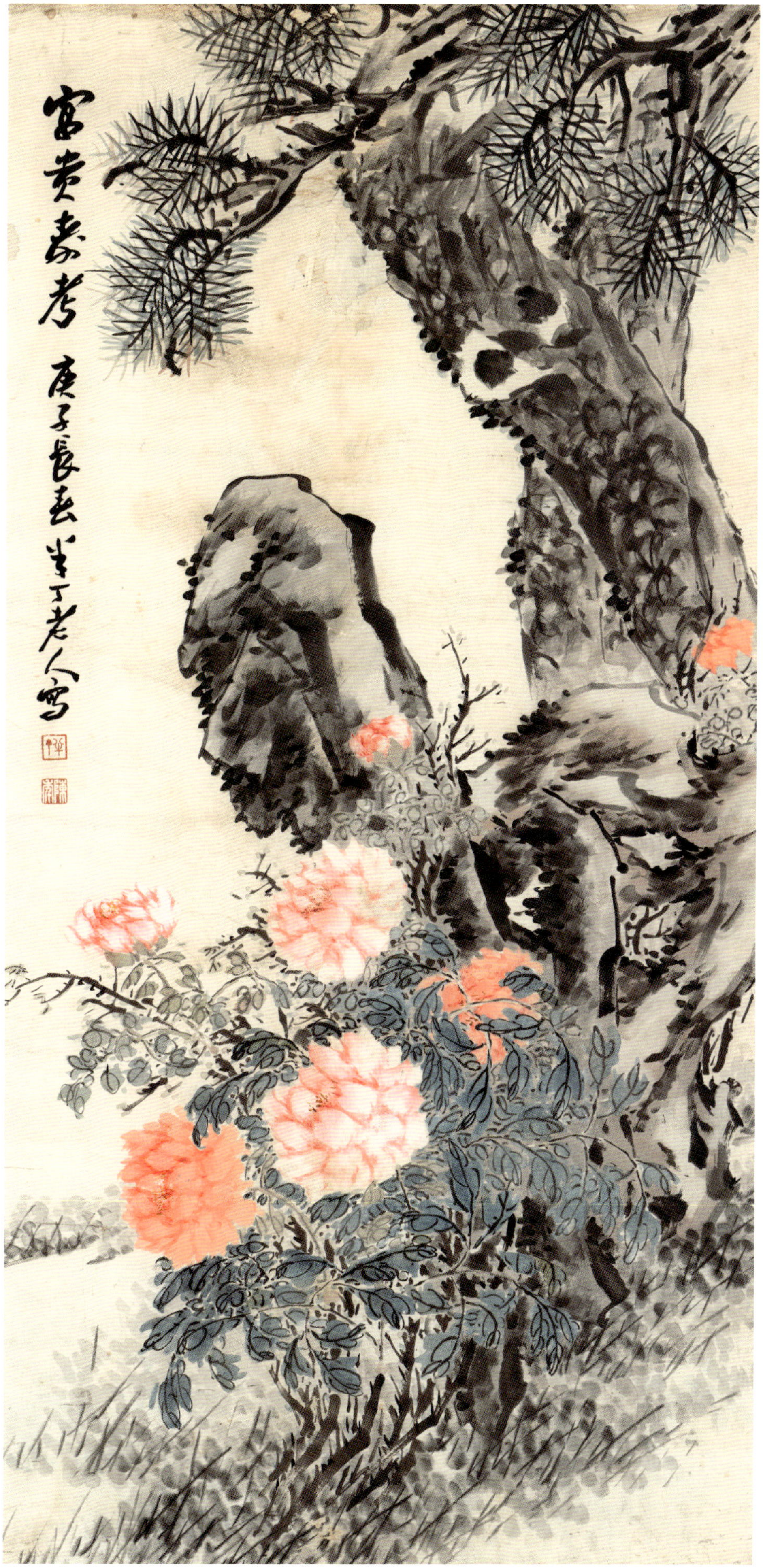

Chen Banding (1876–1970)
Wealth and Longevity handscroll
Ink and colours on paper
Height 142cm, length 67cm
1960

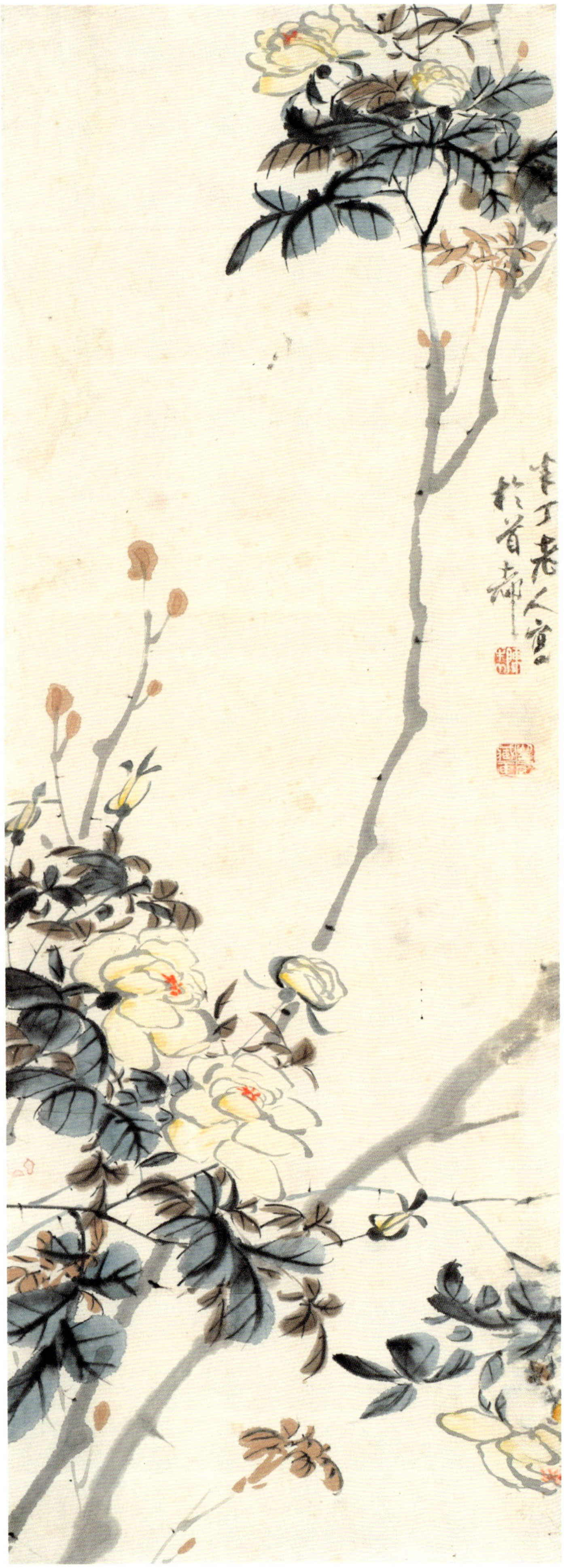

Chen Banding
Rose handscroll
Ink and colours on paper
Height 81cm, length 29cm
Date unknown

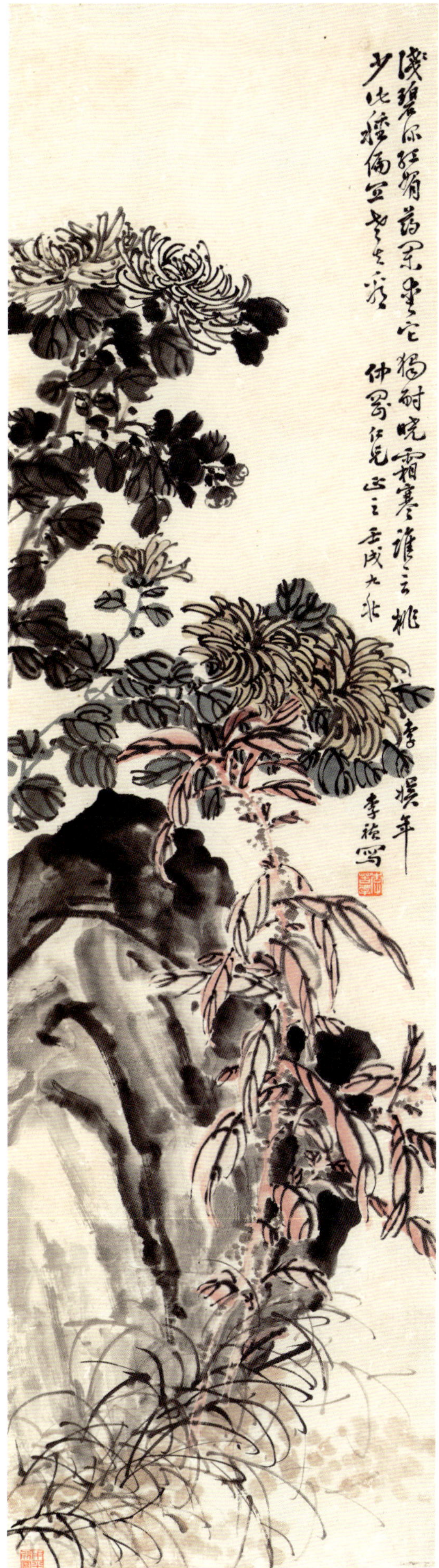

Li Kuli (1877–1929)
Chrysanthemum handscroll
Ink and colours on paper
Height 147cm, length 40cm
1922

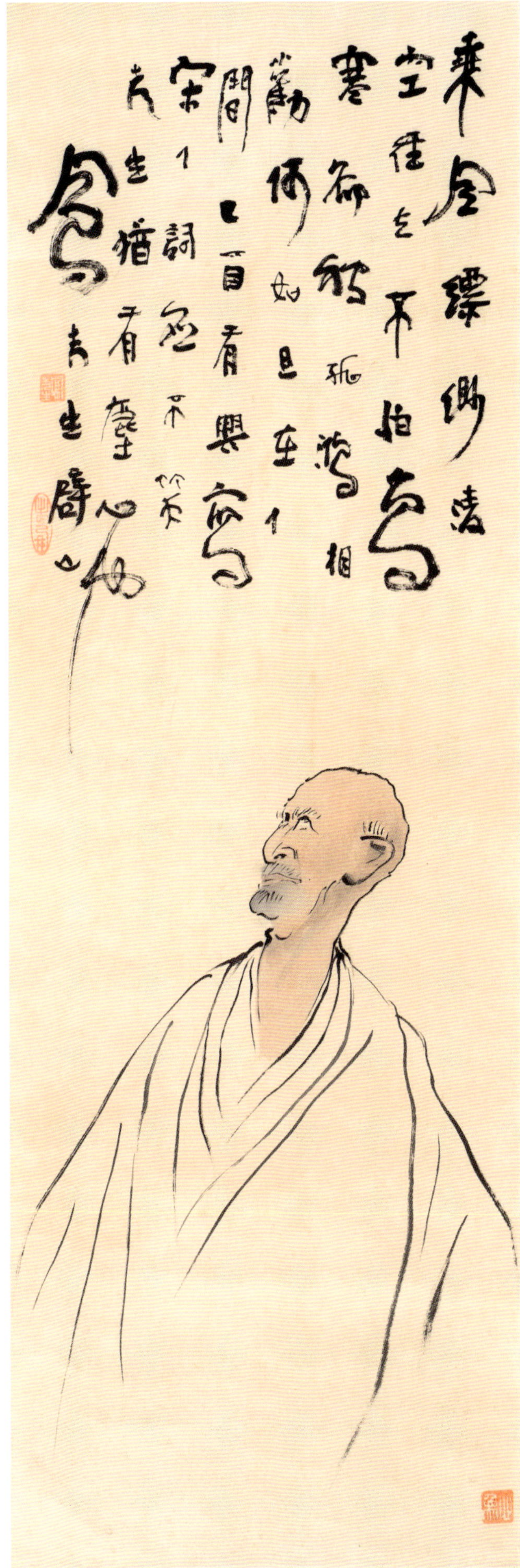

Lǚ Fengzi (1886–1959)
Buddhist Arhat handscroll
Ink and colours on paper
Height 100cm, length 32cm
Date unknown

Liu Haisu (1896–1994)
Two Ducks handscroll
Ink and colours on paper
Height 30cm, length 33cm (top);
height 32cm, length 42cm (bottom)
1936

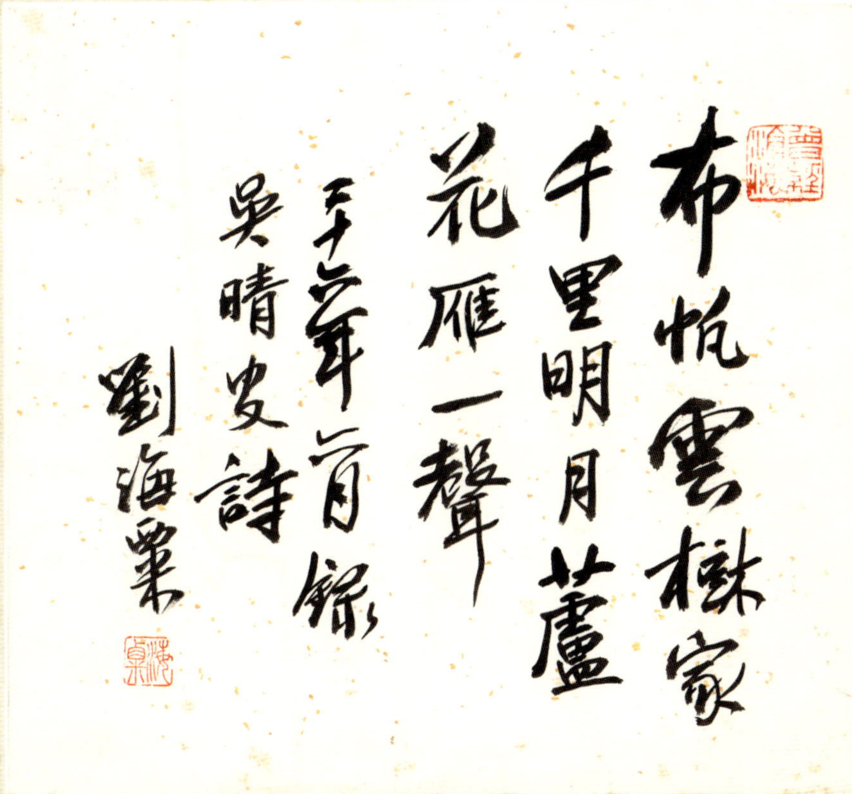
布帆雲樹家
千里明月蘆
花雁一聲
吳晴史詩
劉海粟

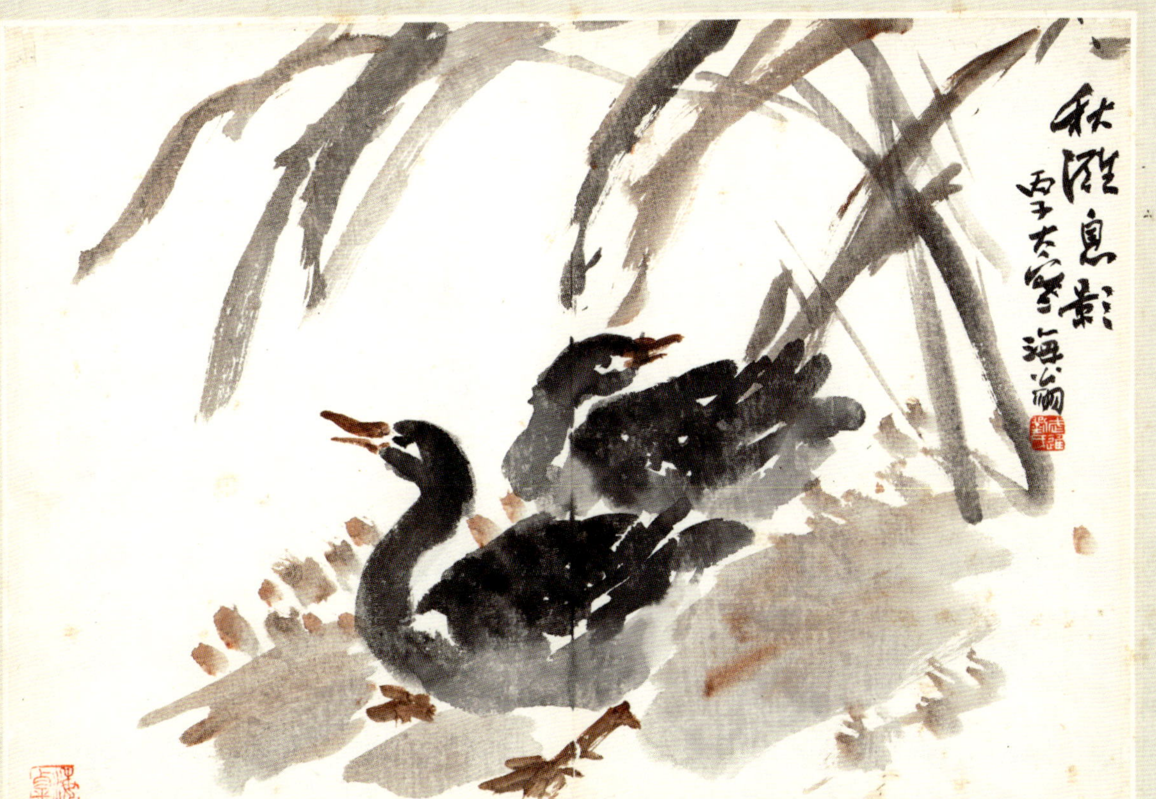
秋灘息影
海翁

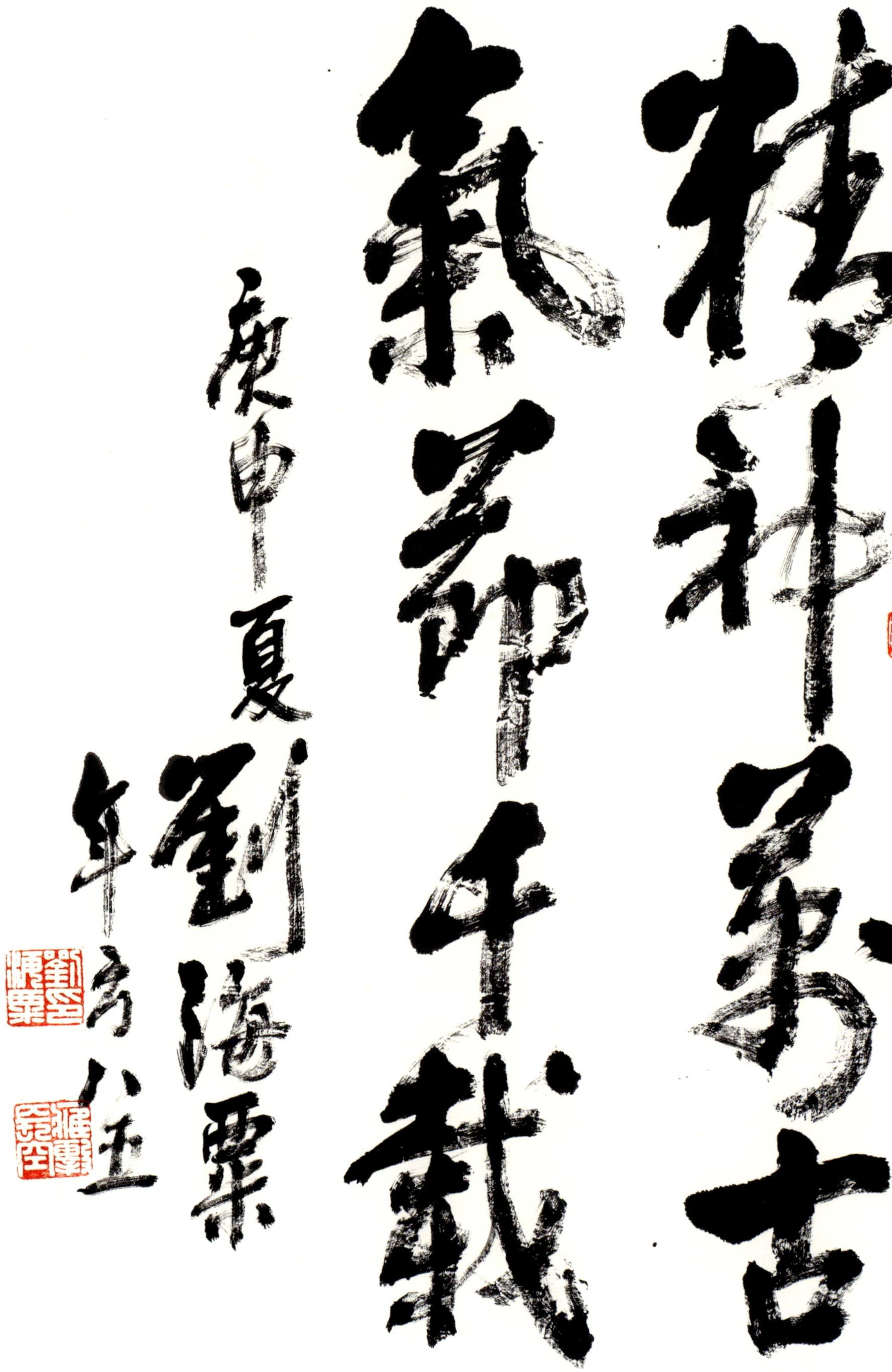
精神萬古
氣節千載
庚申夏
劉海粟
年方八五

Liu Haisu

'Noble spirit lasts forever', calligraphy handscroll (Ziyun Pavilion)
Ink on paper
Height 99cm, length 65cm
1980

Painted by Zhang Tianqi (1901–83) and Zhu Wenyun (1895–1939)
Inscribed by Pan Tianshou (1897–1971)
Birds handscroll
Ink on rice paper
Height 136cm, length 34cm
1925

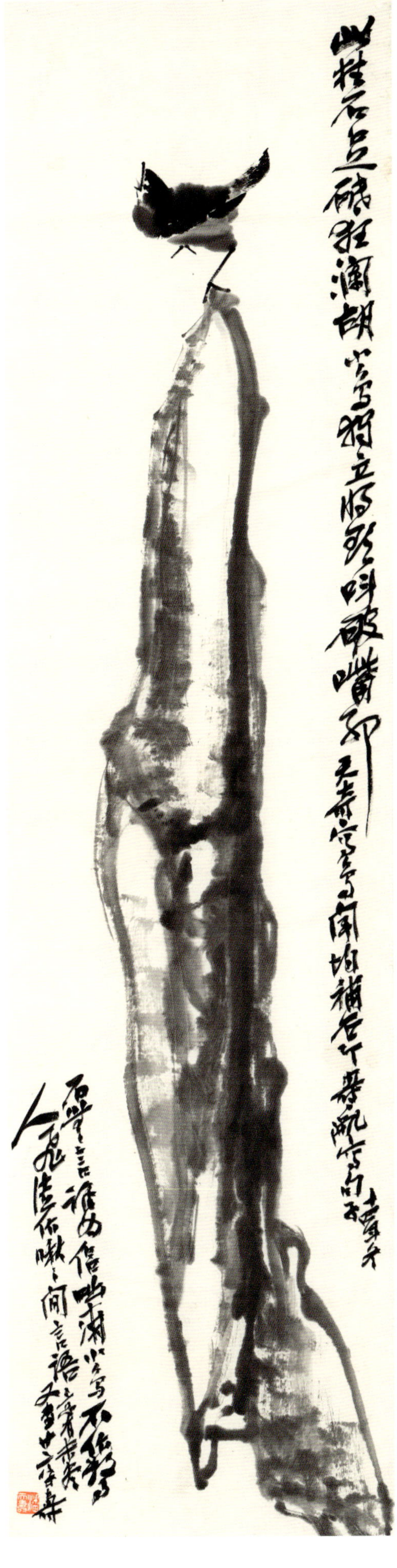

Painted by Xie Gongzhan (1885–1940), Xie Jiezi (1898–1930), Zheng Wuchang (1894–1952), Pan Tianshou, Gao Jianfu (1879–1951) and Ma Mengrong (1890–1932)
Inscribed by Zheng Manqing (1901–75)

Aquatic Animals handscroll
Ink and colours on paper
Height 92cm, length 43cm
1930

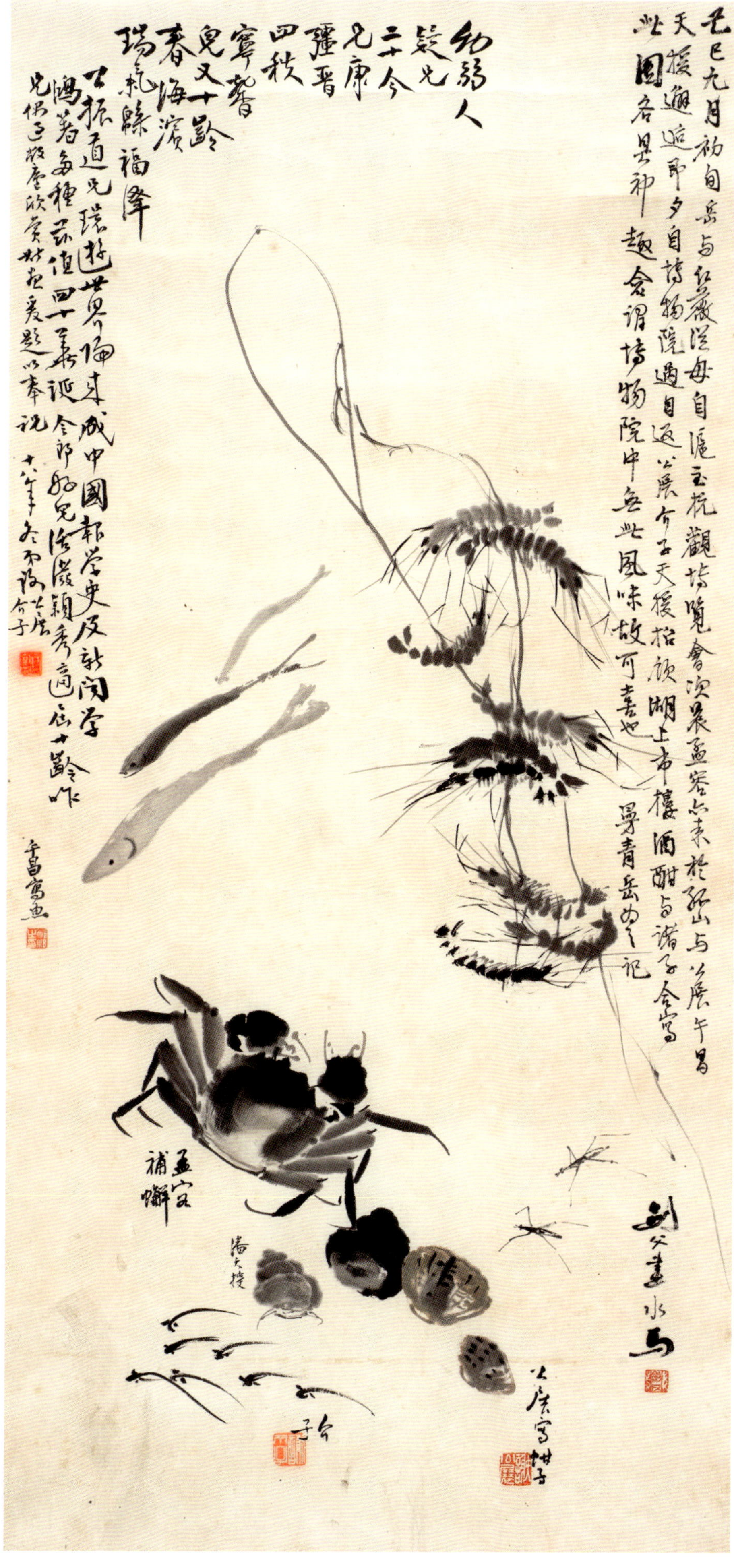

Qian Shoutie (1897–1967)
Bizarre Landscape handscroll
Ink on paper
Height 49cm, length 56cm
Date unknown

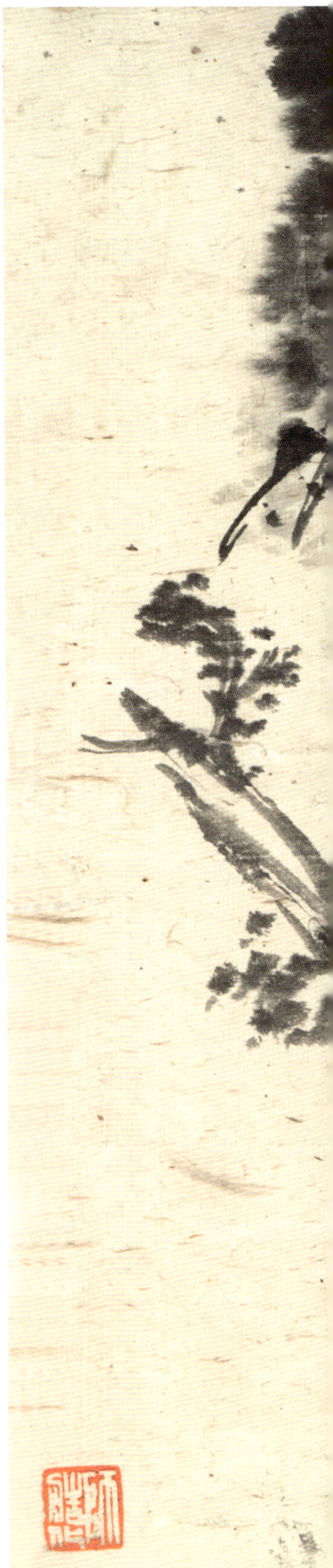

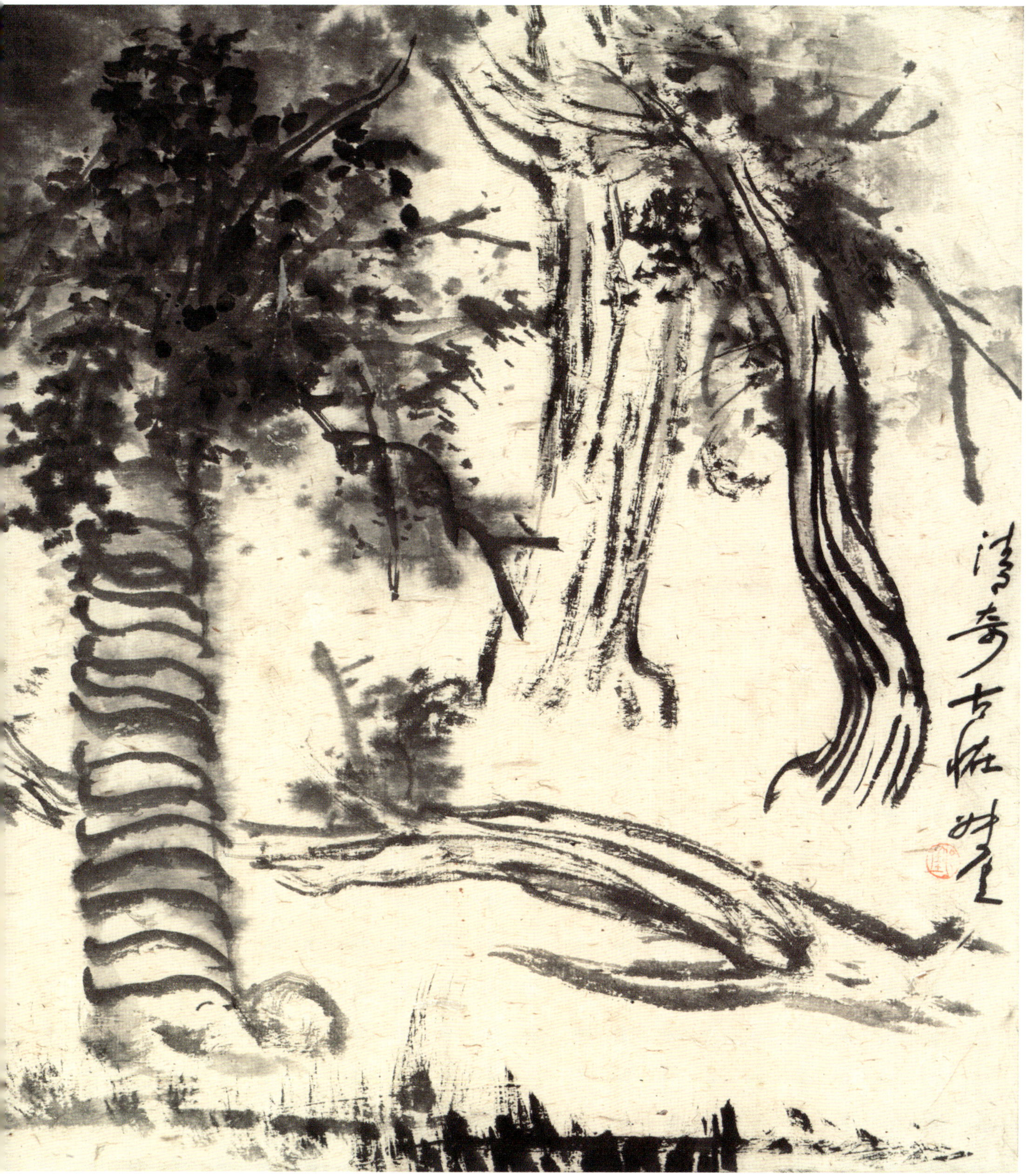

Qian Shoutie
Red Plum handscroll
Ink and colours on paper
Height 47cm, length 25cm
Date unknown

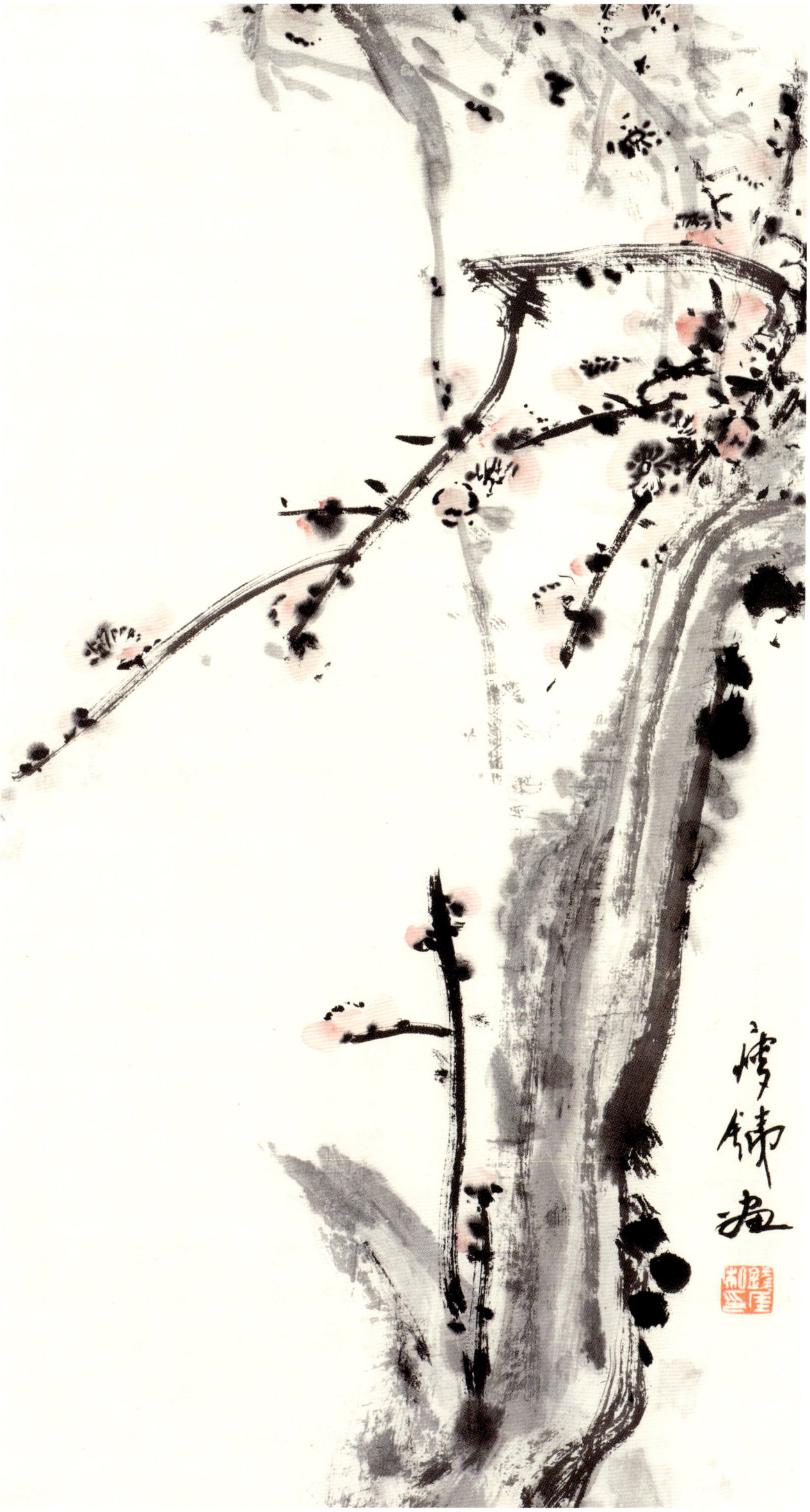

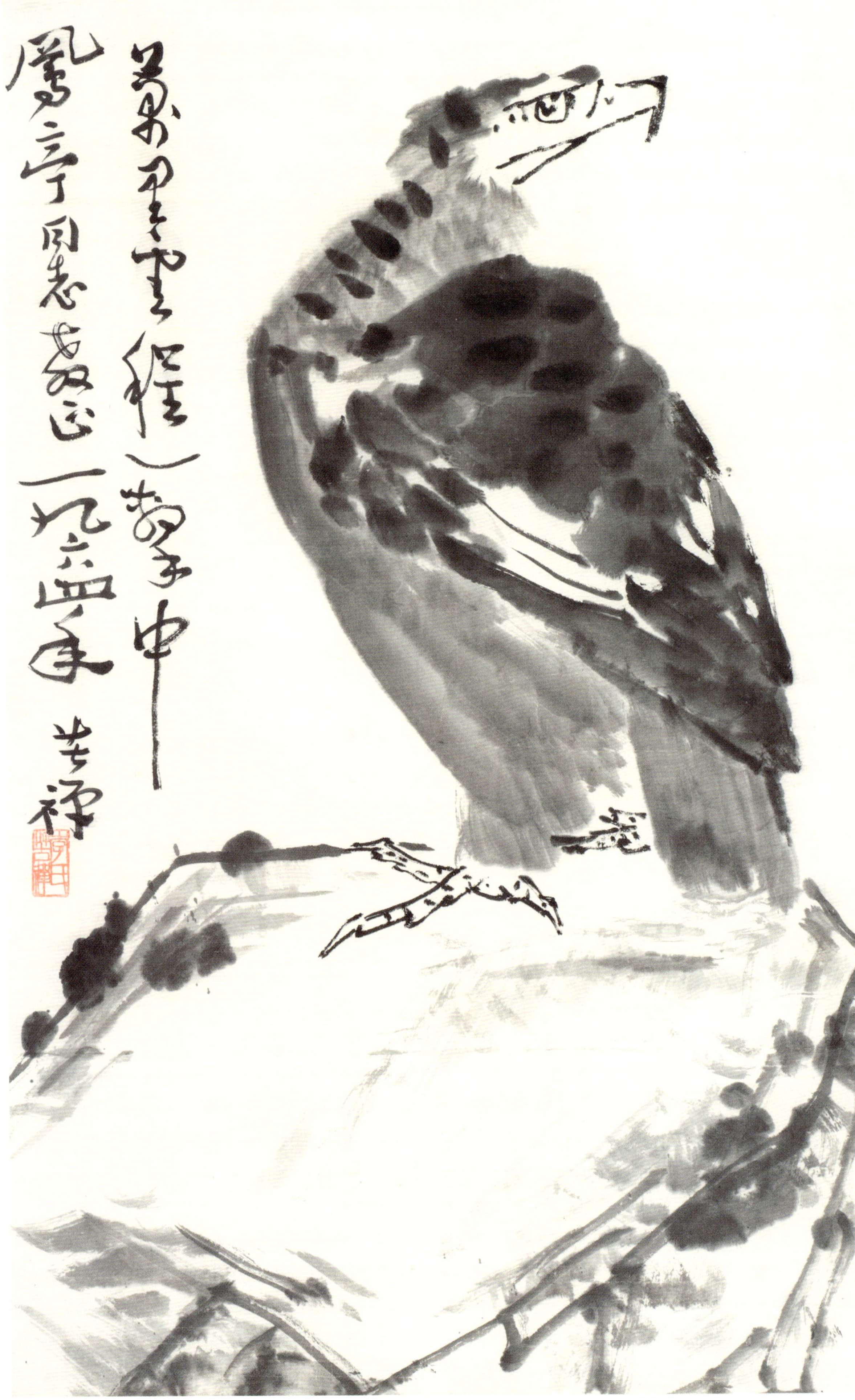

Li Kuchan (1899–1983)
Eagle handscroll
Ink and colours on paper
Height 83cm, length 50cm
1964

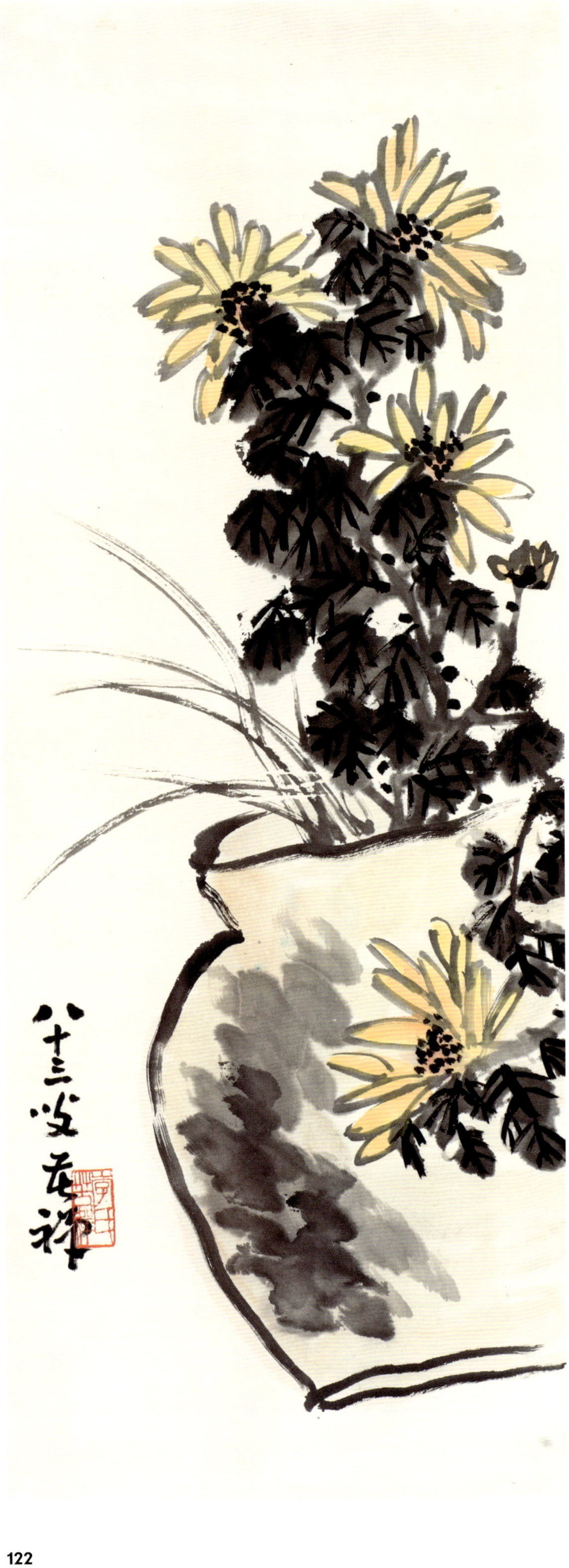

Li Kuchan
Chrysanthemum handscroll
Ink and colours on paper
Height 90cm, length 33cm
1982

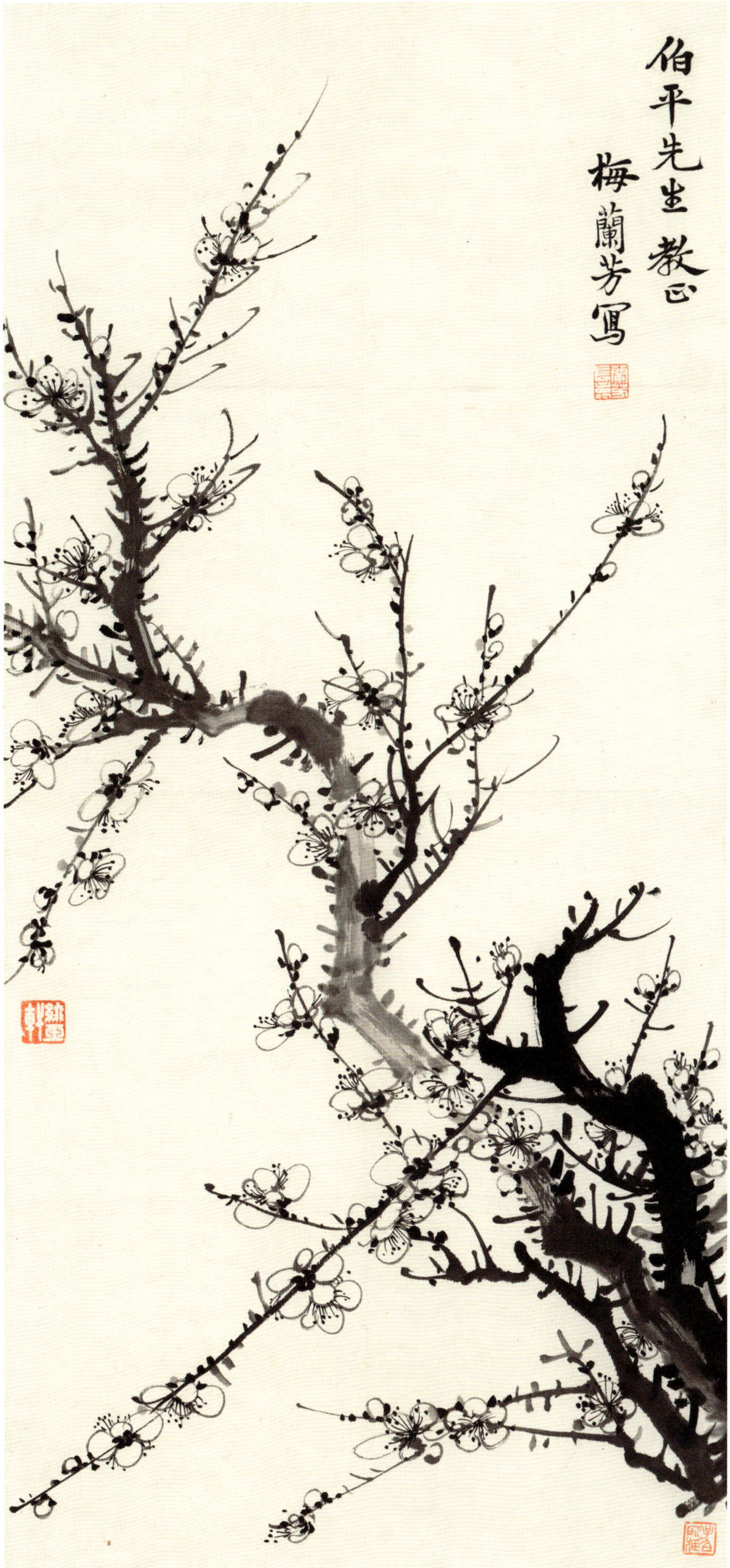

Mei Lanfang (1894–1961)
Plum Blossom handscroll
Ink and colours on paper
Height 72cm, length 33cm
Date unknown

Mr. Mei Lanfang is a great master of Peking opera. At the young age of 20, Mei Lanfang performed in Shanghai for the first time, during which he became acquainted with Wu Changshuo who was at that time, 70 years old. They cultivated a profound friendship despite their large age difference. Whenever Mei Lanfang performed in southern regions of China, he never missed the chance to consult with Wu Changshuo on painting techniques. Although he didn't take up an apprenticeship with Wu Changshuo, he always considered him as his master.

Wu Hufan (1894–1968)
Coloured Landscape handscroll
Ink and colours on paper
Height 61cm, length 40cm
1926

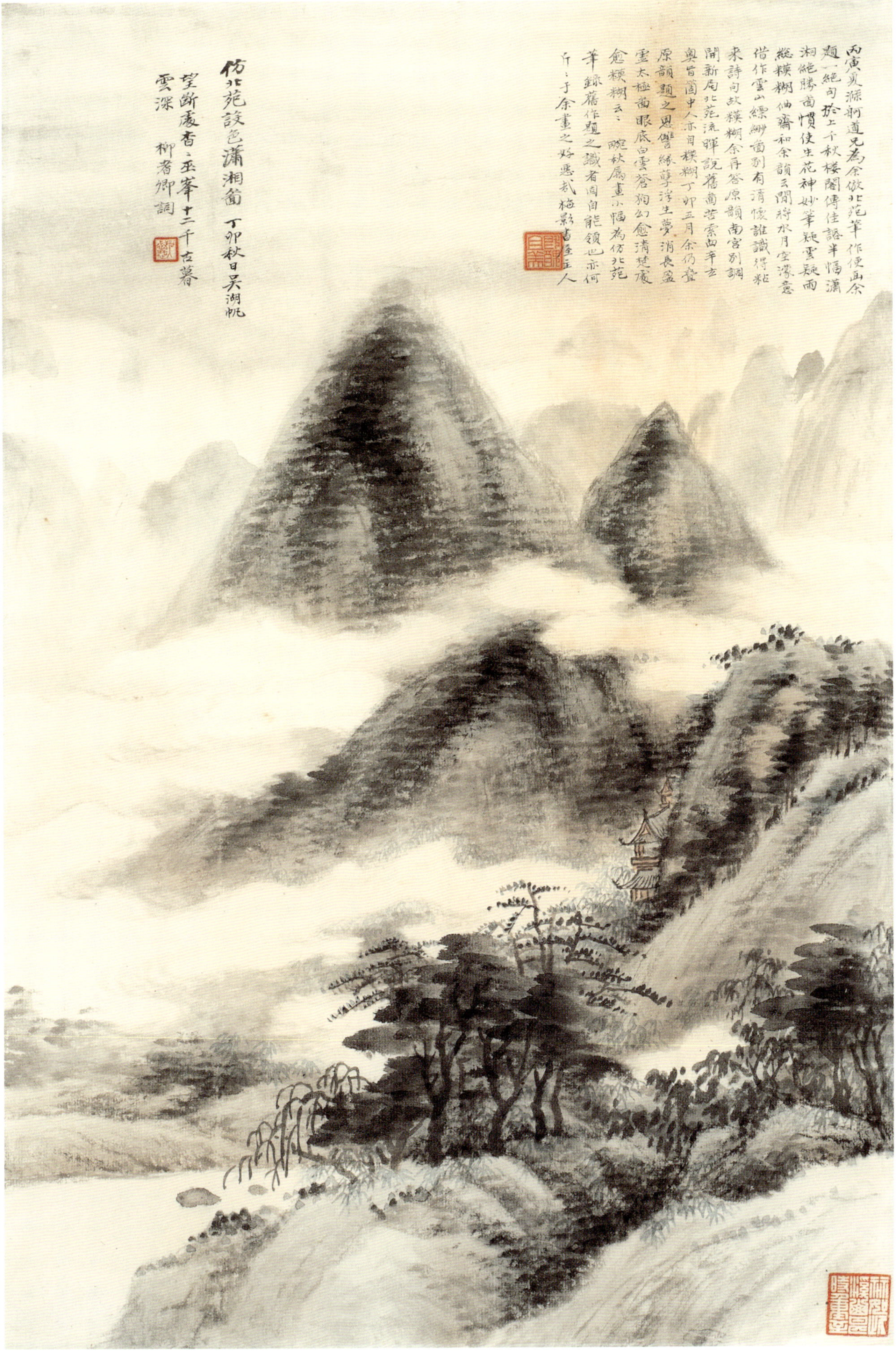
仿北苑設色瀟湘圖 丁卯秋日吳湖帆

花傍瑤林浥露多

吳湖帆

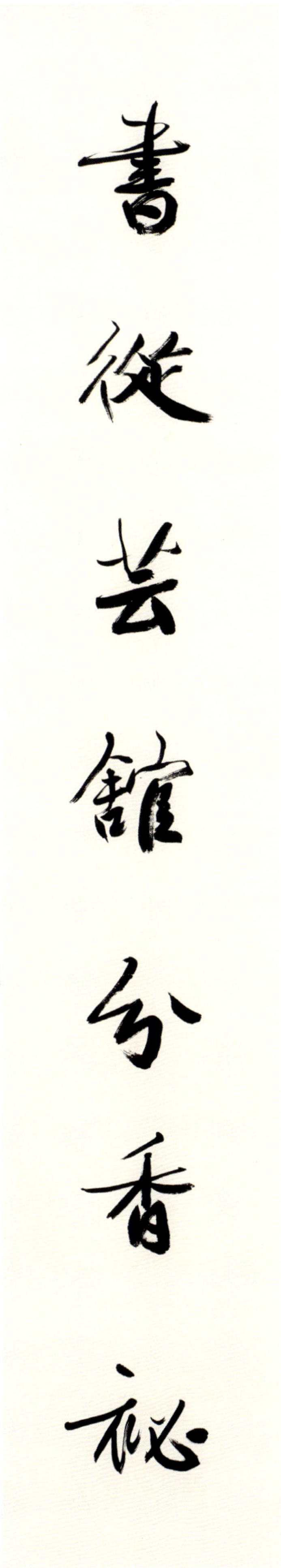

Wu Hufan

Calligraphic couplet
(seven Chinese characters on each piece of rice paper)
Ink on rice paper
Height 146cm, length 26cm
Date unknown

Zhang Daqian (1899–1983)
Layered Stones and Chinese Cherry Apple Flower handscroll
Ink and colours on paper
Height 137cm, length 36cm
1921

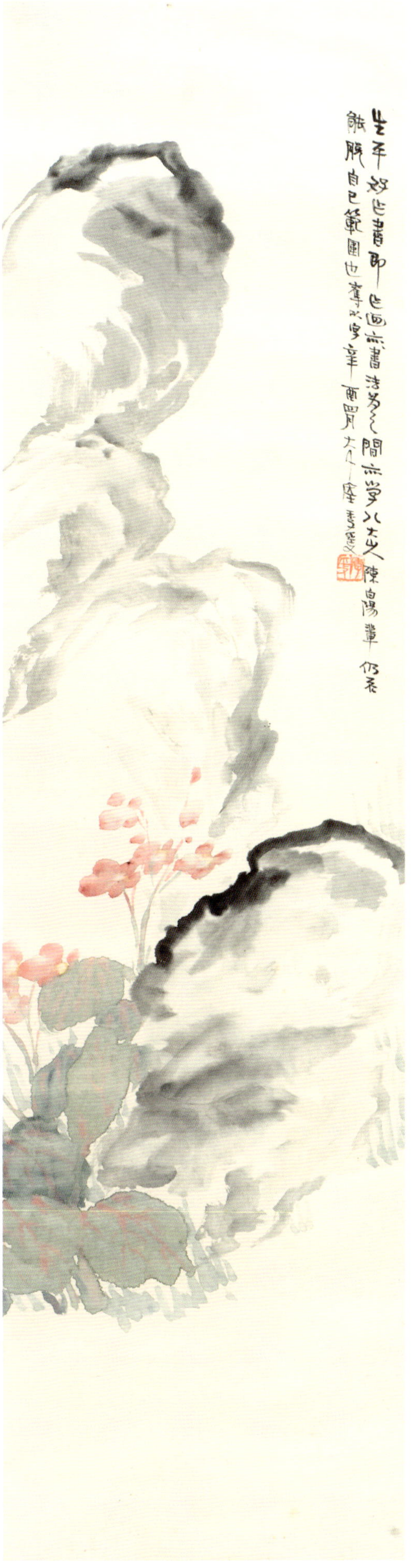

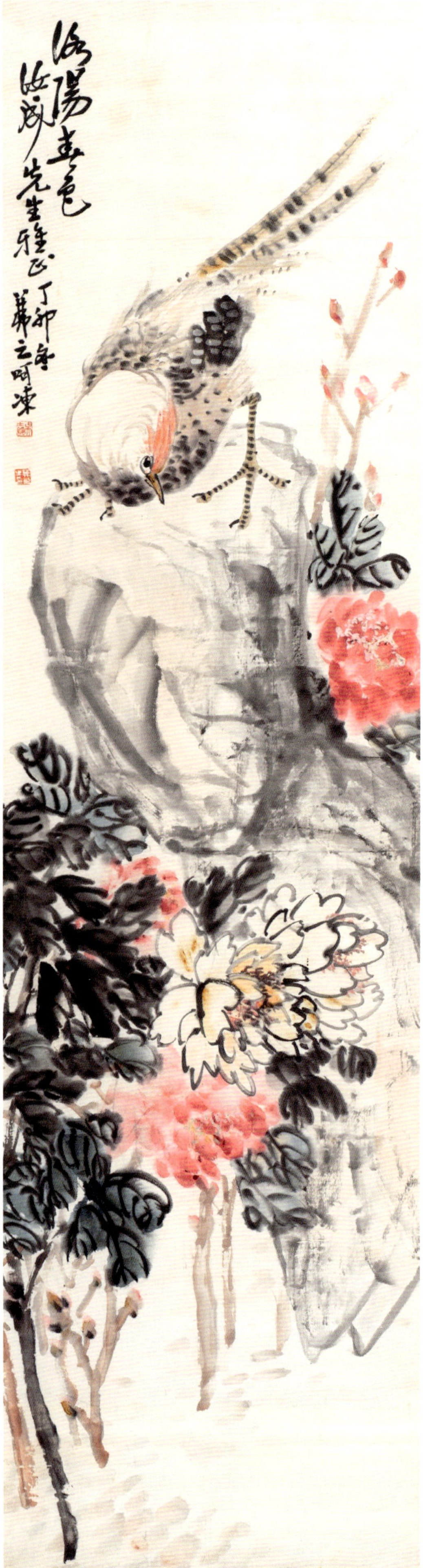

Wu Fuzhi (1900–77)
Peony handscroll
Ink and colours on paper
Height 149cm, length 40cm
1927

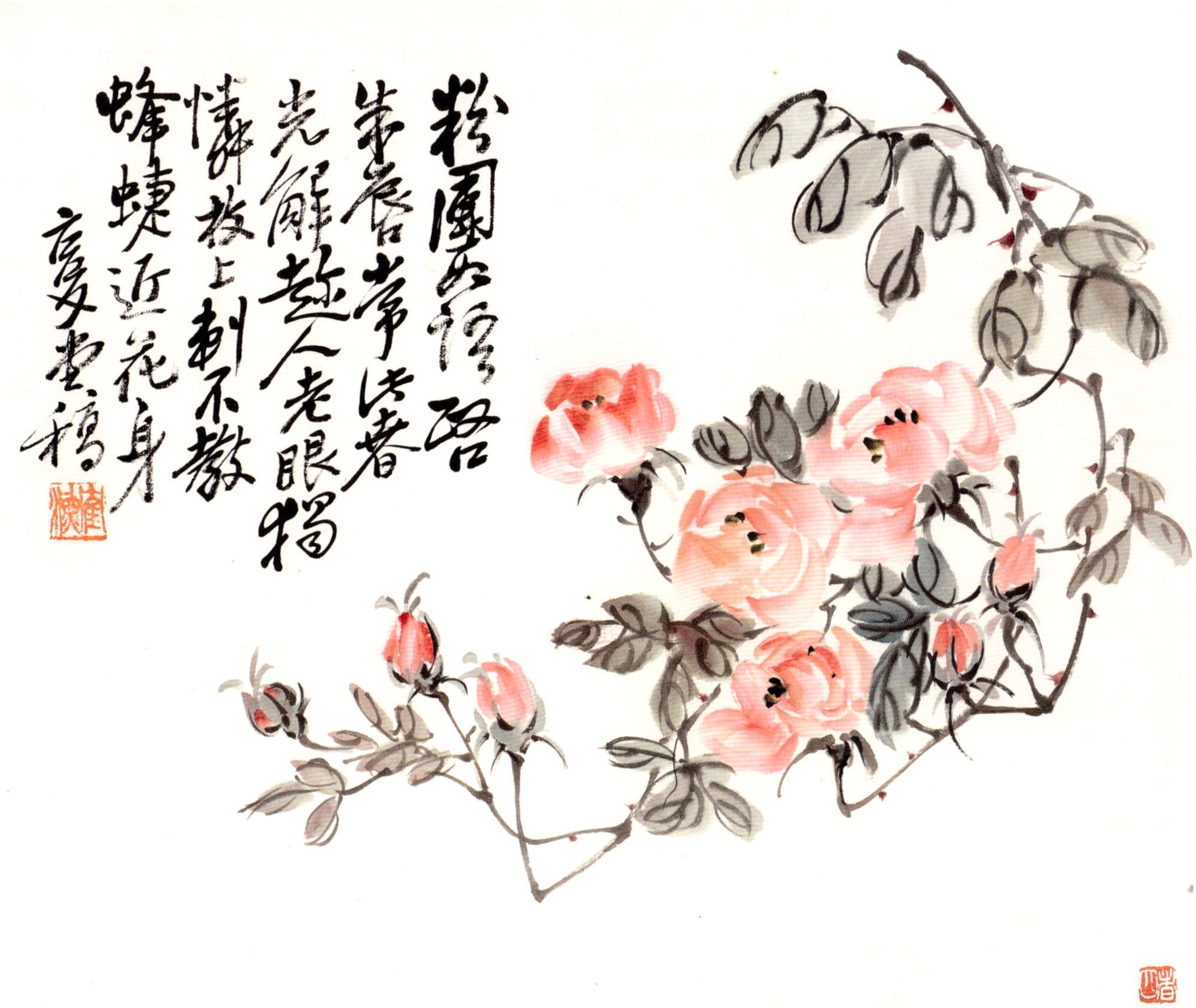

Zhu Lesan (1902–84)
Red Rose handscroll
Ink and colours on paper
Height 28cm, length 34cm
Date unknown

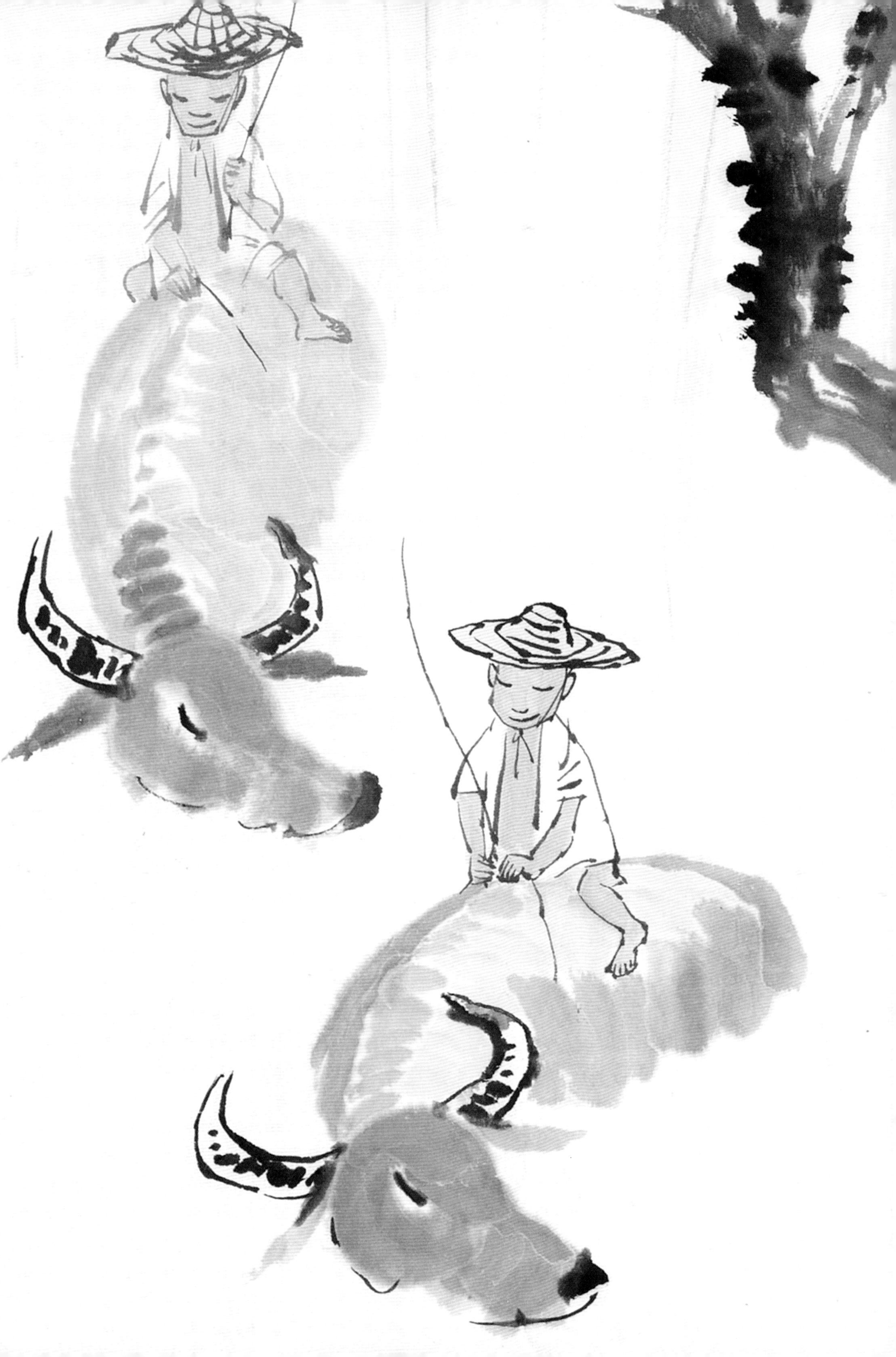

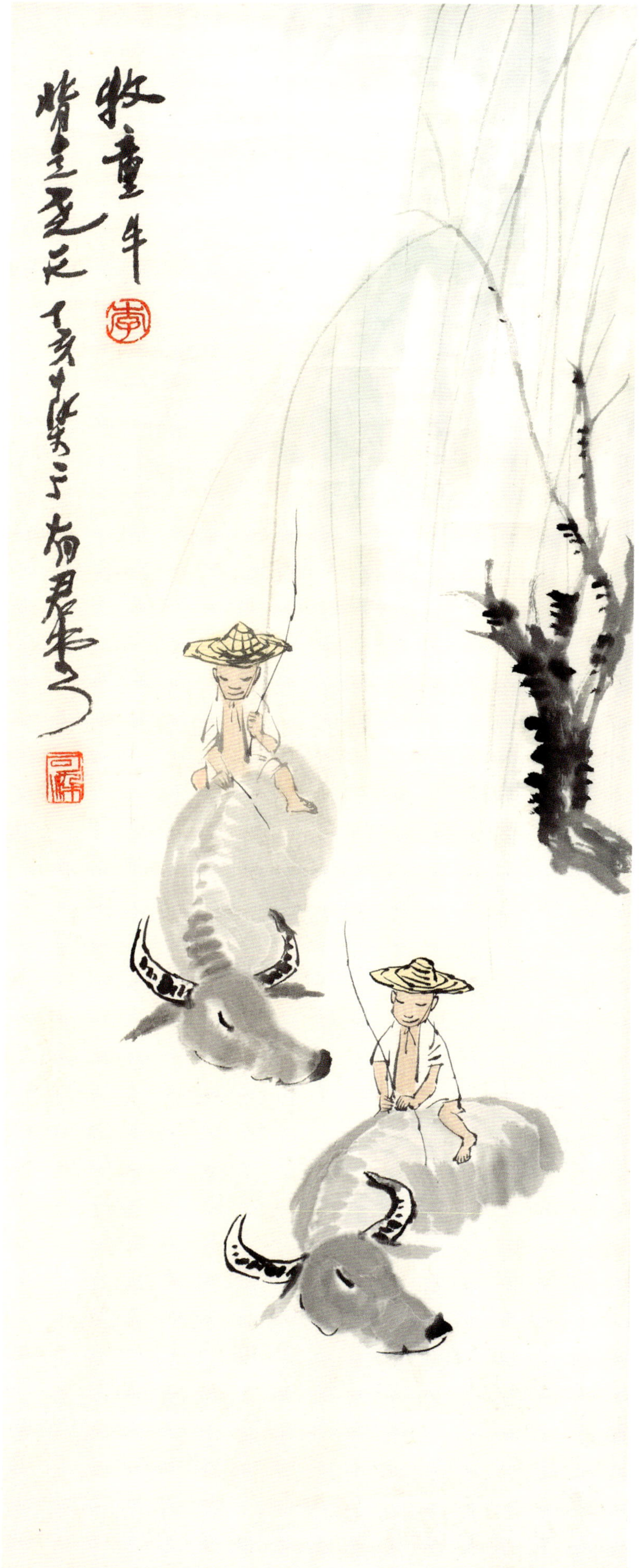

Li Keran (1907–89)
Cowboy Grazing Cattle handscroll
Ink and colours on paper
Height 80cm, length 32cm
1947

Li Keran

'Savouring the way with a pure mind' calligraphy handscroll

Ink on paper

Height 47cm, length 63cm

1984

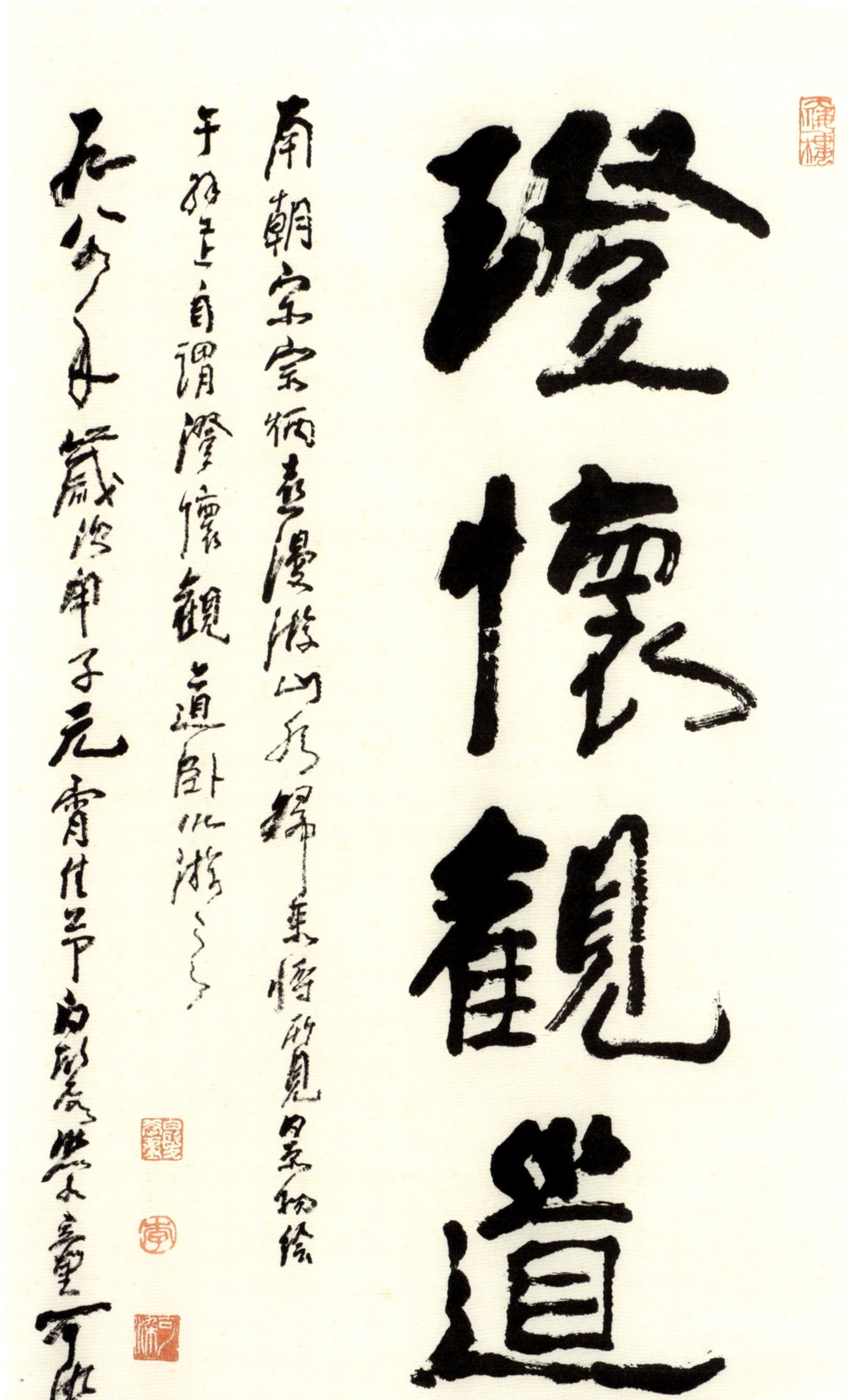
澄懷觀道

Lu Yanshao (1909–93)
Coloured Landscape vertical handscroll
Ink and colours on paper
Height 70cm, length 45cm
1982

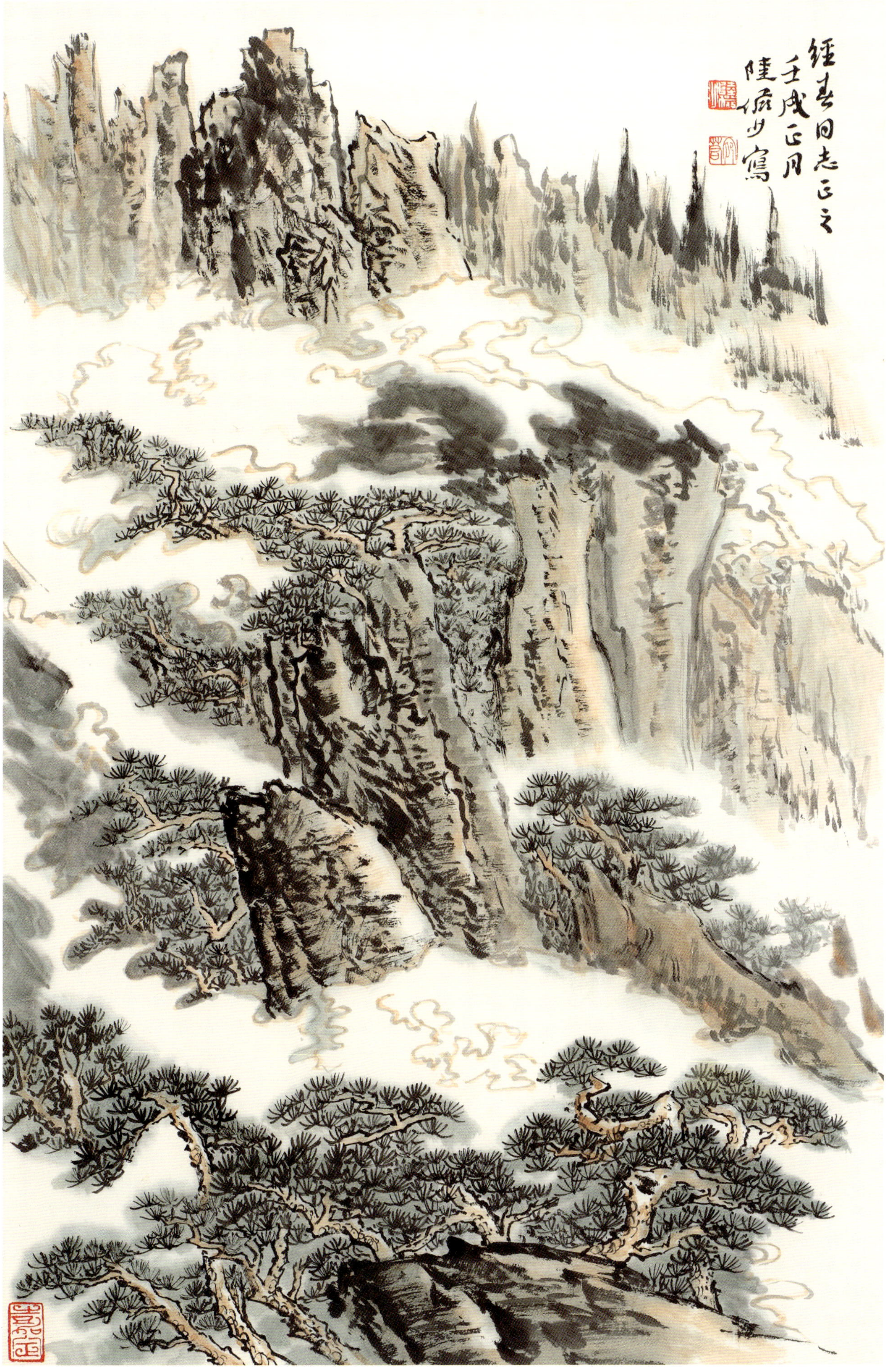
壬戌正月
陸儼少寫

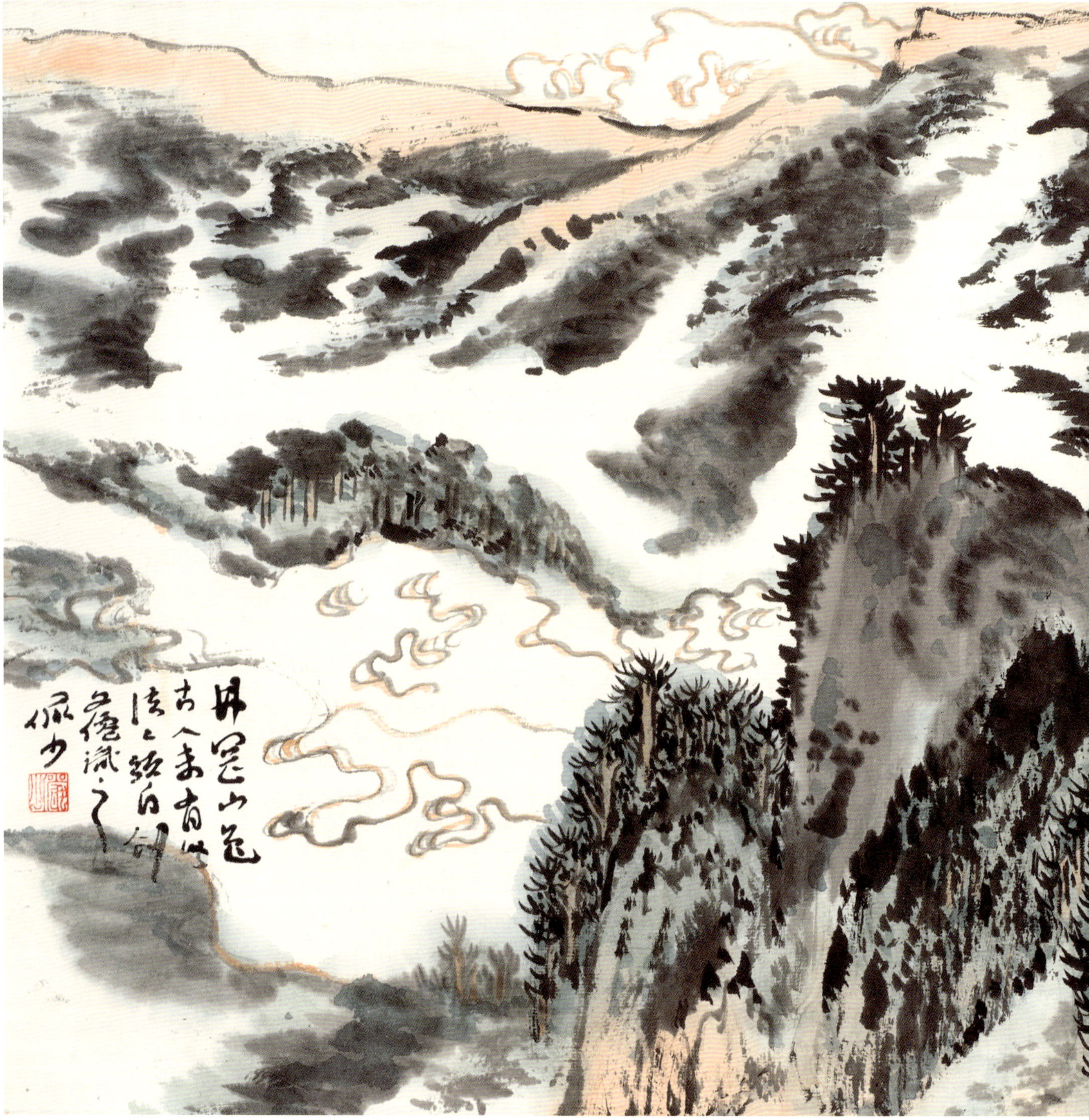

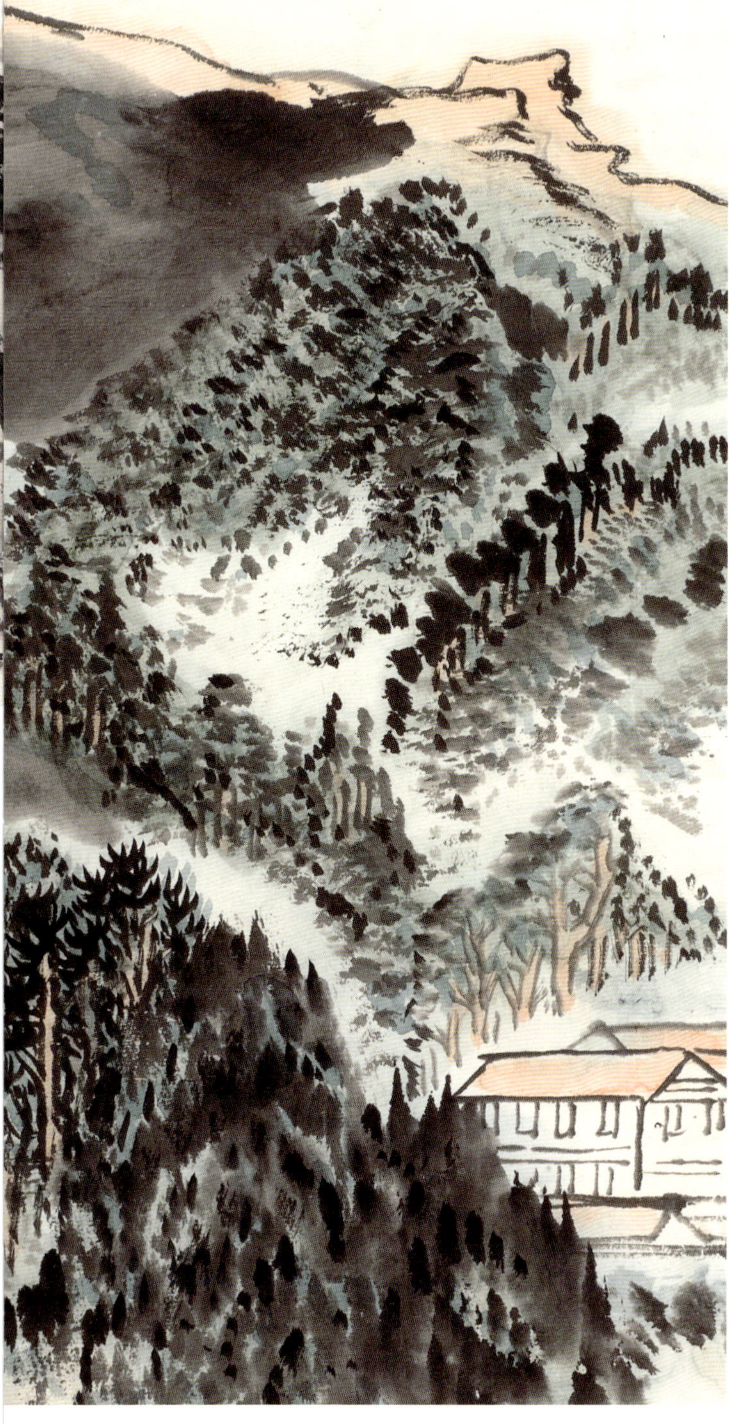

Lu Yanshao
Coloured Landscape horizontal handscroll
Ink and colours on paper
Height 34cm, length 53cm
Date unknown

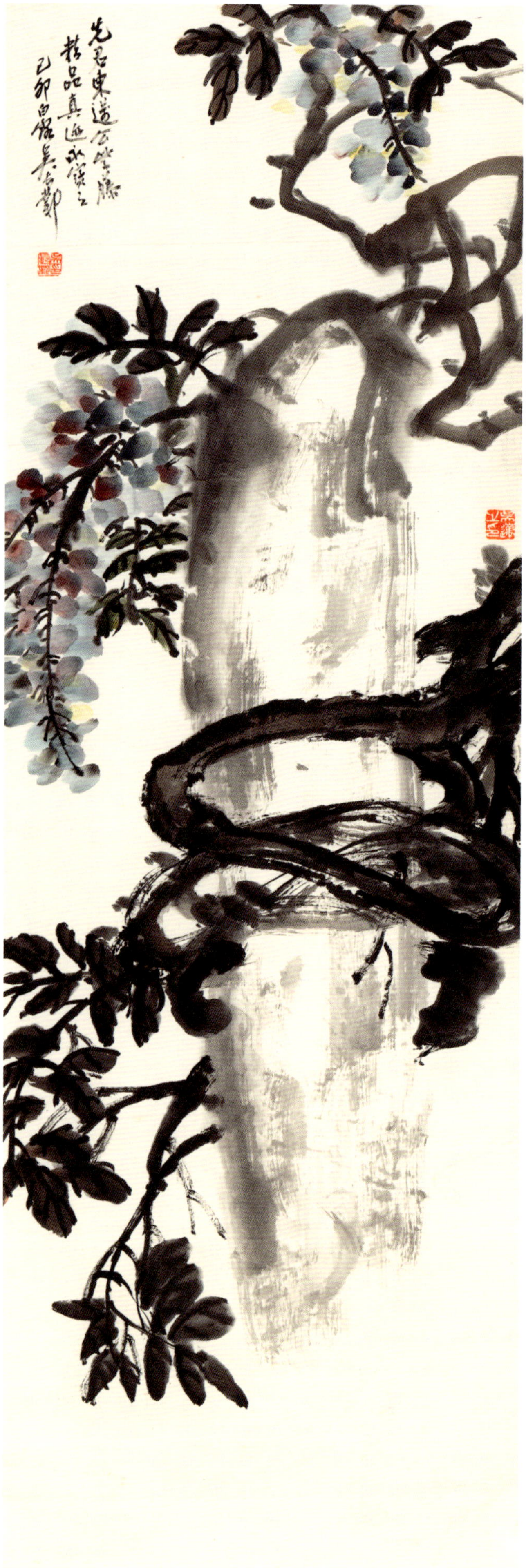

Wu Dongmai (1886–1963)
Wisteria handscroll
Ink and colours on paper
Height 104cm, length 34cm
1939

Wu Han (1876–1927), **Liu Shannong** (1878–1932), **Wu Dongmai and Zhu Wenyun**
Chrysanthemum handscroll
Ink and colours on paper
Height 130cm, length 40cm
Date unknown

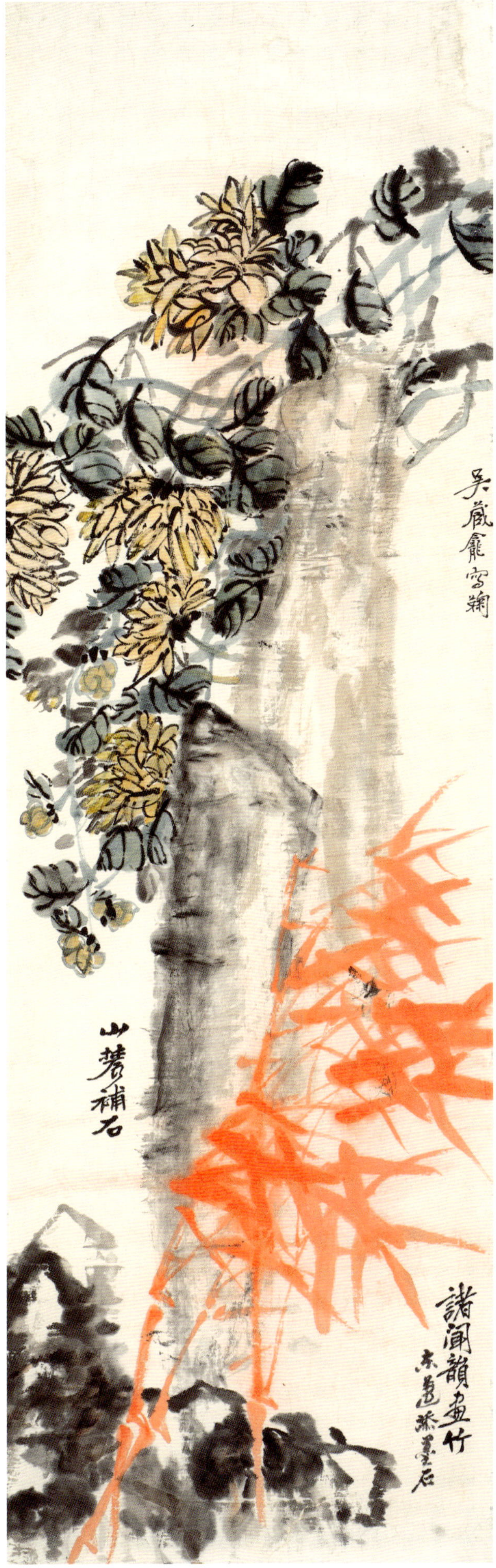

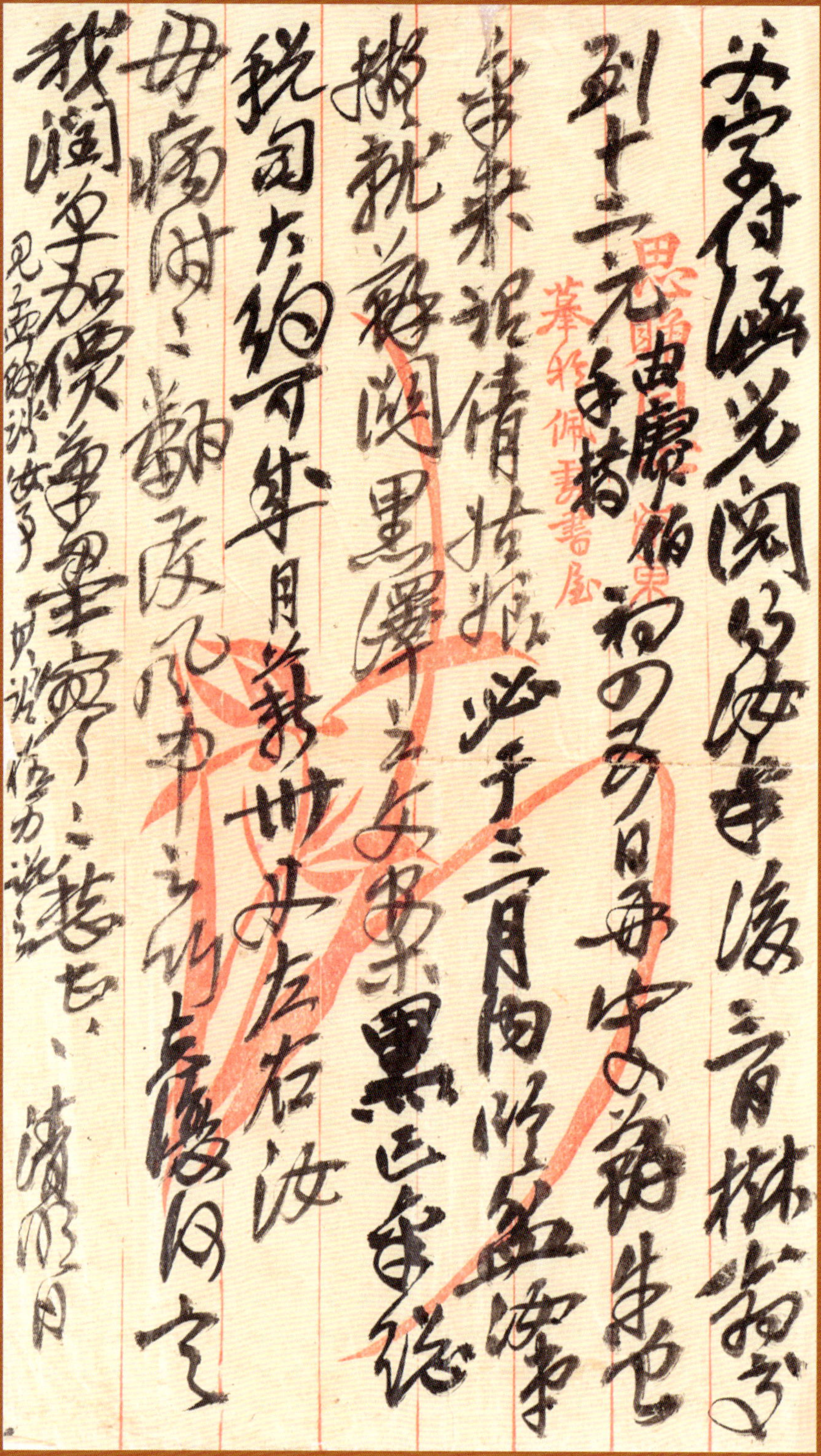

Wu Changshuo

One-page Envelope of Correspondence to My Son Wu Han

Ink on rice paper

Height 22cm, length 12cm

1911

The Wave-Rider: Wu Changshuo's Artistic Revolution and Legacy

Deng Feng

Each age brings forth new genius on this noble land, and each will lead the trend for centuries to come.

In the tide of time, the generations before and after inspired and excelled one another unremittingly. The tide ebbed and flowed. Those who withstood the tide were pioneers of their time; they were the 'wave-riders'.

Looking back on the radical changes in Chinese painting over the last century, Wu Changshuo was undoubtedly a 'wave-rider' and leader of the modernisation of painting. He inherited freehand brushwork techniques and seal engraving aesthetics from the Ming and Qing dynasties. Drawing from this traditional culture, he then incorporated the ancient elements into dynamic brushstrokes, initiating a magnificent new style – a new wave – so as to develop Chinese painting and bring it into the 20th century. This new wave was not only a response to the development of Chinese painting, but also to the cultural and historical spirit of the times.

As a master of this new painting style, incorporating freehand brushwork with the aesthetic of seal engraving, Wu Changshuo brought together the Four Arts of poetry, calligraphy, painting and seal engraving. Beginning with seal engraving followed by calligraphy, he later added poetry and literature. By integrating the Four Arts, Wu gave each of them distinctive contemporary characteristics with a modern outlook. Essentially, he was carrying on the work of his predecessors while enlightening the future with a remarkable influence that would go on to span centuries.

The following facts are laid down in history:

In 1843, Shanghai was formally opened to the rest of the world as a port for commerce, marking the momentum for a tremendous change that moulded Chinese modern society.

In the 1870s, Wu Changshuo made many visits to Shanghai to see his teachers and friends.

Around 1890, Wu Changshuo temporarily moved to Pudong, and then travelled between Suzhou and Shanghai for many years.

In 1913, Wu Changshuo settled in Shanghai, hence the influence of the Shanghai style to the south and north of China and eastward to Japan and Korea.

In 1990, one century after Wu Changshuo formed a connection with Pudong, the one-time fishing village became a new area for development. Over the past 30 years, Pudong New Area, as it became known, is a good example of a 'wave rider'; following the reform and opening-up policy by the Chinese government, it became an important centre for the reform of China's economy.

Though Wu Changshuo, the wave-rider of the painting style of the century, is long gone, his spirit has never faded and 'exists like a firm rock in midstream'.

On the 130th anniversary of Wu Changshuo's connection to Pudong and the 30th anniversary of the founding of Shanghai Pudong New Area, the Jinqiao Being Art Museum organised the 'Tide: 130th Anniversary of Wu Changshuo's Pudong Bond' exhibition. The special exhibition displayed the collection from Shanghai Wu Changshuo Art Museum and was supported by the Wu family. The exhibition brought together more than 100 works – painting, calligraphy, seal engraving and literature – many of which were on display for the first time. The exhibition began with Wu Changshuo's painting *Pudong Peony*, which was painted when he 'crossed the Huangpu River in a storm'. It continued with 'Lonely Journey with Company of Friends' – an introduction of his teachers and friends from the Shanghai-style painting school. This was then followed by the painting style's influence on the 'convergence of the South and the North', and finally showcased the research publications on Wu Changshuo, displayed on bookcases with Chinese characters printed on the walls to demonstrate how the style of the century was forged. Meanwhile, an interactive exploration area was set aside for an elaborate display of Wu Changshuo's smaller seal engravings alongside large modern installations. This had a twofold objective: first, it allowed viewers to perceive the fusion and transition between brush and knife when appreciating and comparing works of calligraphy and seal engraving; second, modern interactive projection screens were used to present elements from Wu Changshuo's work for the enjoyment of viewers, providing them with an immersive experience.

What are the legacies of Wu Changshuo? Is it his fascinating classic seal engraving or his calligraphy and painting? Or is it his bold, remarkable personality that continues to live on, or his humble appearance despite his incredible achievements? It is all these things, and when we put them all together and observe them, there is a clear vitality surging within.

So, let's walk through the exhibition and ride the waves that Wu Changshuo has created for us.

Being Art Museum Academic Host: Deng Feng
October 2020

Ancient Brick Inscriptions and Their Influence on Wu Changshuo's Art

Mei Song

A new trend in epigraphy emerged during the late Qing dynasty, as collectors shifted their focus from bronzeware and steles to inscribed bricks from the Han and Jin dynasties. This shift was driven by the expansion of categories in the epigraphical collections influenced by Han learning (an intellectual movement that reached its height in the middle of the Qing dynasty). Bricks are also known as 叀 (zhuān), 甎 (zhuān), 塼 (zhuān), and 墼 (jī), and referred to as 甓 (pì) in the book *Yunhui*. Those that were particularly favoured by late Qing collectors were predominantly from the Han and Jin periods, mainly sourced from tomb chambers. According to the custom of the late Han period in southern China, elite officials and scholars used specially crafted bricks for their tombs. These bricks were thick and weighty, often engraved with burial dates, the name of the deceased, descendants responsible for the burial, or auspicious phrases and patterns. Such inscriptions and designs captivated antiquarians in the late Qing dynasty. Following the reign of Qianlong and Jiaqing Emperors, a culture of collecting and appreciating inscribed bricks gradually developed in the Jiangsu and Zhejiang regions. Key figures in this movement included Ruan Yuan (1764–1849) and Zhang Tingji (1768–1848).

1. The Connoisseurship of Inscribed Bricks in Jiangsu and Zhejiang Regions

Inscribed tomb bricks were sporadically unearthed during the Song dynasty but were not widely appreciated until the Qianlong and Jiaqing periods, when scholars such as Ruan Yuan, Zhang Tingji, Zhang Yanchang (1738–1814) and Chen Nanshu amassed extensive inscribed tomb bricks and formally introduced this category into epigraphical research. Just as Ruan Yuan had his *Bazhuan Yinguan* (a studio with eight bricks), Zhang Tingji had the *Bazhuan Jingshe* (a study with eight bricks) and Xie Qikun (1737–1802) had the *Bazhuan Shufang* (a riverboat with eight bricks), it is evident that the collection of ancient bricks had become a prevailing trend at that time. In Zhang Tingji's *Inscriptions and Postscript of the Qingyi Pavilion Collections* (清仪阁题跋), it reads:

> 'When I was younger, I read Hong Shi's *Continued Records of Calligraphy* and aspired to acquire a few ancient bricks from Luoyang or Chang'an to study their ancient architectural styles, but this ambition

> remained unfulfilled. In March of the 16th year of the Qianlong reign (1795), while travelling in Haiyan County, I came across several bricks from the Han and Jin dynasties among the ruins by the sea, exposed by the retreating tides. I bought them for a hundred coins. The next day, I returned and found another dozen or so pieces through local intermediaries. Selecting the finest among them, I named my study *Bazhuan*, meaning "eight bricks study".'

In the early years of the Jiaqing era (1796), the current Minister of Education Ruan Yuan came to inspect the Zhejiang academies and inscribed a plaque for my study. At that time, Xie Qikun of Suzhou had the *Bazhuan Shufang* to commemorate his eight Yongping bricks. Ruan Yuan, having assumed office in Zhejiang, collected bricks with inscriptions such as 'Five Phoenixes' and 'Yellow Dragon' and named his study *Bazhuan Yinguan*, engraving each brick with 'One of Ruan's Eight Bricks' to distinguish them from mine and Xie's collections. For the past 30 years, notable figures from my hometown and beyond, such as Cao Zhongshui, Xu Aishan, Li Jinlan, Ge Suru of Xiushui, Zhang Yanchang of Haiyan, Huang Jiaosheng, Guo Shenchui, Chen Nanshu, Lang Shan, Tian Houcun of Pinghu, Zhao Luosheng of Renhe, Xu Wenqu of Qiantang, Xu Shouyu of Haichang, Xu Xiongfei of Wukang, Zhu Shimei of Wujiang, Chen Baozhi, Wang Erqiao, and Niu Chongxi of Wuxing, each presented their prized bricks.

Additionally, Wen Suizhi of Shunde in Guangdong wrapped his bricks in felt and brought them from thousands of miles away. The scholar Weng Fanggang from Daxing often mentioned my name while composing poems about ancient bricks. More recently, my friend Liuzhou of Haichang and Wu Kangfu of Tongcheng have shown great enthusiasm, often exchanging letters and gifts. The accumulated collections and extensive viewing over the years far exceed the records of Lu Jiannan (Lu You, a poet in the Song dynasty) and Yue Juanweng. The land is generous with its treasures, and people are fortunate to connect with these ancient relics, truly a great blessing. However, residing in the countryside, still dressed in humble attire, and having only flower bricks to muse over, sometimes makes me a subject of ridicule. This engenders in me a mix of pride and embarrassment.

> 'Zhuru, you are a distinguished scholar and literatus who frequently traverses the elegant halls. You see these eight bricks as a precursor to future literary achievements. Hastily written and sent from afar, this letter aims to reconnect with you, such a distinguished individual. Written on the 28th day of the intercalary ninth month of the 12th year (1832) of Emperor Daoguang's reign.' (Zhang Tingji's inscription on Han and Jin bricks collected by Pan Zhuru in *Inscriptions and postscript of the Qingyi Pavilion Collections*, compiled by Wei Jiashun and Ding Licheng)

In this postscript, Zhang Tingji references numerous individuals, essentially providing a comprehensive record of collectors from the Jiangsu and Zhejiang regions during the Qianlong and Jiaqing eras. Ruan Yuan was a pioneer in the appreciation and collection of early bricks. His collection of Eight Bricks – bricks inscribed with 'Five Phoenixes', 'Yellow Dragon', 'Eternal Happiness', 'Master of Shu', 'Heavenly Book', 'Great Prosperity', 'Universal Harmony' and 'Prosperous Peace' – were housed in Jiguzhai, his treasure gallery, which was subsequently named *Bazhuan Yinguan* (meaning 'a studio of eight bricks'). This impressive collection inspired the creation of a two-volume work titled *Poetry Collection of the Bazhuan Yinguan*. Due to Ruan Yuan's high social status and far-reaching influence on elite officials and scholars, it's evident that his advocacy played a crucial role in fostering the brick-collecting culture in the Jiangsu and Zhejiang provinces. Zhang Tingji, Xu Xiongfei and Chen Jing, all mentioned in this postscript, were Ruan Yuan's disciples. Xu Aishan's father once served as an instructor in Wukang (now Deqing County), and among the renowned bricks in the Qingyi Pavilion's collection, the 'Luo Daoren' inscribed brick was acquired from Deqing before being gifted to Zhang Tingji. Wang Yu was a close friend of Weng Fanggang, who wrote a poem on the bricks in Baoding Jingshe (Wang's private museum). Monk Liuzhou, originally from Haining, served as the abbot of Yanjiao Temple in Huzhou, where he also left his mark in the pursuit of early inscribed bricks. Liuzhou was closely connected with notable figures such as Ruan Yuan, Zhang Tingji, Yang Xian and Qian Song, and had considerable prestige and influence within the epigraphy community. Revered by Ruan Yuan as the 'Epigraphy Monk', Liuzhou is said to have encountered over three thousand types of ancient brick and amassed a collection of several hundred. The sheer abundance of his collection underscores its richness. With such a diverse group of inscribed brick collectors, one can easily envision the vibrant and bustling scene of brick collecting during that period.

After the Qianlong and Jiaqing periods, as the appreciation of ancient bricks became increasingly popular, many collectors began to compile their collections into published volumes. For instance, Ling Xia mentioned numerous examples in the foreword to Lu Xinyuan's *Illustrations and Explanations of Ancient Bricks from the Qianpi Pavilion* (千甓亭古砖图录, 2011):

> 'Since the Qing dynasty, interest in collecting ancient bricks has grown significantly, leading to extensive searches and studies. Chu Jun compiled *Records of Ancient Bricks* (古砖录), which contains many rare pieces but was never published. Later, various works on ancient bricks were compiled, including Zhang Yanchang's *Records of Ancient Bricks from the Three Wu Regions* (三吴古砖录), Feng Dengfu and Monk Liuzhou's separate *Records of Zhejiang Bricks* (浙江砖录), Zhou Zhongfu's *Catalogue of Ancient Bricks from Hangzhou, Jiaxing and Huzhou* (杭嘉湖道古砖目). Xu Xiongfei's *Records of Observed Ancient Bricks* (古砖所见录), Chen Zongyi's *Records of Ancient Brick Inscriptions* (古砖文录), Ding Ruimo's *Study of Han and Jin Dynasty Brick Inscriptions* (汉晋砖文考略), Chen Huang's *Records of Ancient Bricks from Ze Gu Studio* (泽古堂古砖录), Wang Yu's *Catalogue of Ancient Bricks from Baoding Jingshe* (宝鼎精舍古砖录), Niu Chongxi's *Collection of Brick Inscriptions from Baitao Studio* (百陶楼甓文集录), Wu Tingkang's *Illustrated Records of Ancient Bricks from Mutao Pavillion* (慕

陶轩古砖图录), Yan Fuji's *Collection of Yan's Ancient Bricks* (严氏古砖存), Lv Quansun's (1806–59) *Study of One Hundred Bricks* (百砖考), Ji Dafu's *Appraisal of Ancient Bricks* (古砖品), Song Jingshe's *Records of Bricks* (瓴甋录) and, more recently, Lu Zengxiang's *Records of Bricks from Bi Brick Inkstone Studio* (皕砖砚斋砖录). These works have all become significant references for the collection and study of ancient bricks.'[1]

Chu Jun, who made his living selling rubbings of steles, created the *Illustrated Catalogue of Epigraphical Works*, a notable work featuring reproductions of famous inscriptions from various dynasties. Feng Dengfu, a disciple of Ruan Yuan, was particularly distinguished in Chinese classical studies. Zhou Zhongfu, who studied at the Gujing Academy, was also a top student of Ruan Yuan. The Lv family – comprising Lv Quansun, his father Lv Ziban, and one brother – were all passionate about ancient bricks. Feng Dengfu once served as a professor under Lv Ziban. As Feng and the Lv family shared a passion for collecting ancient bricks, they likely fostered private exchanges and held discussions about their collections.

According to my incomplete statistics from the Qing dynasty to the Republic of China, collectors of ancient bricks from the Jiangsu and Zhejiang regions authored as many as 40 to 50 works on the subject. In Huzhou alone, there were 16 such collectors, including Cai Fangyi, Xu Xiongfei, Zhang Jian, Zhou Zhongfu, Chen Jing, Ding Ruimo, Wang Yu, Niu Chongxi, Pan Zhouzun, Zhang Shouxian, Yang Xian, Yu Yue, Lu Xinyuan, Wu Changshuo, Wang Chengtian, and Wang Xiu. These collectors produced 12 notable works, such as Xu Xiongfei's *Records of Observed Ancient Bricks* (古砖所见录), Zhang Jian's *Notes on Ancient Bricks* (古甓记), Zhou Zhongfu's *Catalogue of Ancient Bricks from Hangzhou, Jiaxing and Huzhou* (杭嘉湖道古砖目), Chen Jing's *Illustrated Catalogue of the Epigraphy Collection of Qiugu Studio* (求古精舍金石图), Ding Ruimo's *Study of Han and Jin Brick Inscriptions* (汉晋砖文考略), Wang Yu's *Catalogue of Ancient Bricks from Baoding Jingshe* (宝鼎精舍古砖录), Niu Chongxi's *Collection of Brick Inscriptions from Baitao Studio* (百陶楼甓文集录), Lu Xinyuan's *Catalogue of Bricks from Qianpi Pavilion* (千甓亭砖录) and its sequel *Illustrated Explanation of Ancient Bricks from Qianpi Pavilion* (千甓亭古砖图录), Wang Chengtian's *Memorial Album of Brick Inscriptions from Xinglou* (邢楼砖刻纪念册) and Wang Xiu's *Catalogue of Bricks from Han'an Hall* (汉安甋庼砖录). This extensive body of work vividly depicts the rich culture of ancient brick collecting in the Jiangsu and Zhejiang regions.

2. Wu Changshuo's Artistic Practices Influenced by Ancient Brick Inscriptions

The brick-collecting trend that flourished in Jiangsu and Zhejiang regions since the Qianlong and Jiaqing periods undoubtedly provided a practical model for Wu Changshuo, whose limited finances and deep passion for antiquities made brick collecting an ideal pursuit. Wu himself admitted to having a 'brick obsession', with a significant collection of bricks from the Han and Jin dynasties. In his *Notes on Ancient Bricks*, Shi Yusheng remarked that

1
Lu Xinyuan, *Illustrated Explanation of Ancient Bricks from Qianpi Pavilion*, preface by Ling Xia, Zhejiang Ancient Books Publishing House, 2011, title page.

Wu's collection included 13 notable bricks: five from the Eastern Wu period, including 'Five Phoenixes', 'Eternal Peace', 'Phoenix', and two 'Heavenly Chronicles', and eight from the Jin dynasty – such as two 'Yuankang', two 'Yongjia', and one each of 'Jianxing', 'Xianhe', 'Taiyuan' and 'Taishi' bricks (Shi Yusheng, *Jinzhong Shanfang Collection, Posthumous Work of the Shi of Anji County*, Vol.1, 1891, block-printed edition). Several factors drove Wu Changshuo's dedication to brick collecting. First was his inherent passion for it; second, his limited financial resources; third, the modest profits he could earn to supplement his income; and fourth, the mutual influence of fellow brick enthusiasts like Yang Xian, Lu Xinyuan and Jin Jie. For Wu, the true value of these ancient bricks lay in their potential for artistic expression. He incorporated the inscriptions into his calligraphy and seal engraving, created rubbings with accompanying commentary, and used the bricks in his *Bogu* (meaning 'ancient erudition') paintings. Additionally, he crafted brick inkstones and inscribed them, merging his artistic pursuits with his collection.

Incorporating ancient brick inscriptions into seal engraving was one of the artistic practices influenced by the brick-collecting trend of the Qianlong and Jiaqing periods, guided by the concept of seeking inspiration beyond traditional seal script. Under this philosophy, seal carvers expanded their sources of inspiration to include ancient scripts from bronze vessels, Han dynasty mirrors and coins, integrating these into their work. Examples include Wu Rangzhi's adaptation of Han stele inscriptions, Huang Shiling's mimicry of bronze inscriptions, and Zhao Zhiqian's incorporation of characters from Han mirrors and coins. These practices have been well-documented by scholars and need no further elaboration here.

However, seal carvers' use of ancient brick inscriptions has not received the same level of academic attention. Among them, eight specialists from the Seal Engravers' Society of Xiling were particularly notable for experimenting with brick inscriptions in their seal designs. They drew inspiration from the archaic seal Mouzhuan script (缪篆 , a variation of small seal script) of ancient bricks, layout, and the aesthetic of deliberate imperfections created by the carving process, which have an evident influence on their distinctive seal styles. This article will use Wu Changshuo as an example to explore how he applied ancient brick inscriptions in his calligraphy and seal engraving.

(1) Integrating Ancient Brick Inscriptions into Calligraphy

The inscriptions on ancient bricks are uniquely styled and highly varied, reflecting the rustic charm and artistic spirit of folk calligraphy. From a historical perspective, Han dynasty brick inscriptions predominantly feature the Mouzhuan script, which closely resembles the script used in Han seals. This similarity is a primary reason why seal engravers often drew directly from ancient brick inscriptions. The inscriptions on Six Dynasties bricks, however, display a greater diversity, incorporating both seal scripts and clerical scripts, often with a rougher execution and an increase in orthographic errors. Bricks from the Three Kingdoms period exhibit characteristics that fall between these styles. They include both the standard Mouzhuan script and other regional styles. For instance, a recently unearthed brick from Shaoxing city inscribed with 'Fenghuang Sannian' (凤皇三年) features a script typical of the Stele of Divine Prophecy Revealed from God (天发神讖碑), aligning with the calligraphic style of the Eastern Wu.

Wu Changshuo's incorporation of ancient brick inscription into seal carving began with his use of these inscriptions in calligraphy. Wu frequently mentioned this in his poetry and prose, emphasising the importance he placed on these ancient scripts. For instance, in his works, he wrote lines such as: 'Foulu's[2] path lies in embracing the inscriptions on broken bricks'[3]; 'Tiles and bricks fortunately carry the spirit of Qin and Han, their way persists through time' (*Xiaogulu Seal Stamps Collection, Collection of Foulu*, Vol. 2); 'The great calamity of book burning by the Qin Shi Huan[4] spared the essence of the inscriptions in tiles and bricks' (*Dunhe's*[5] *Pottery Seal Stamps Collection, Collection of Foulu*, Vol. 3); 'Recognising an almost perfect script from Chiwu Brick[6], admiring the ancient elegance of the brushworks' (The 'Endless Happiness' Inscript, Specially Made for Nagao Uzan, Collection of Foulu, Vol. 2); and 'The script of "Tianji" on a brick, coiling like clouds and thunder, is as precious as a stele script to me'[7]. These passages illustrate Wu Changshuo's reverence for ancient brick inscriptions, equating them with Qin and Han steles and viewing them as remnants of a culture that survived Qin Shi Huang's infamous book burning.

Historically, others also directly incorporated ancient brick scripts into their calligraphy. For example, Pan Zhouzun's Wu Pi Studio housed a brick inscribed with 'Auspicious year, eternal blessings, longevity, and prosperity without end', which Wu Tingkang admired and frequently imitated in his lifetime, resulting in multiple extant pieces. Similarly, the monk Liuzhou and Xu Lian produced calligraphic couplets based on brick inscriptions. These examples demonstrate that since the Qianlong and Jiaqing periods, calligraphers and seal carvers have continuously expanded their sources of inspiration, with ancient brick inscriptions becoming a direct reference.

As a calligrapher and seal engraver, Wu Changshuo naturally created works imitating Han dynasty brick inscriptions. One notable example is 'Longevity akin to gold and stone'. His approach, characterised by capturing the essence rather than merely the form, exemplifies his profound understanding and mastery of calligraphy.

(2) Adapting Ancient Brick Inscriptions into Seal Carving

Beyond integrating ancient brick inscriptions into his calligraphy, Wu Changshuo also followed in the footsteps of the Xiling Society's artists, infusing these inscriptions into his seal carving. This continuous

2
Foulu is one of the alternative names of Wu Changshuo.

3
The 'Endless Happiness' Inscript, Specially Made for Nagao Uzan, Collection of Foulu, Vol. 2, the 9th Year of the Republic of China, Modern China Historical Materials Series, Vol. 8, Wenhai Publishing House, Photocopy.

4
Qin Shi Huang was the founder of the Qin dynasty and the first emperor of China.

5
Dunhe is one of the alternative names of Wu Yin.

6
Chiwu (238–251 AD) is the fourth regnal title of Sun Quan of the Eastern Wu.

7
Inscription of the Tianji Inkstone Brick, *Poems of Foulu* in the 2nd Collection of Foulu, the 19th year of the Emperor Guangxu, block-printed edition.

8
Wu Dacheng, *Poems of Kezhai*, Proofread by Yin Xiaofeng, Huadong Normal University Press, 2009, p.138.

9
Collection of Wu Changshuo's Artworks, Vol. 2 of *Carving*, edited by Zou Tao, Shanghai Painting and Calligraphy Publishing House, 2017, p. 57.

10
Letters to Zhang Ziqing, No.3, *Collected Letters of Liang Lei Xuan*, Vol. 7, *Modern China Historical Materials Series*, Vol. 27, Wenhai Publishing House.

connection with ancient bricks significantly enriched his artistic creations. Wu Dacheng described Wu Changshuo's approach in his *Inscription on Wu Changshuo's Seal Stamps Collection*: 'Mysterious ancient scripts from vessels and bells, meticulously studied and refined, merged with the inscriptions from ancient bricks of the Six Dynasties, resembling the grand stele inscriptions of the two capitals'[8]. This clearly illustrates Wu Changshuo's practice of drawing from ancient bronzes, pottery seals, brick inscriptions and Han dynasty stele inscriptions. According to my knowledge, Wu Changshuo's works that directly draw from ancient brick inscriptions include several notable examples:

'Longevity': Wu Changshuo carved two versions of this seal. One bears the inscription, 'Imitating Han brick script by Junqing' [9]. The other reads, 'Wu Jun imitated Han brick script, at Mid-Autumn Festival in 1875' (Collection of Wu Changshuo's Artworks, Vol. 1 of *Carving*, p. 12). Both seals closely resemble the inscription 'Longevity and prosperity for descendants' from Lu Xinyuan's *Illustrated Explanation of Ancient Bricks from Qianpi Pavilion*, Vol. 29.

'Humble Success': the inscription on this seal reads, 'In 1885, in the Eastern Wu area, I obtained a precious ancient brick and imitated it. A person of truth in ancient times neither sought greatness nor was arrogant. October 1885, Cangshuo' (Collection of Wu Changshuo's Artworks, Vol. 1 of *Carving*, p. 79).

'Cangshi': the inscription reads, 'Obtained a brick with the character "Cang" in Yancheng City, imitated it. Carved by Foudaoren in Yuanpu County (now Huaiyin County, Jiangsu Province), Spring of 1900' (Collection of Wu Changshuo's Artworks, Vol. 1 of *Carving*, p. 163).

'Eight Hundred Guests from the Heavenly Realm in a Cave': the inscription reads, 'Imitating Han brick script by Dalong' (Collection of Wu Changshuo's Artworks, Vol. 2 of *Carving*, p. 331).

'Longevity and Wealth for Noble Lords': Wu Changshuo carved three versions of this seal, with one inscription reading, 'Imitating Qian Naiqing ' (Collection of Wu Changshuo's Artworks, Vol. 2 of *Carving*, p. 24). Wu likely noted that the style of this seal closely matched that of Qian Song (1818–60) after his work was done, thus inscribing it as 'Imitating Qian Naiqing'. This indicates the profound influence of ancient brick inscriptions on the Xiling Society's artists. Additionally, a letter from Wu Yun to Zhang Zhiwan mentions the other two seals:

> 'The "Longevity and Wealth for Noble Lords" brick was carried across the river by a scholar to celebrate Ruan Yuan's eightieth birthday. He was delighted and commissioned skilled seal carvers to engrave the brick and a "Qihou urn", featuring the "Longevity" painting. Viewing the manuscript still evokes the joy and grandeur of that moment. Wu Yun and Wu Changshuo crafted two seals that mirrored the inscriptions on the ancient brick and urn, presenting them as a gift to Ruan Yuan.' [10]

This confirms that Wu Changshuo carved two versions of the 'Longevity and Wealth for Noble Lords' seal, both based on the ancient brick inscriptions.

Lastly, Wu Changshuo created a small seal for Fei Nianci. In one of the six poems written to Li Zi'ao about the seal, he writes: 'I carved a seal for the use of Xili [the pen name of Fei Nianci] reviewing books. The joy of carving seals is boundless. Searching for inscriptions and collecting fragments of bricks and tiles has been my passion for thirty years'.[11] Sadly, it's unclear whether this seal still exists today.

(3) Capturing the Beauty of Imperfection from Ancient Bricks

Infusing the weathered, fragmented charm of ancient brick inscriptions into seal carvings, Wu Changshuo not only embraced but celebrated their unique patina, imbuing his seals with an aura of historical depth and venerable beauty. This distinctive quality is particularly prominent among the works of the eight masters in the Xiling Society, marking a signature element of the Zhejiang School of seal carving with its unmistakable regional character.

Yet, the influence of ancient bricks on Wu Changshuo's art extends far beyond mere imitation. While many scholars attribute Wu's penchant for a fractured aesthetic to his exposure to sealing clay, the reality is more nuanced. Wu's direct interaction with sealing clay was quite limited, having primarily relied on the collections of fellow connoisseurs like Wu Yun, Wu Dacheng and Pan Zuyin. Furthermore, it was through the collections of Wu Yun and Wu Dacheng that Wu Changshuo encountered the rubbings of sealing clay gifted or exchanged by Chen Jieqi. While these sealing clay works undoubtedly influenced his seal engraving aesthetic, they paled in comparison to the profound impact of ancient bricks on his work. Also, collecting ancient bricks was easier for him. His genuine engagement with the tactile and visual aspects of ancient bricks – evident in his collecting, handling and rubbing practices – offered him a profound appreciation for their imperfect allure. This personal immersion, more than any other external influence, deeply shaped Wu's aesthetic sensibilities and contributed significantly to his distinctive style. This aspect of Wu Changshuo's artistic development remains a crucial yet often overlooked facet of his oeuvre. The impact of ancient bricks on his work is not just a footnote in his artistic journey but a cornerstone of his creative expression, underscoring the essential role these artifacts played in his enduring legacy.[12]

Mei Song: executive director of Wu Changshuo Research Association of Anji County

11
Chronicle of Wu Changshuo, edited by Zhu Guantian, Zhejiang Ancient Books Publishing House, 2014, p.143.

12
For a more detailed exploration, see Mei Song's *The Dao in Bricks and Tiles: Wu Changshuo's Collection of Ancient Bricks and His Artistic Practice*, Sanlian Press, 2017

Artists Contributing to the Establishment of Shanghai Wu Changshuo Art Museum

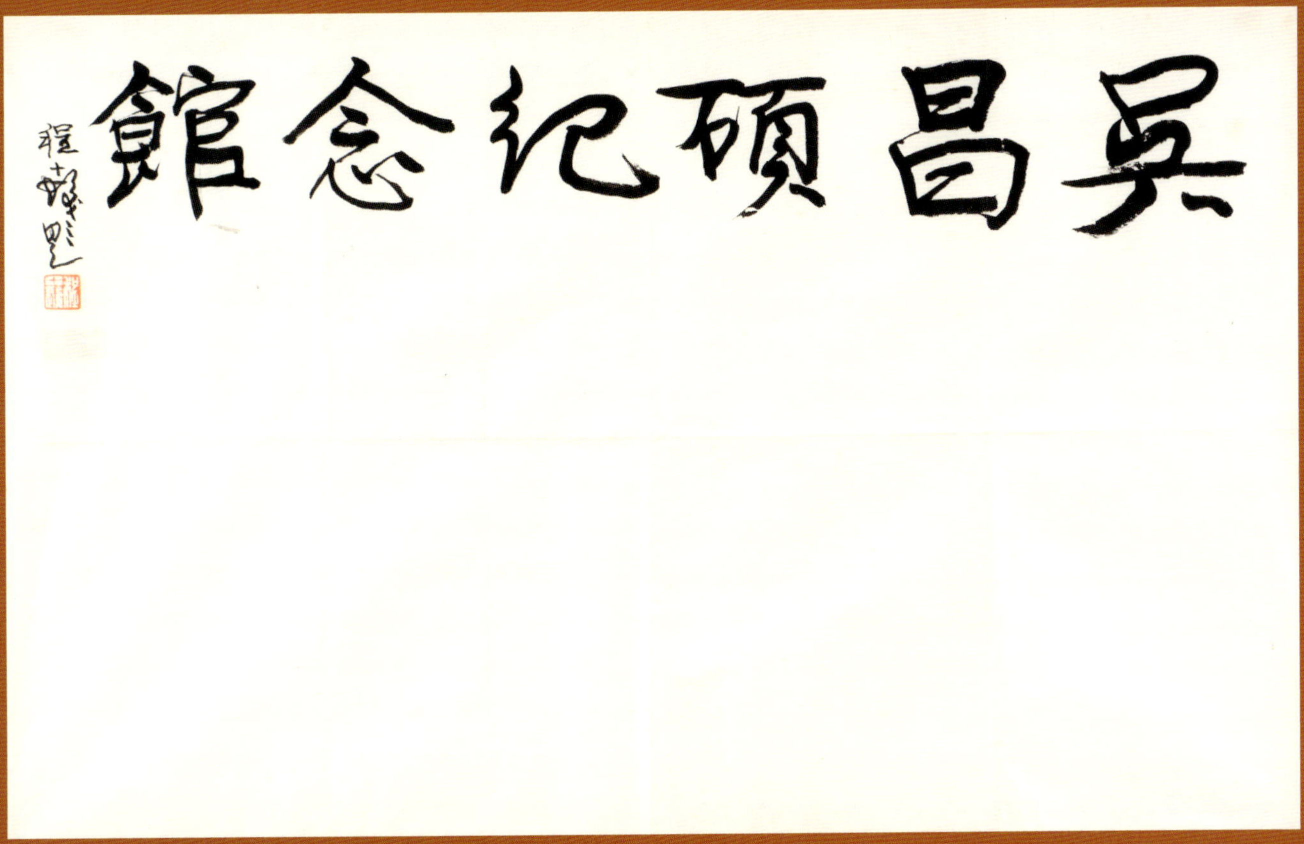

Cheng Shifa (1921–2007)
Calligraphy work (Wu Changshuo Art Museum)
Ink on paper
Height 69cm, length 45cm
1994

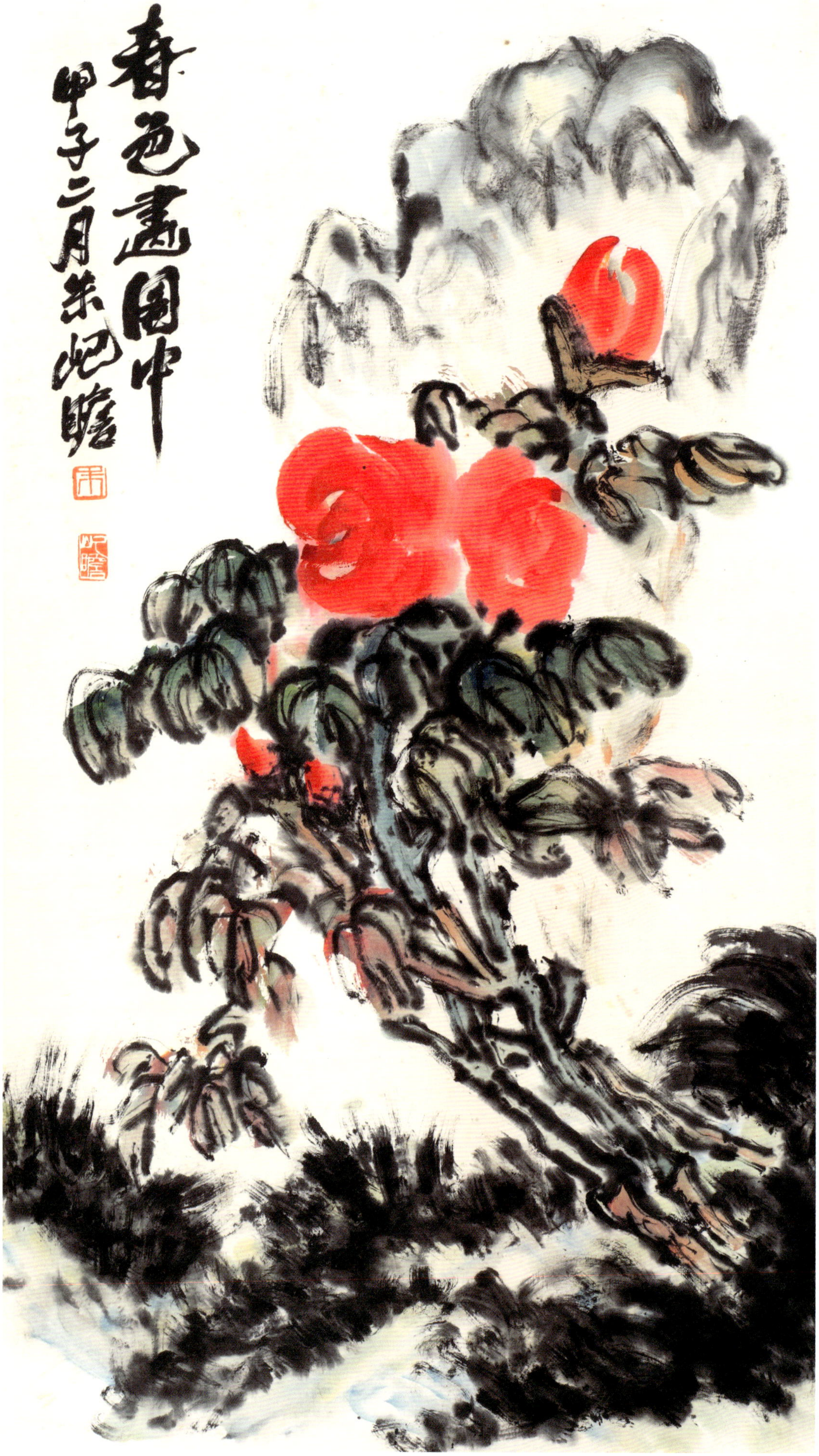
春色滿園中
甲子二月朱屺瞻

Zhu Qizhan (1892–1996)
Peony handscroll
Ink and colours on paper
Height 88cm, length 50cm
1984

Sha Menghai (1900–92)
Handscroll of poetry by Su Shi in running and cursive scripts
Ink on paper
Height 69cm, length 34cm
1991

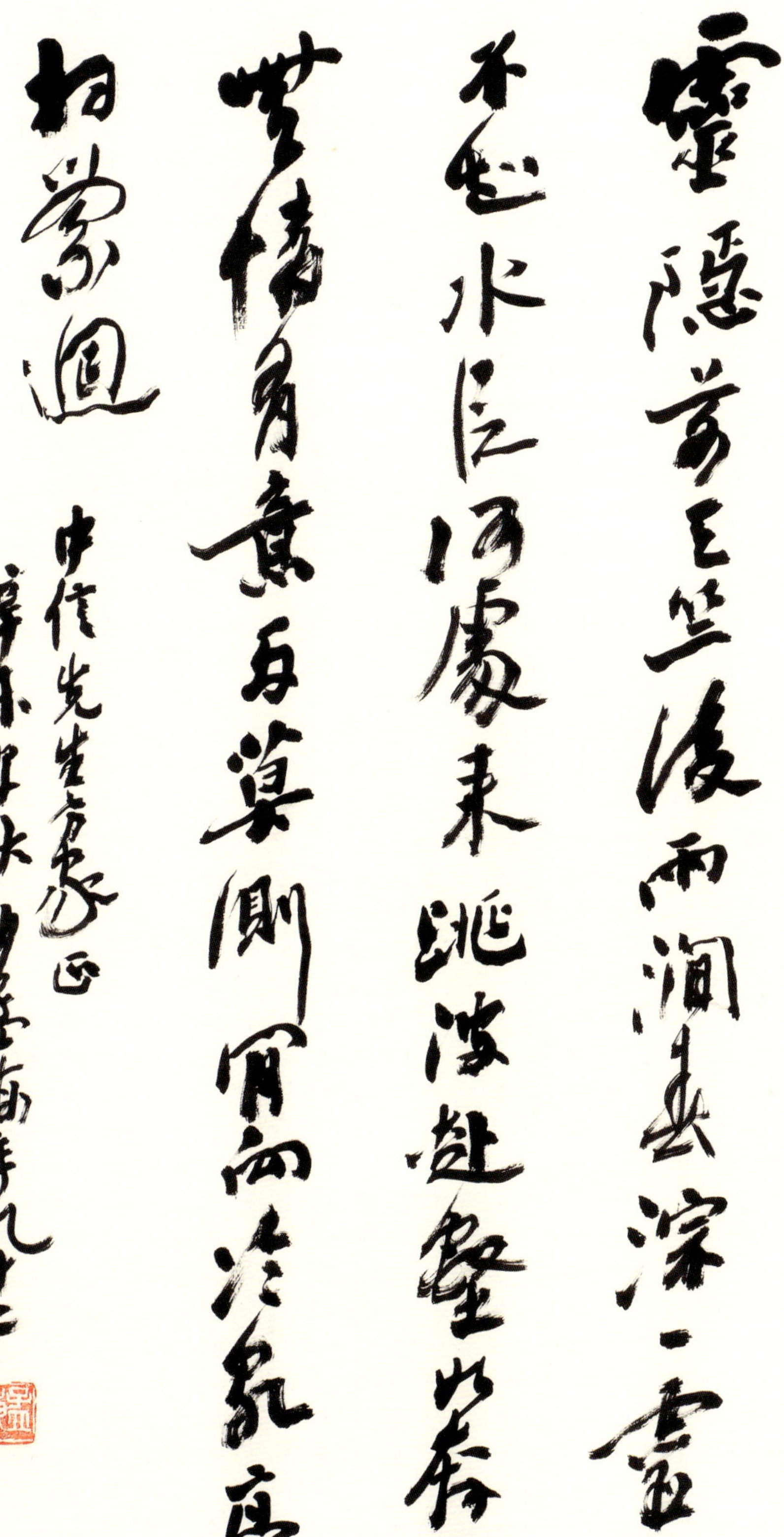
靈隱前三竺後兩澗春淙一靈鷲
不知水從何處來跳波赴壑如奔雷
無情有意兩莫測肯向冷泉亭下
相盤桓
中信先生方家正
辛未中秋 沙孟海年九十二

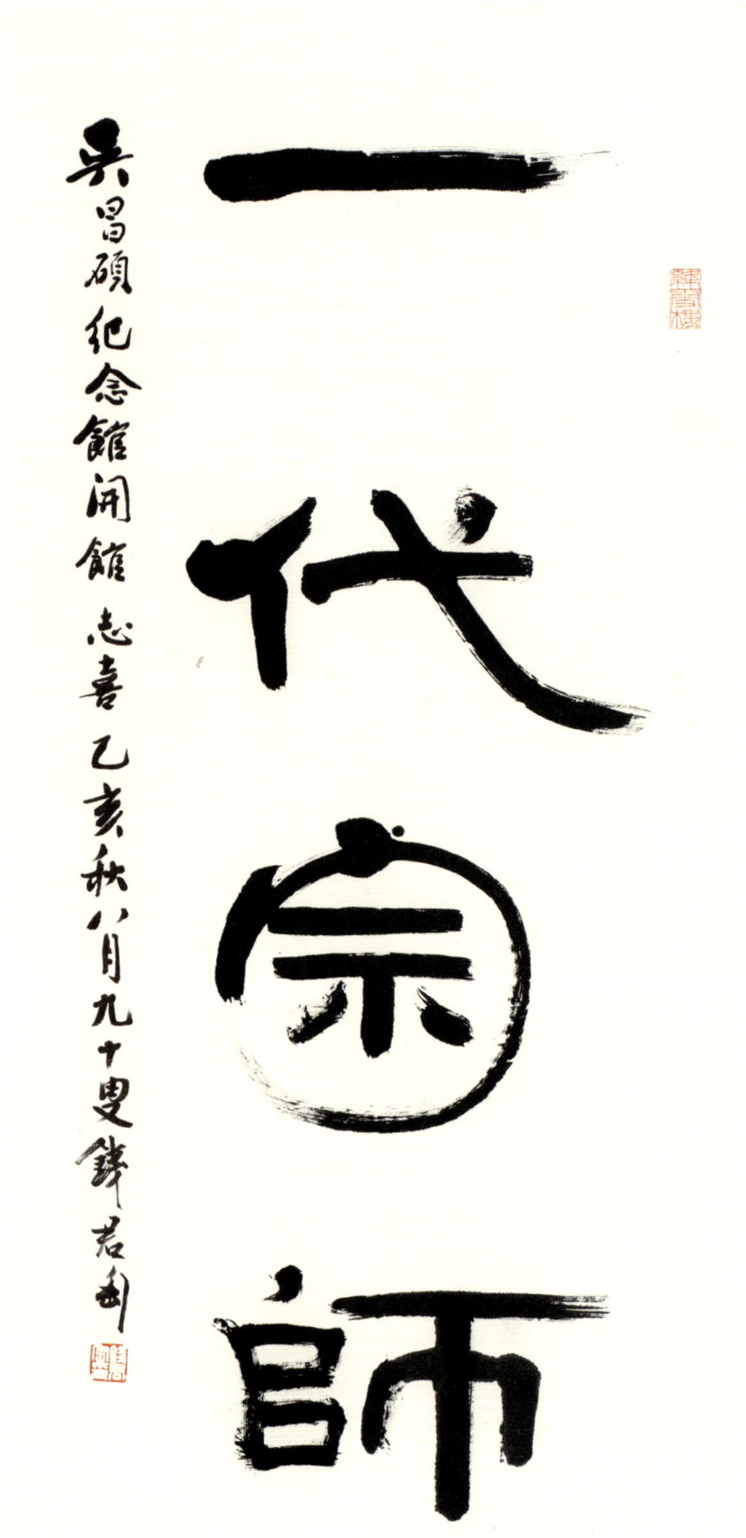

Qian Juntao (1907–98)
'Epoch-making Great Master' calligraphy handscroll
Ink on paper
Height 136cm, length 67cm
1995

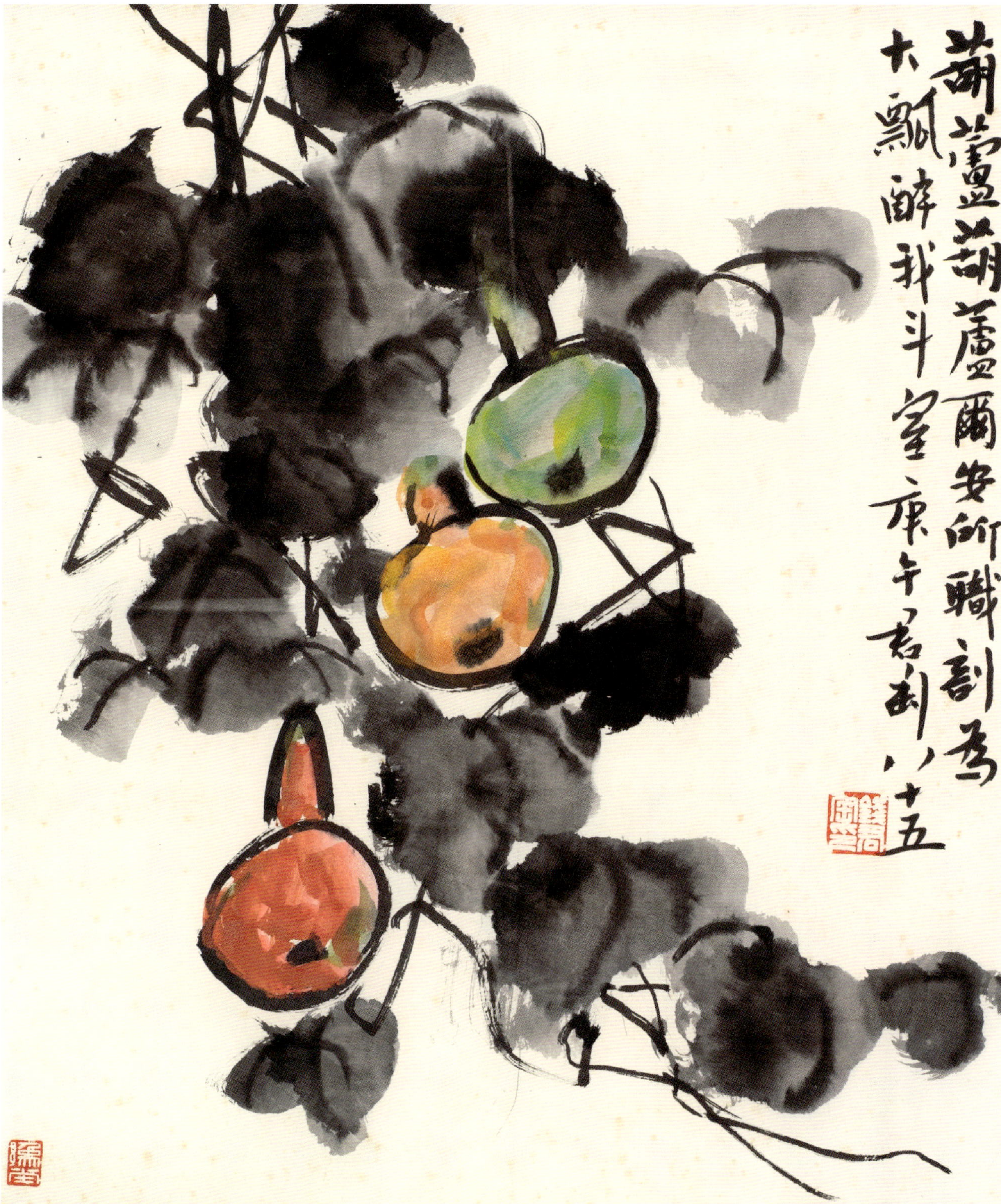

Qian Juntao
Calabash handscroll
Ink and colours on paper
Height 66cm, length 55cm
1990

Zhao Puchu (1907–2000)

Handscroll of the poem *'A Visit to Lion Rock in Qujiang District in Guangdong Province'* in running and cursive scripts
Ink on paper
Height 133cm, length 56cm
1986

洞裏觀湖更看山，置身十二萬年前。
漫誇子壽文章好，馬壩人羣是祖先。（張九齡曲江人字子壽）
石器舊新相去遠，古來進化路漫漫。
那知电子今時代，換斗移星剎那間。
溫故知新知未來，勤勞攻造勉吾儕。
殘枝片石須珍重，無盡星河自此開。

一九八六年三月遊曲江獅子岩訪馬壩故址有作 趙樸初

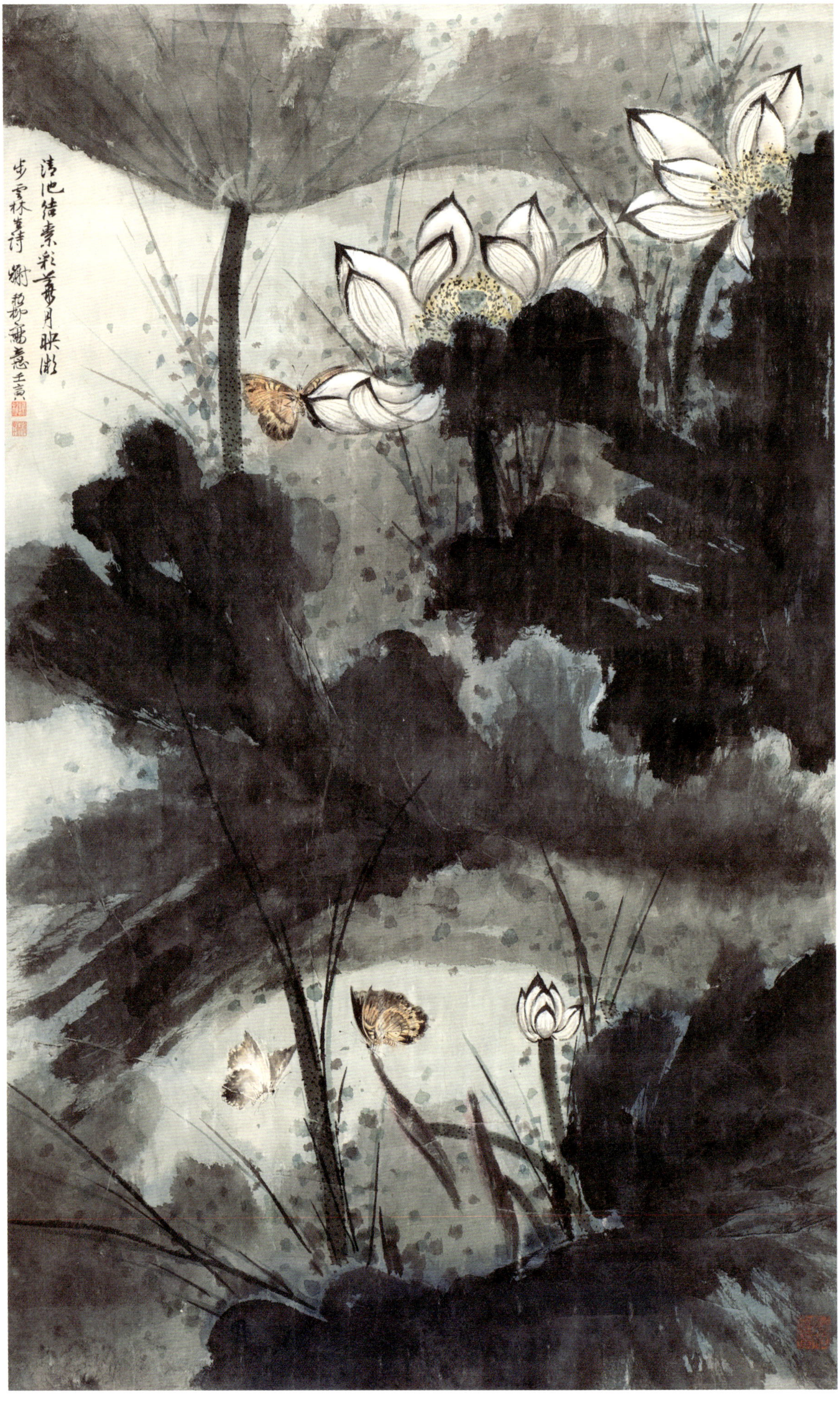

Xie Zhiliu (1910–97)
Lotus handscroll
Ink and colours on paper
Height 87cm, length 52cm
1962

Cao Jianlou (1913–2005)
Spring Welcoming handscroll
Ink and colours on paper
Height 95cm, Length 42cm
1980

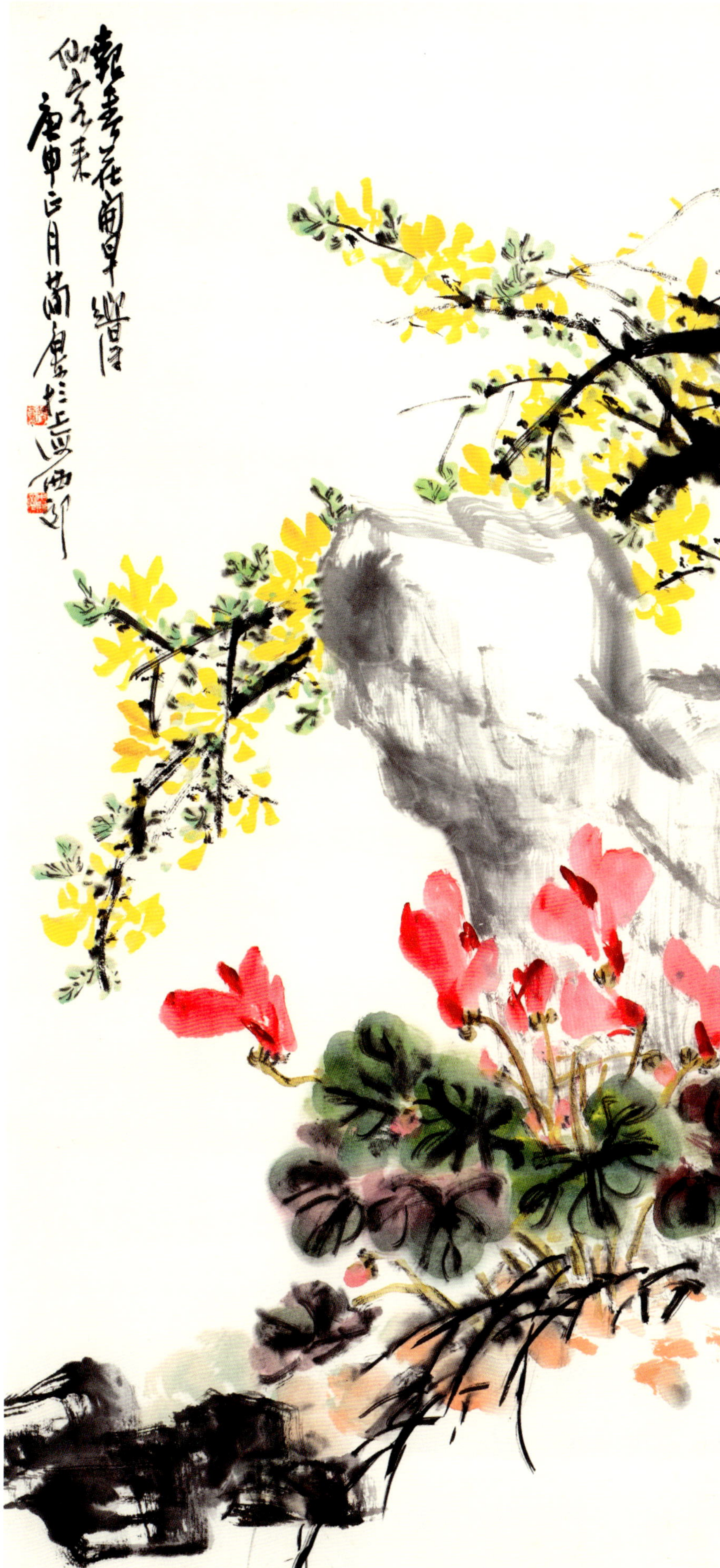

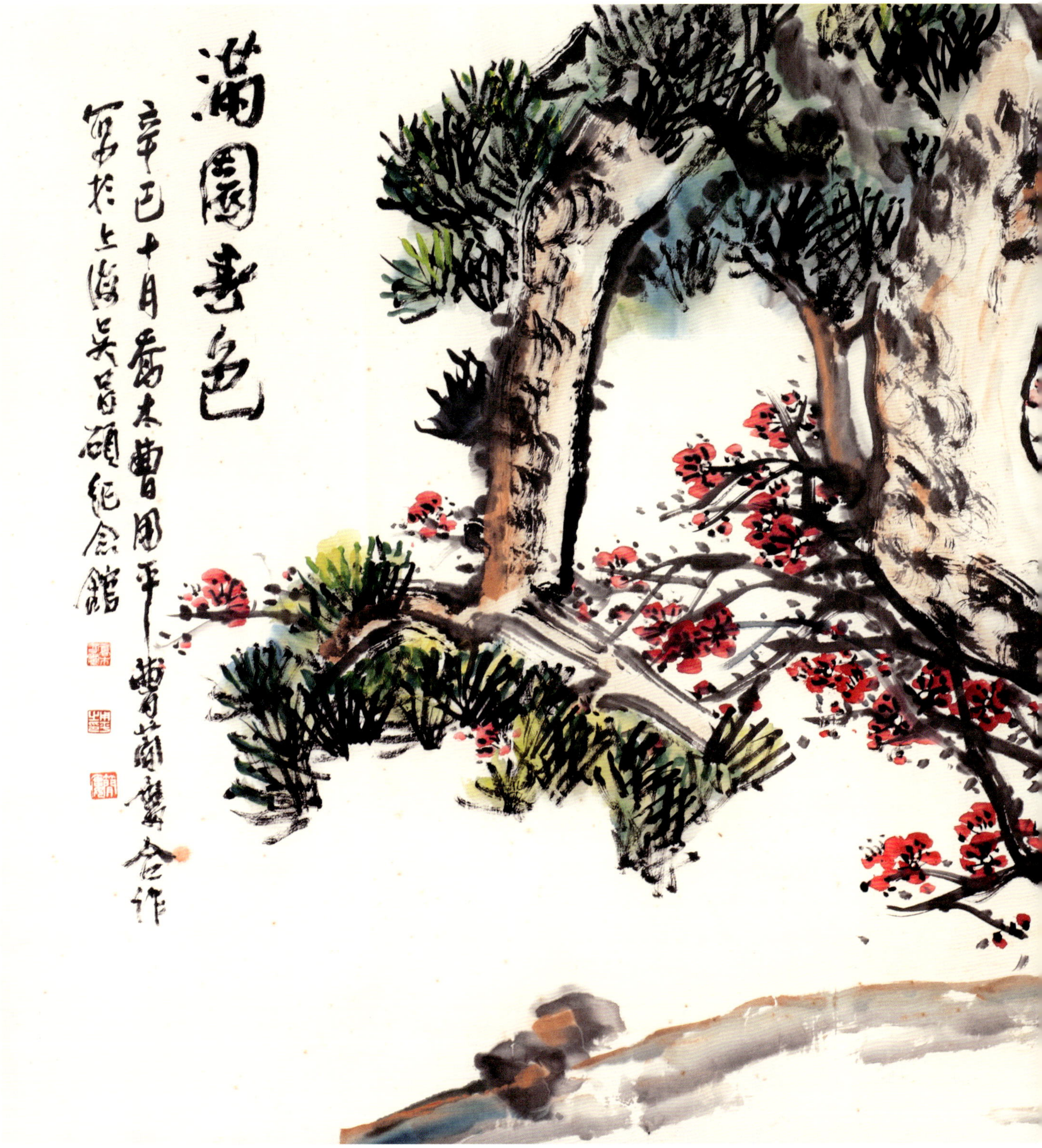
滿園春色
辛巳十月喬木曹用平 曹簡樓合作
寫於上海吳昌碩紀念館

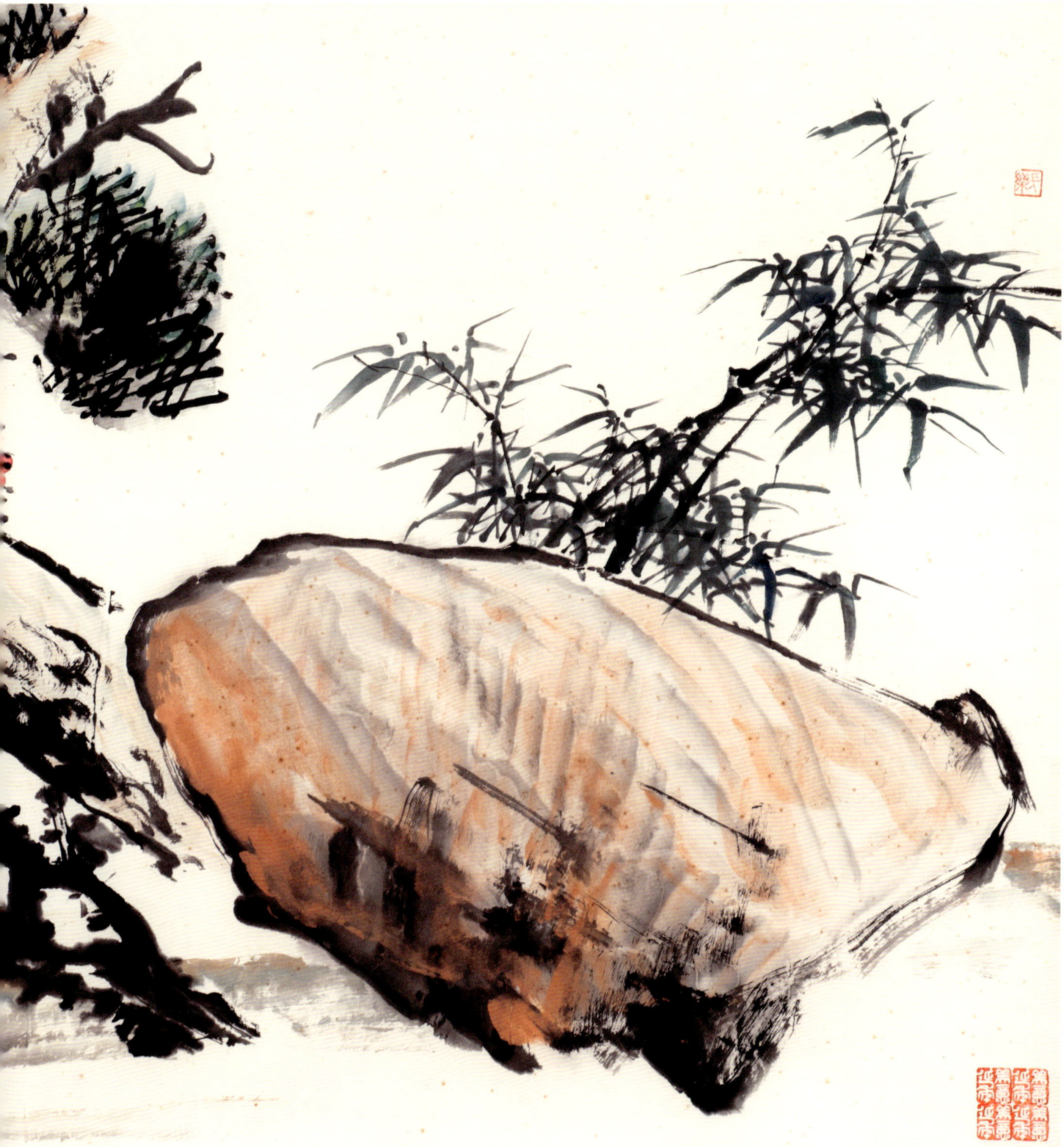

Cao Jianlou, Qiao Mu (1920–2002), Cao Yongping (1922–2018)
Floral
Ink and colours on paper
Height 140cm, Length 180cm
2001

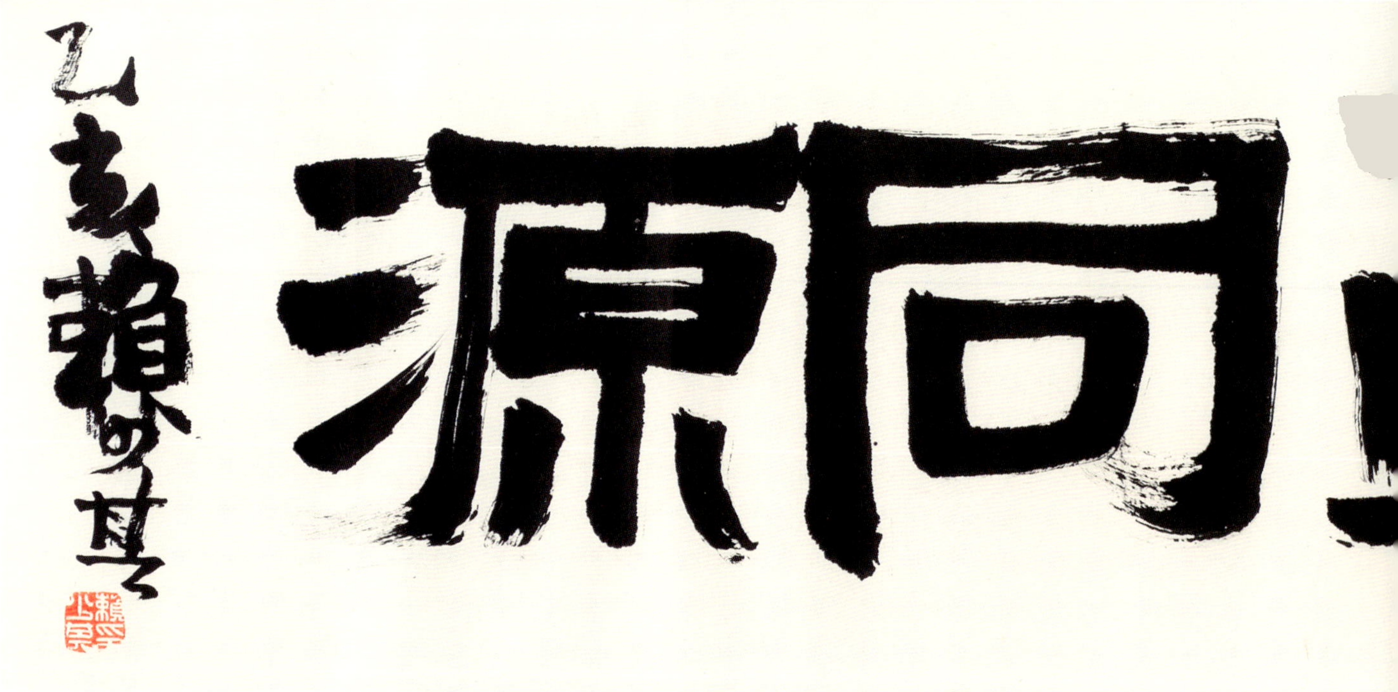

Lai Shaoqi (1915–2000)
Calligraphy handscroll
Ink on paper
Height 33cm, length 135cm
1995

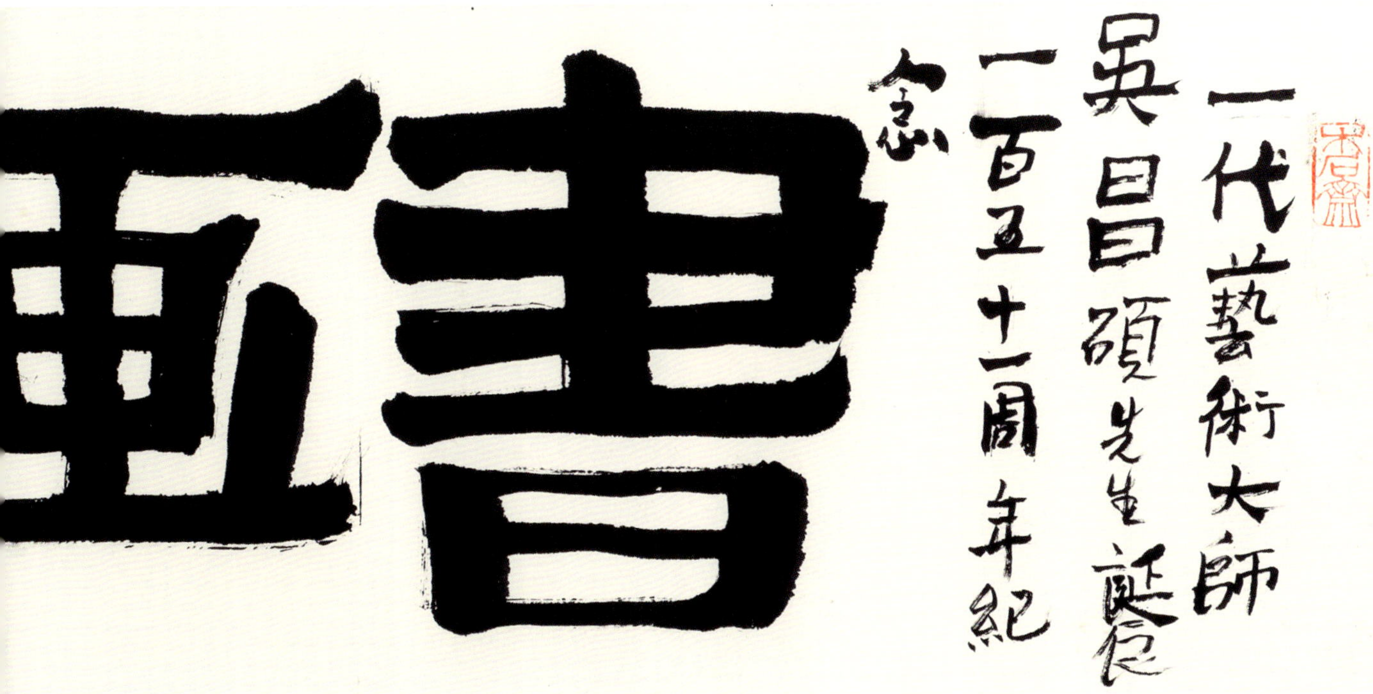

The work was to commemorate the 151st anniversary of the birth of Wu Changshuo, one of the greatest art masters.

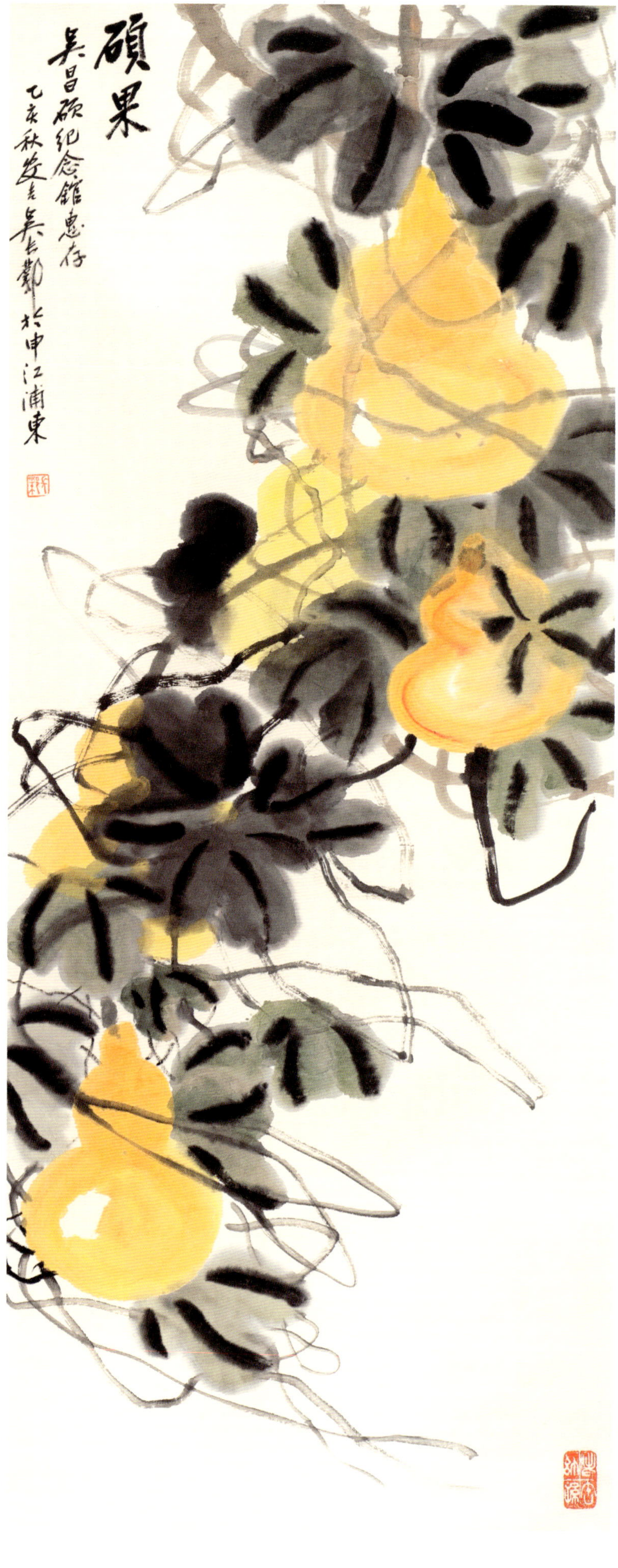
碩果
吳昌碩紀念館惠存

Wu Changye (1920–2009)
Gourd handscroll
Ink and colours on paper
Height 120cm, Length 48cm
1995

Gao Shixiong (1921–2019)
Handscroll with poetry in pre-Qin script
(engraved on stones and the Yu cottage)
Ink on paper
Height 100cm, length 60cm
1995

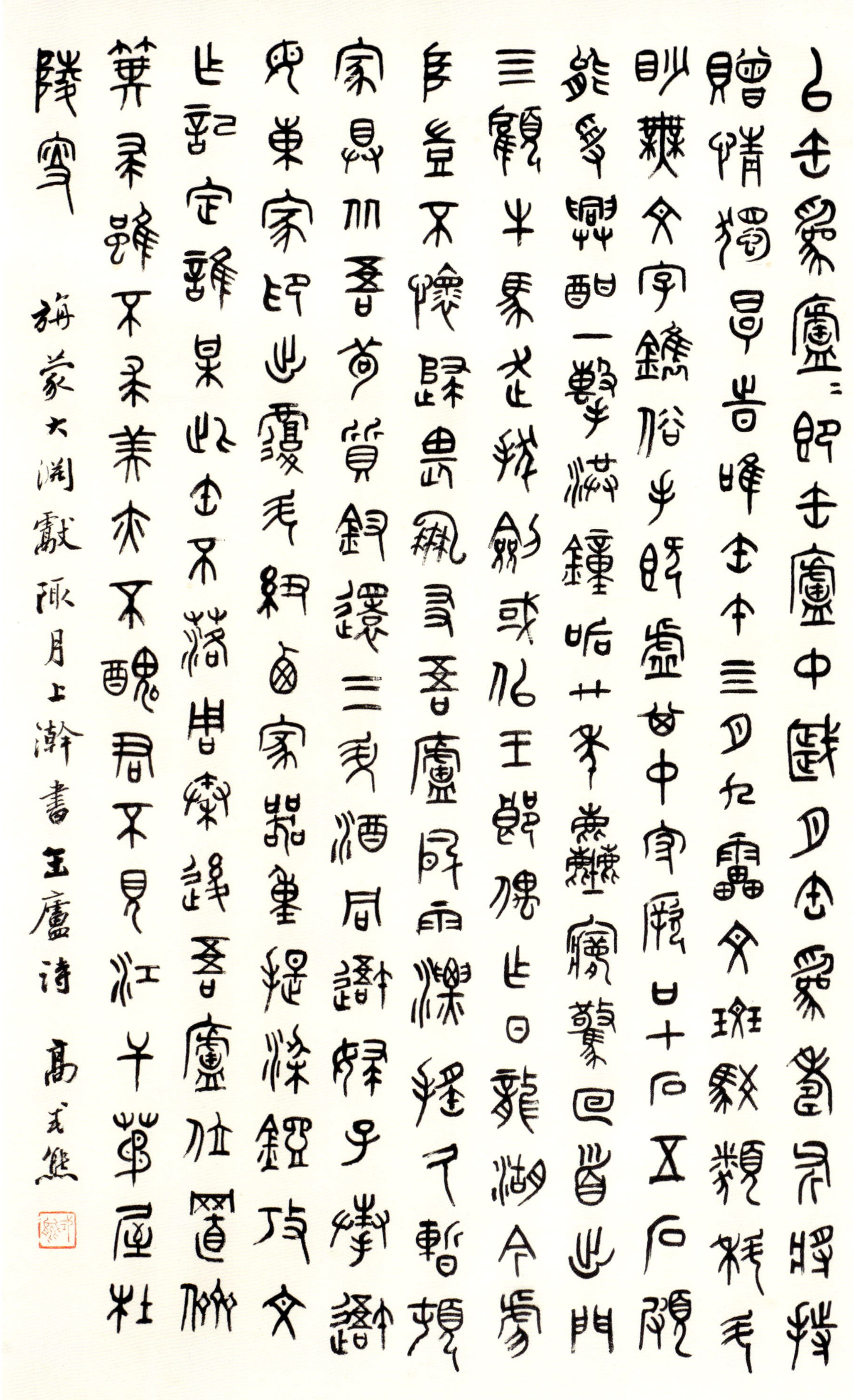

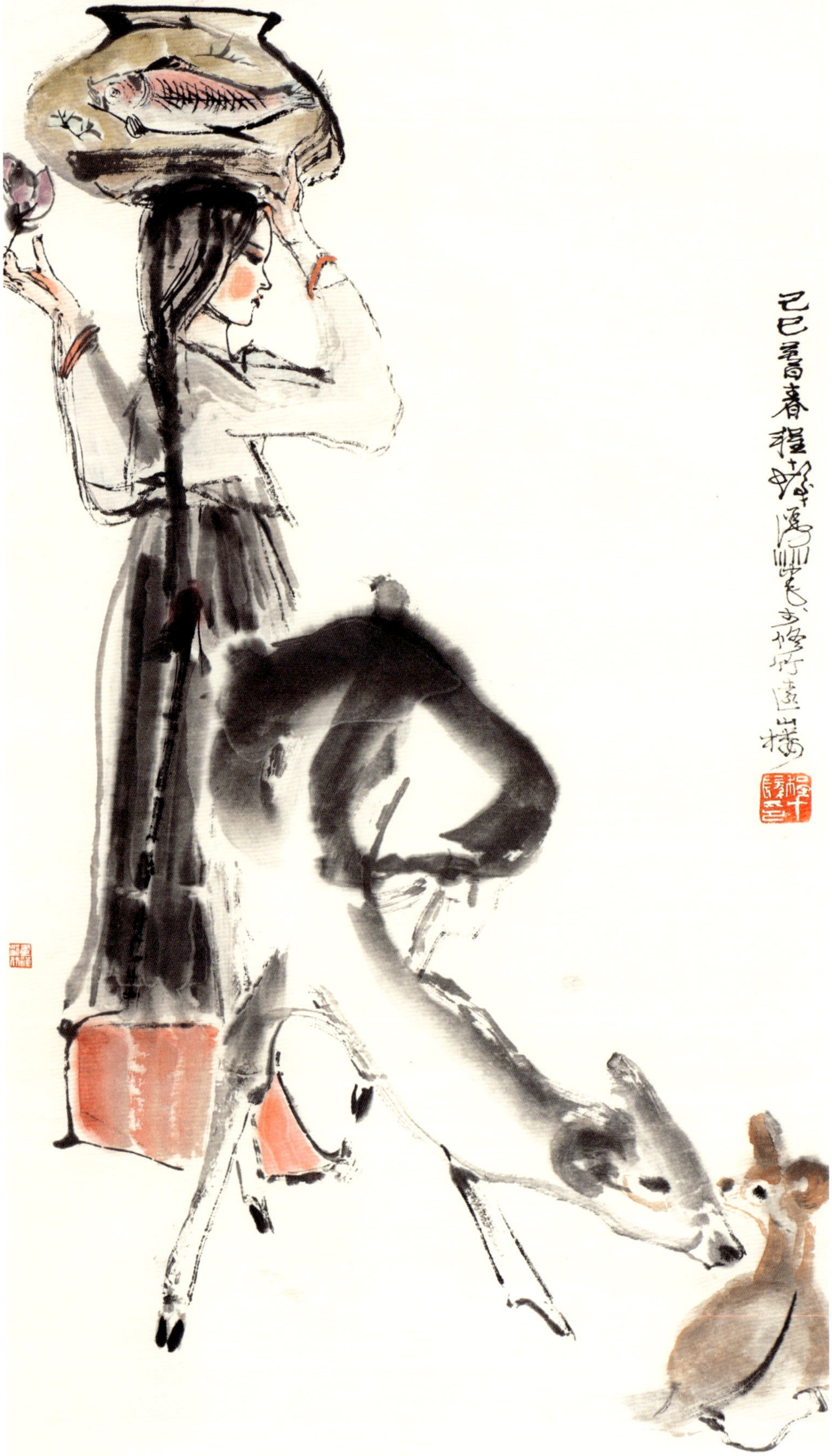
己巳暮春程十髮寫

Cheng Shifa (1921–2007)
A Young Woman and Two Deers handscroll
Ink and colours on paper
Height 126cm, length 88cm
1989

Cheng Shifa

Cao Cao Watching the Sea handscroll
(a powerful warlord and dictator in ancient China)
Ink and colours on paper
Height 39cm, length 41cm
Date unknown

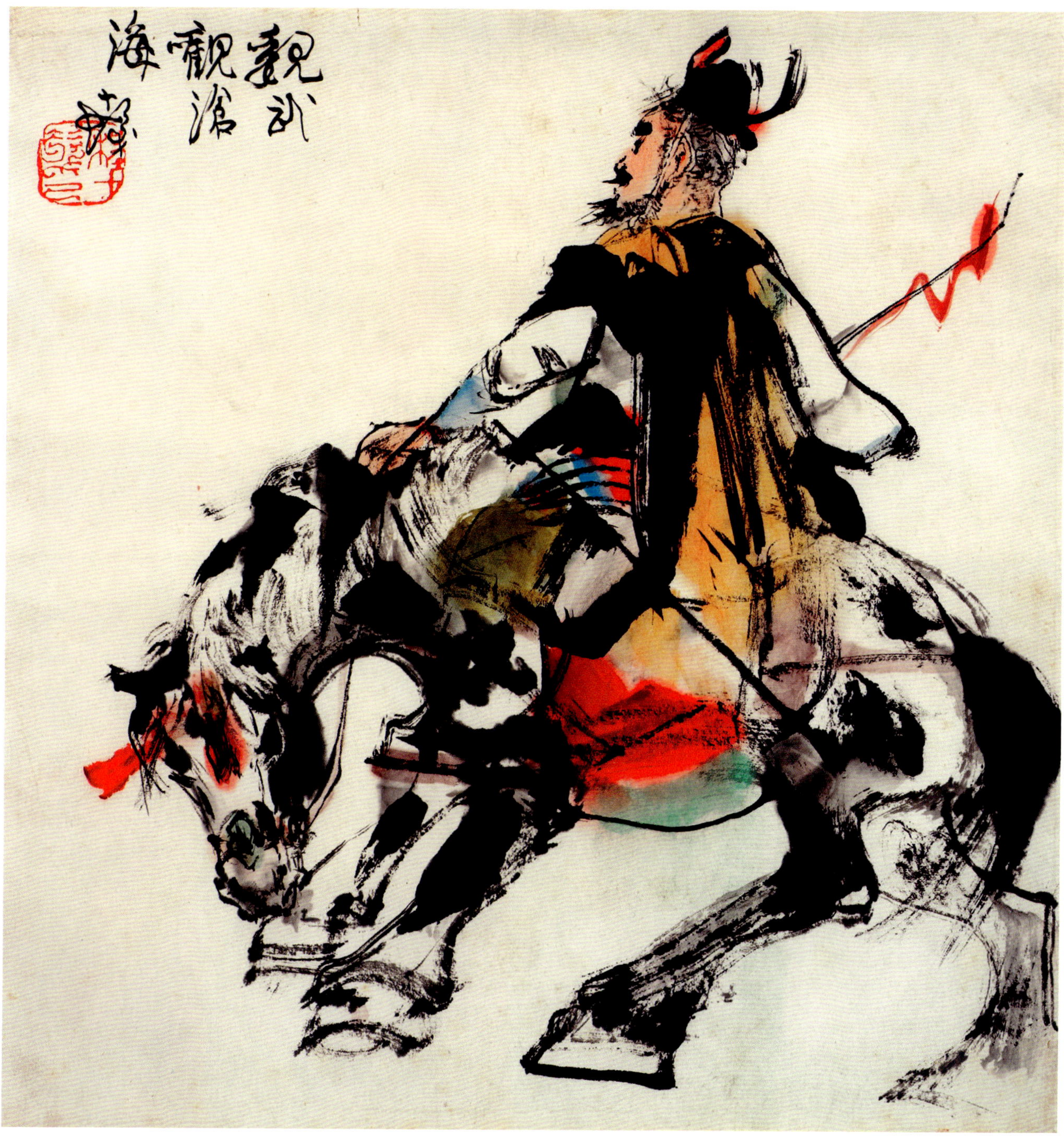

Chen Peiqiu (1922–2020)
Hazy Landscape handscroll
Ink and colours on paper
Height 68cm, length 60cm
Date unknown

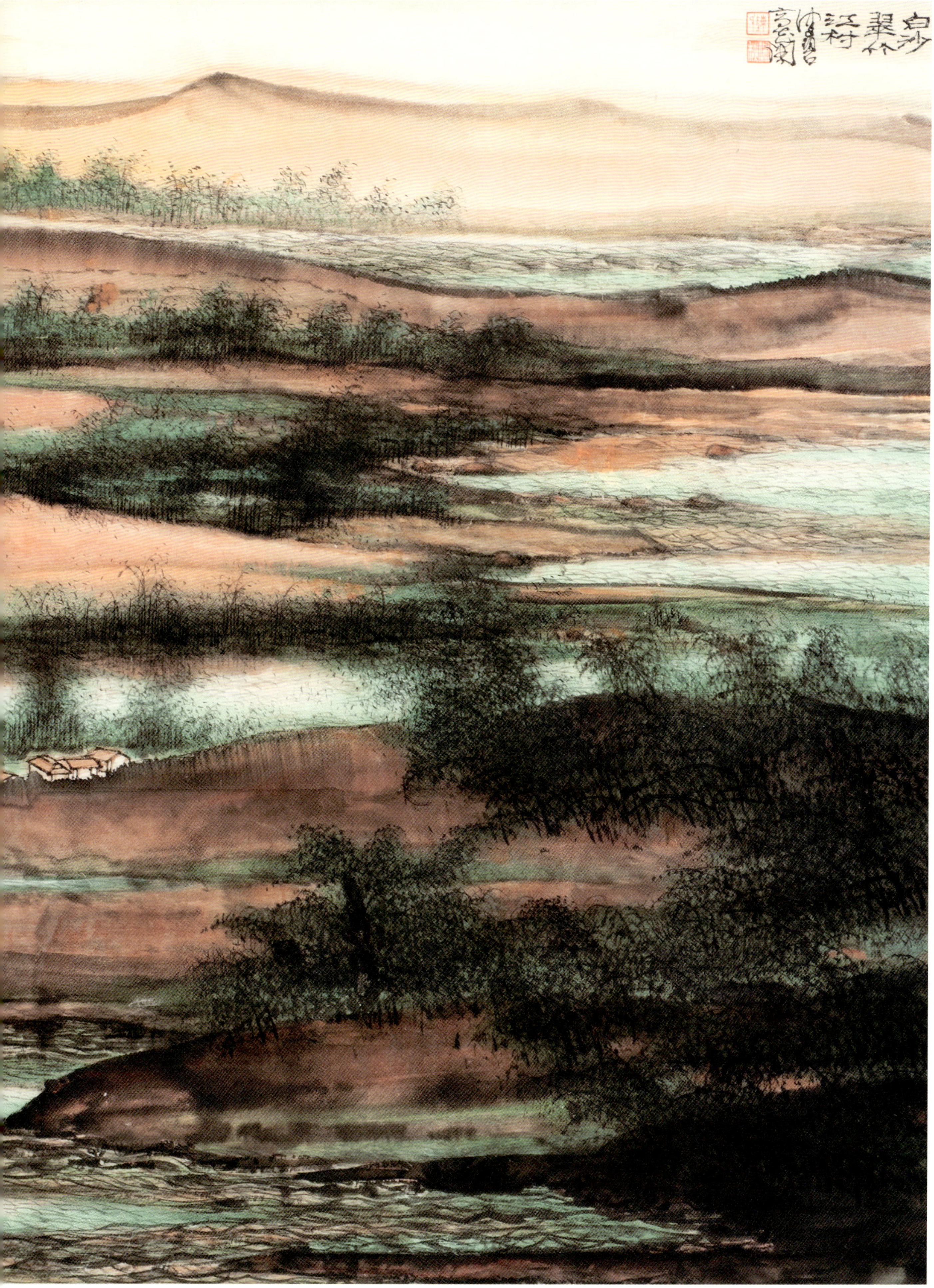
白沙翠竹江村

Han Tianheng (1940–)

Calligraphy handscroll ('Wu is a great master and role model for future generations')
Ink on paper
Height 90cm, length 48cm
1995

Han Tianheng created this calligraphy handscroll to celebrate the establishment of the Shanghai Wu Changshuo Art Museum in 1995.

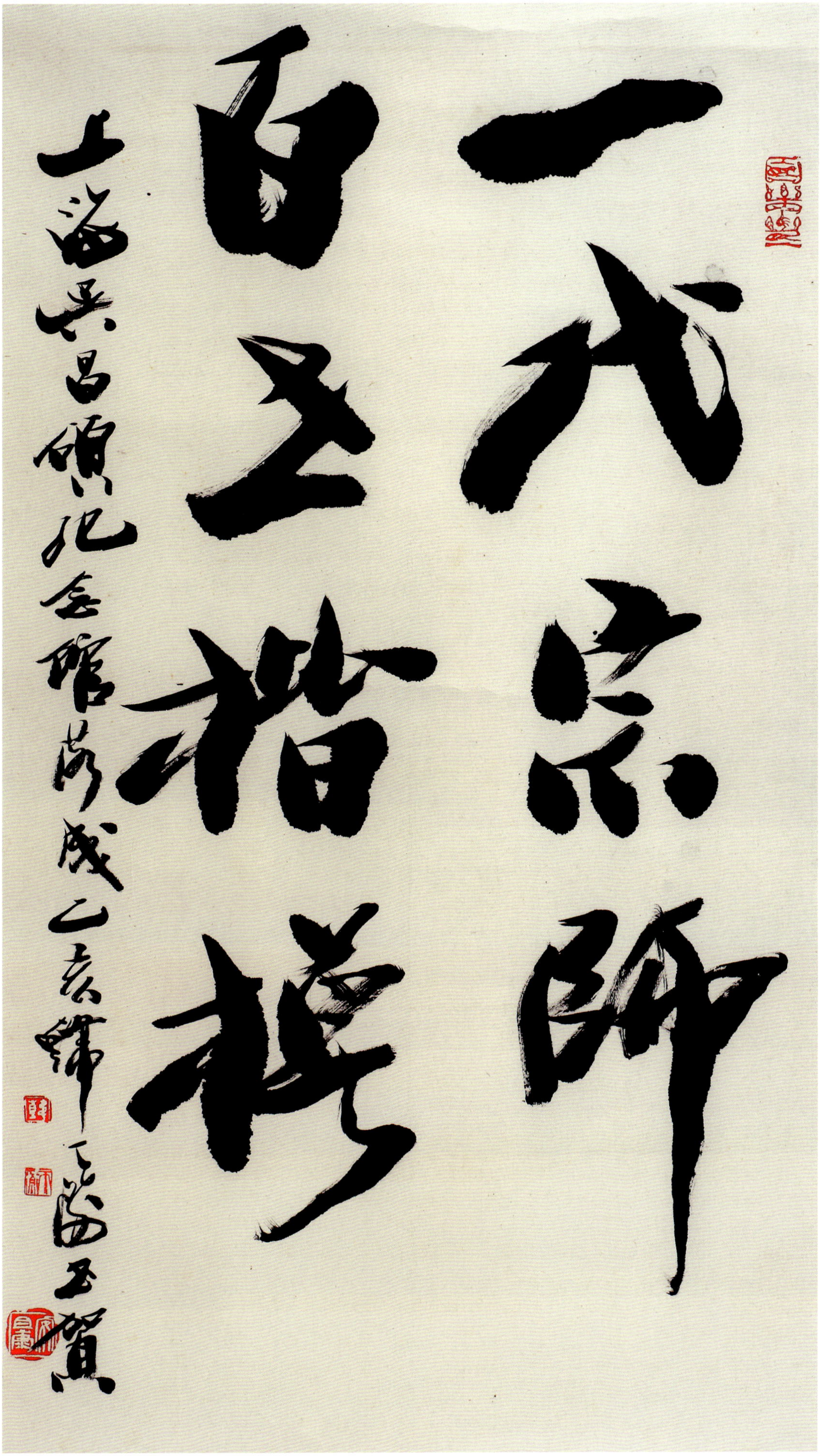
一代宗師
百世楷模
上海吳昌碩紀念館落成

Han Tianheng
Palm Tree handscroll
Ink on paper
Height 86cm, length 38cm
Date unknown

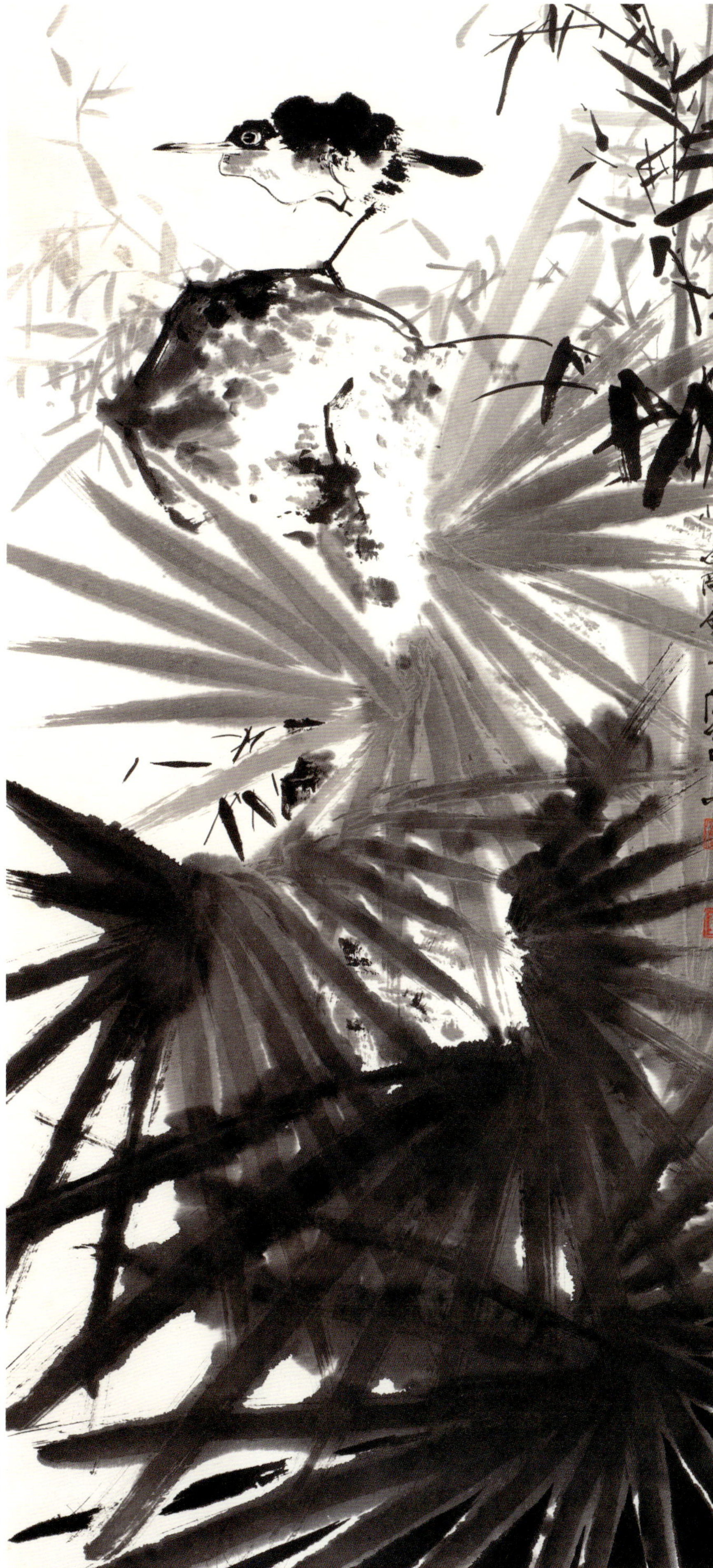

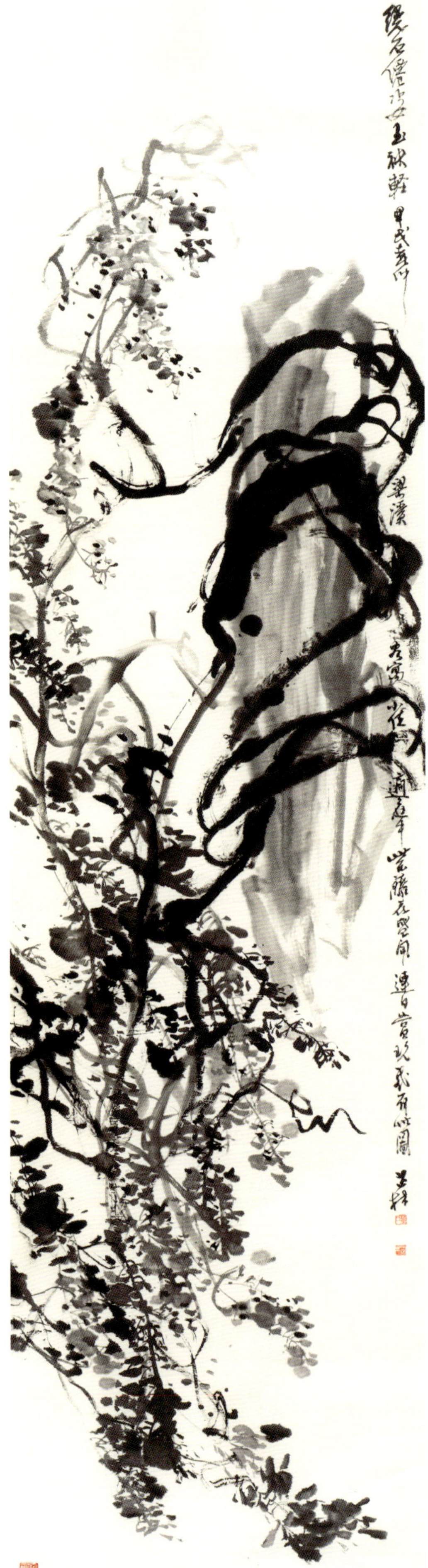

Dong Zhilin (1945–)
Ink Wisteria handscroll
Ink on paper
Height 258cm, Length 67cm
1994

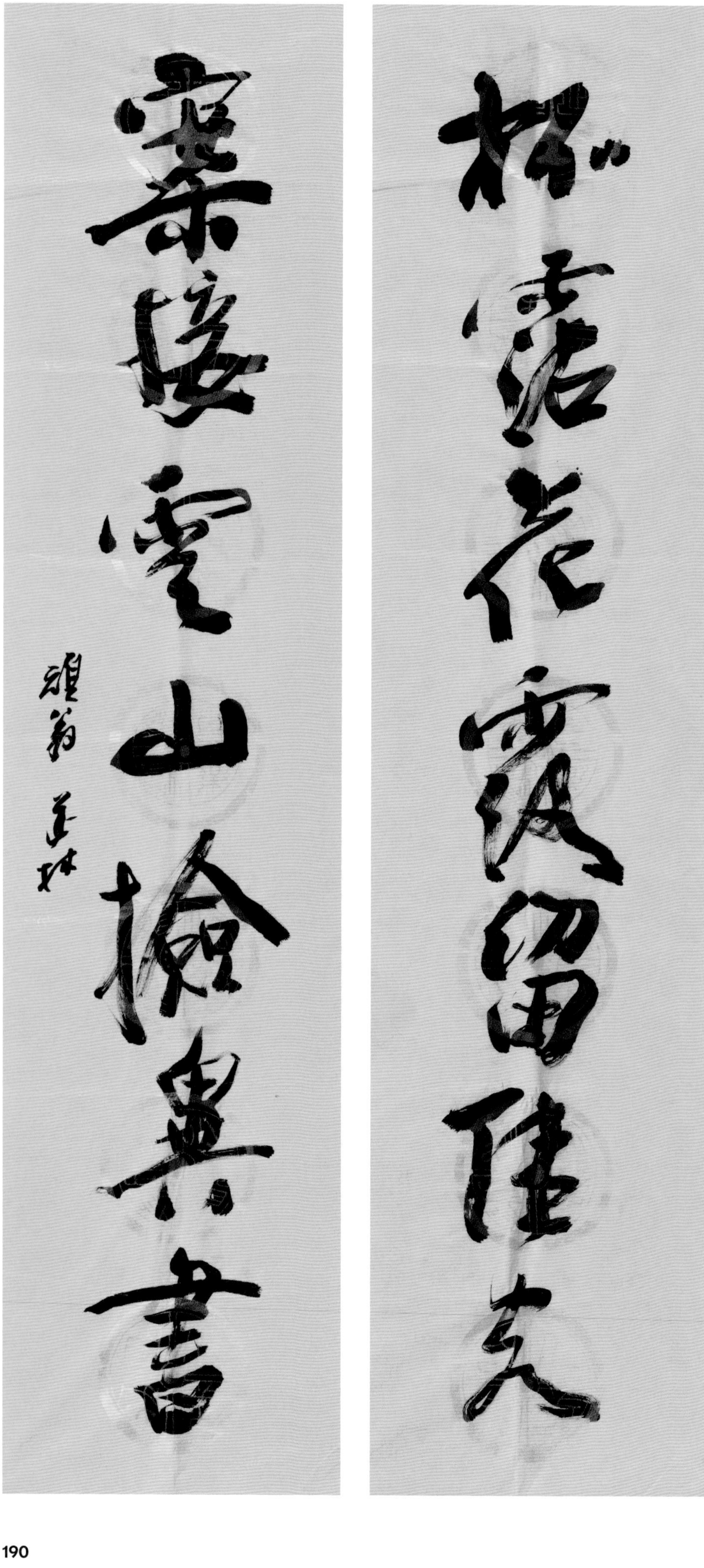

Dong Zhilin

Running script, seven-character couplets
Ink on paper
Height 137cm, Length 35cm
Date unknown

Tong Yanfang (1946–)
Clerical Script, Five-Character Couplets
Ink on paper
Height 130cm, Length 30cm
1998

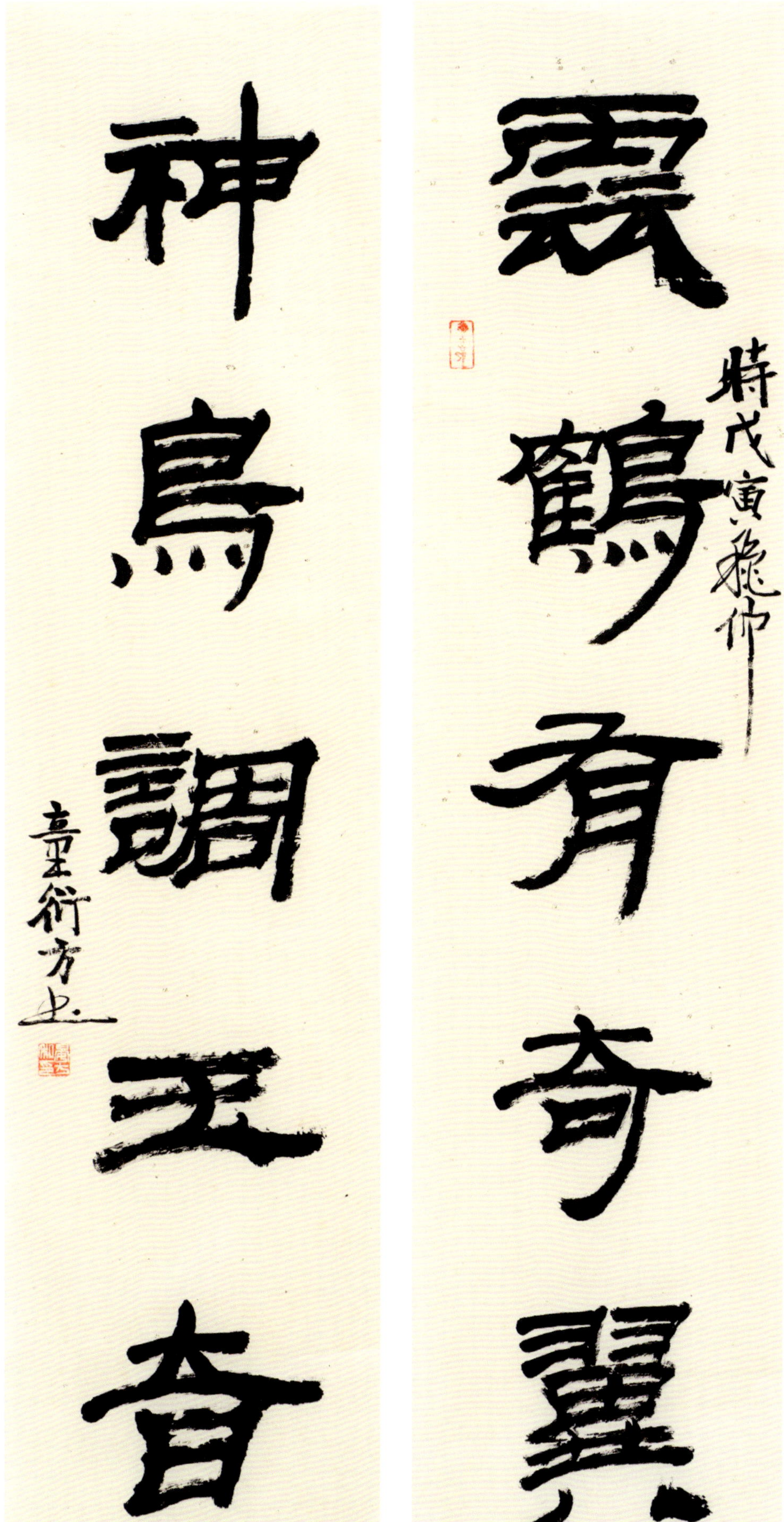
雲鶴有奇翼
神鳥調玉音

3
EXHIBITIONS

Since its reopening to the public in January 2023, the Wu Changshuo Art Museum, a municipal-level protected cultural site, has launched a total of nine public exhibitions featuring fine art from the Shanghai School of Art as of October 2024. These exhibitions aim to create a contextualised art exhibition space centred around the cultural circle of Wu Changshuo, attracting over 80,000 visitors.

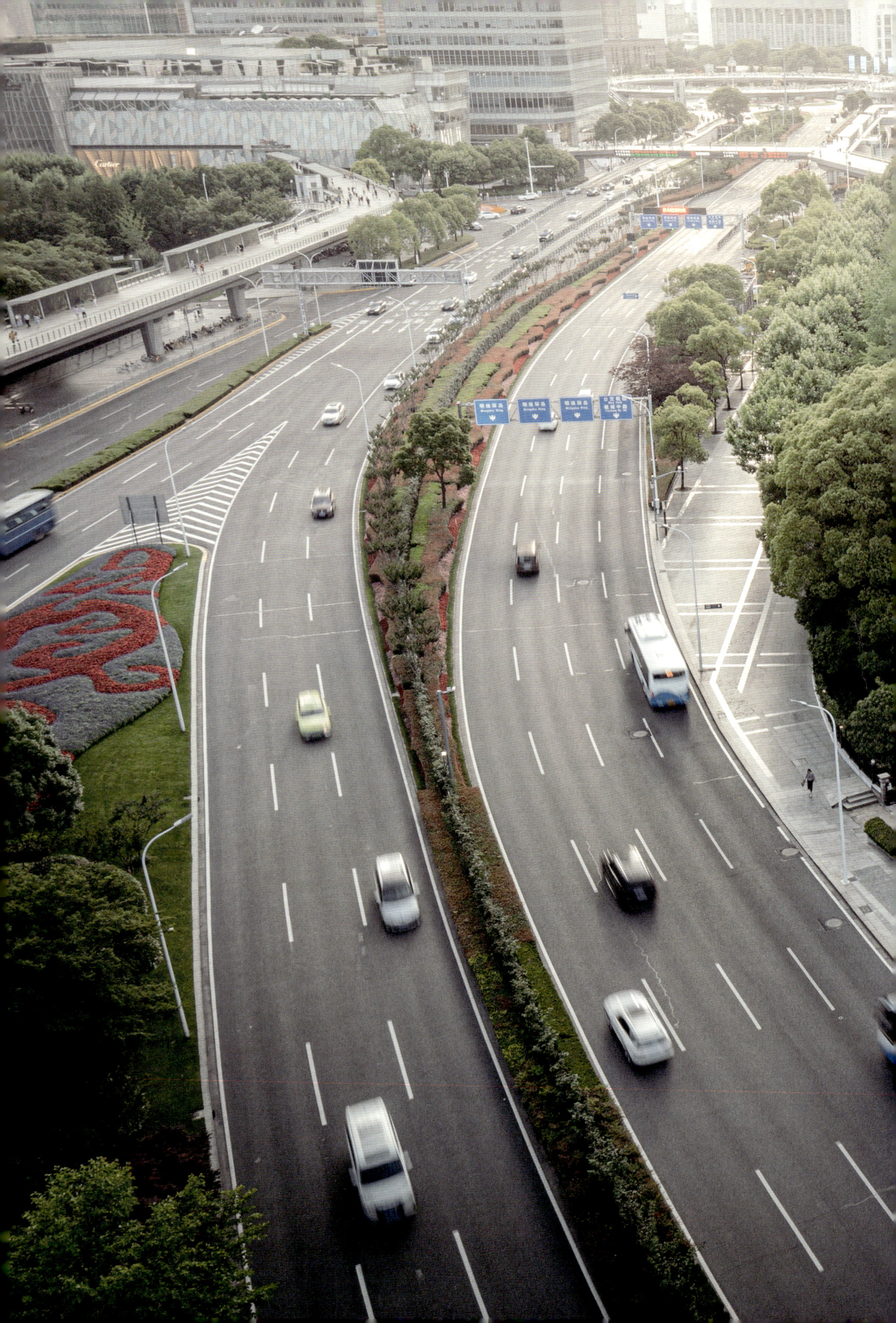

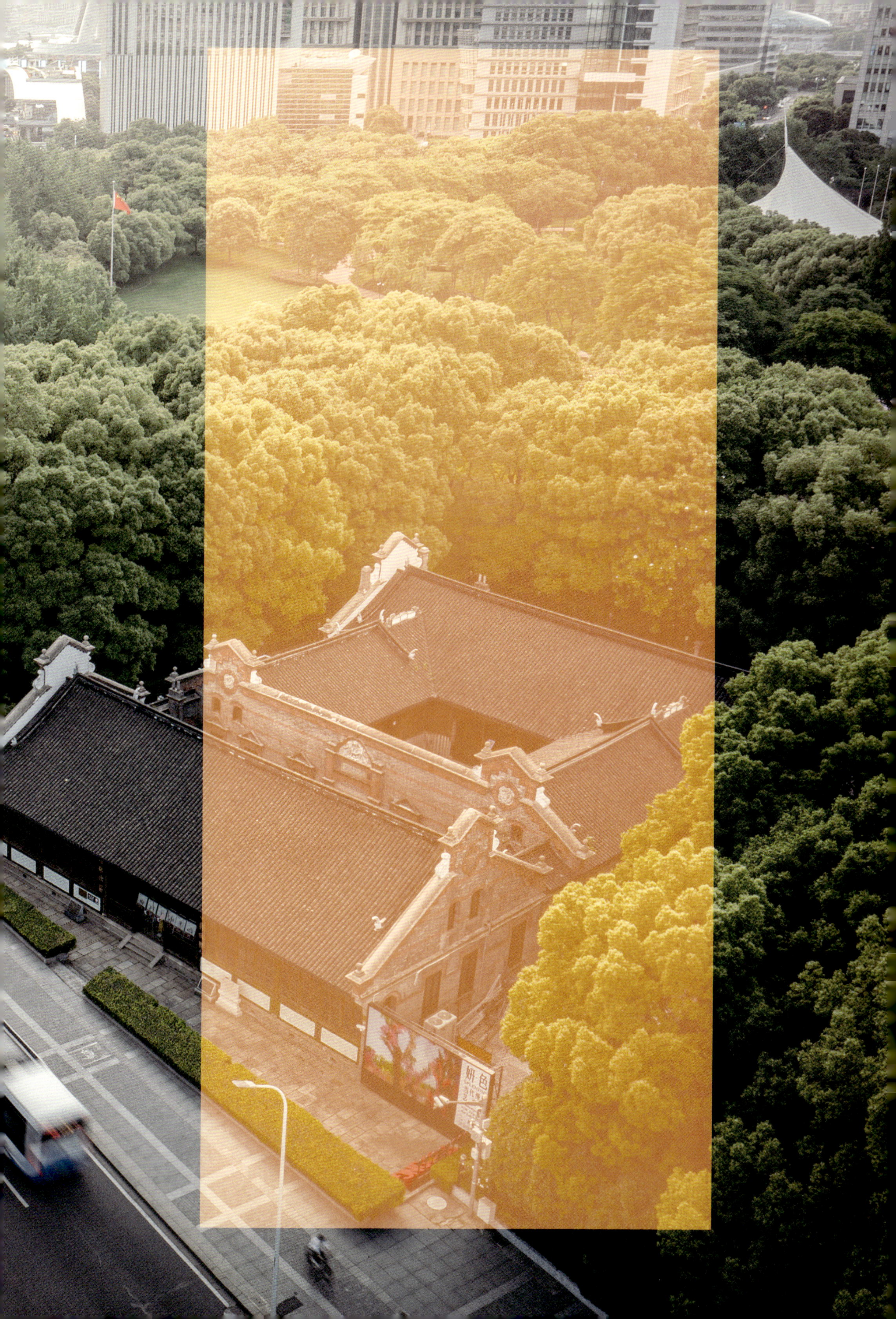
妍色

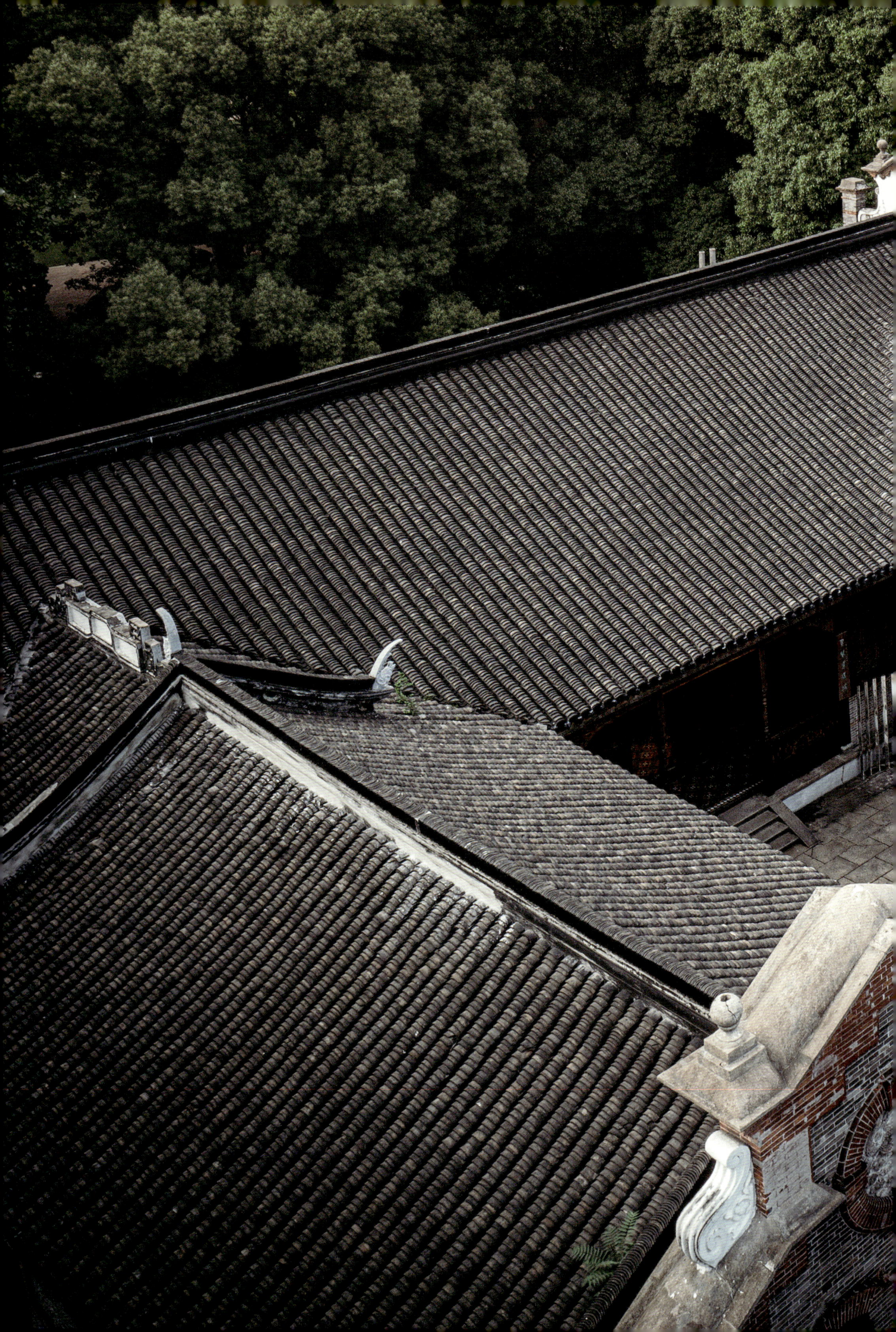

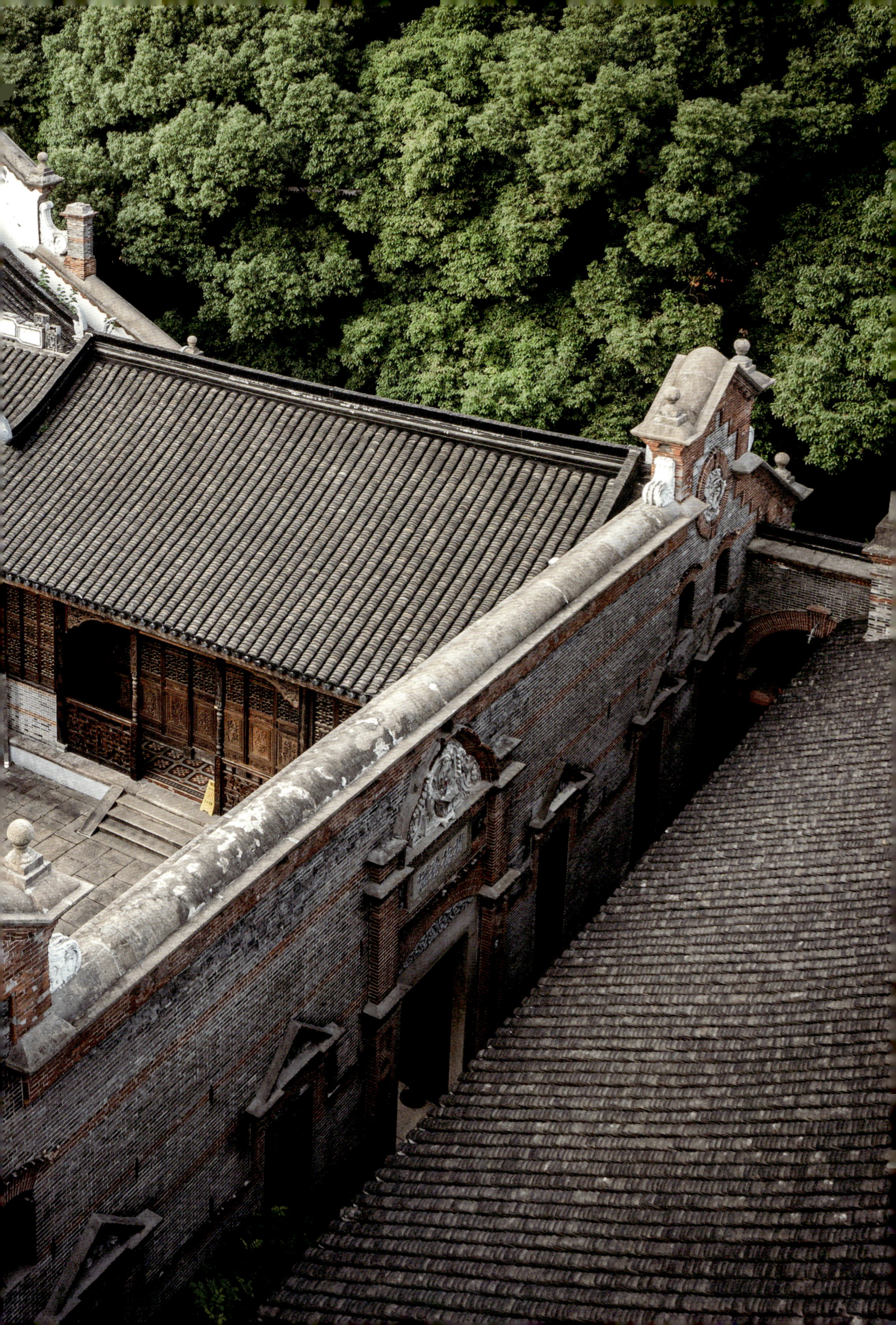

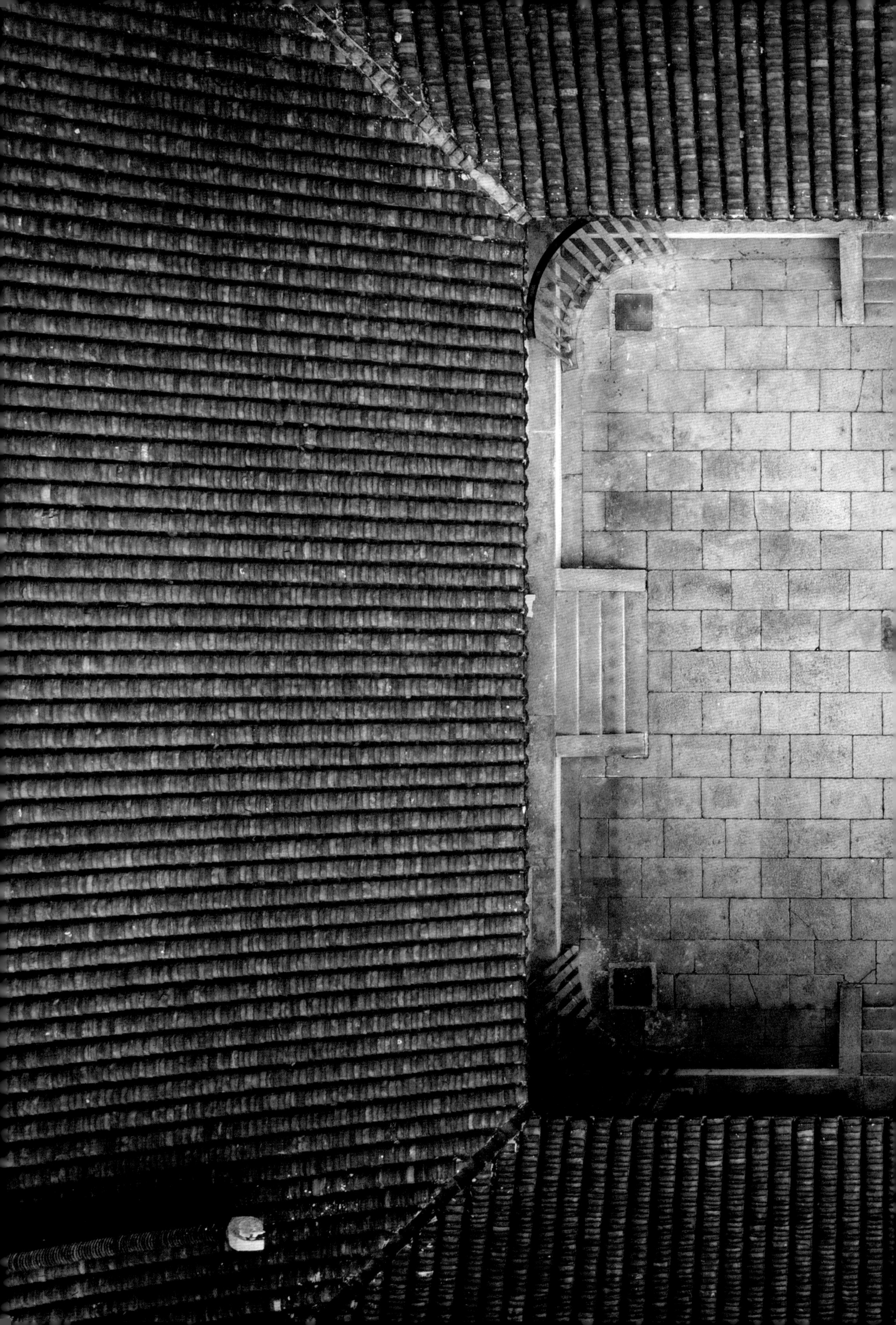

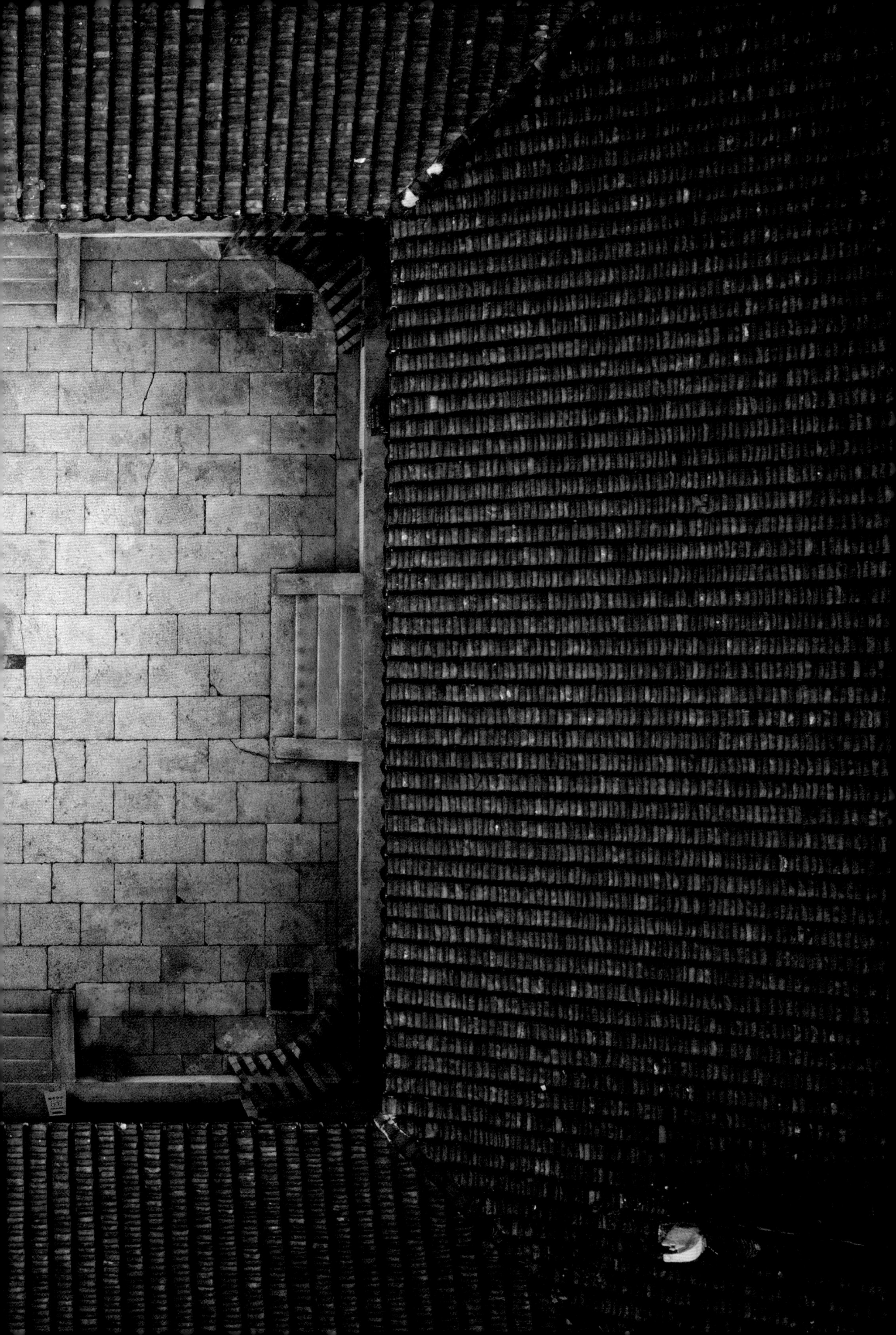

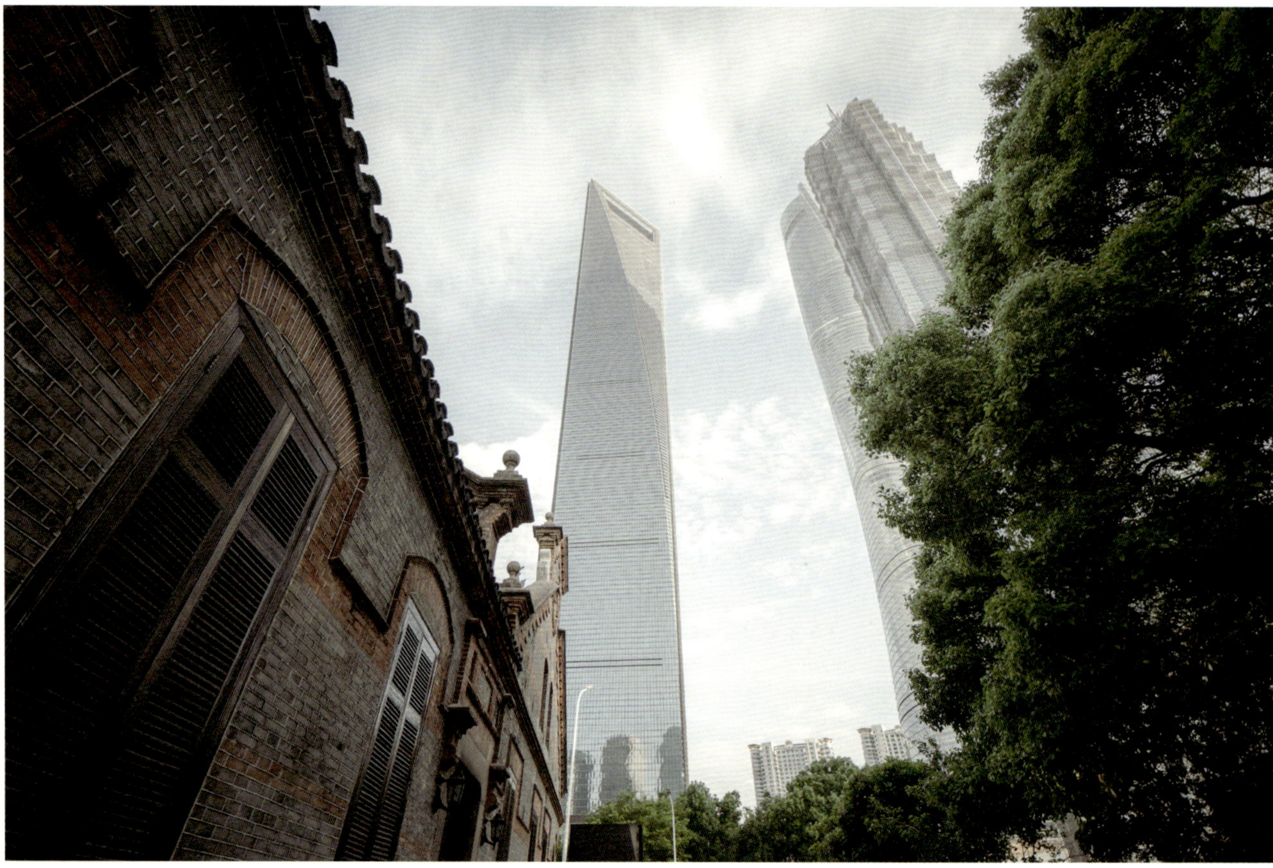

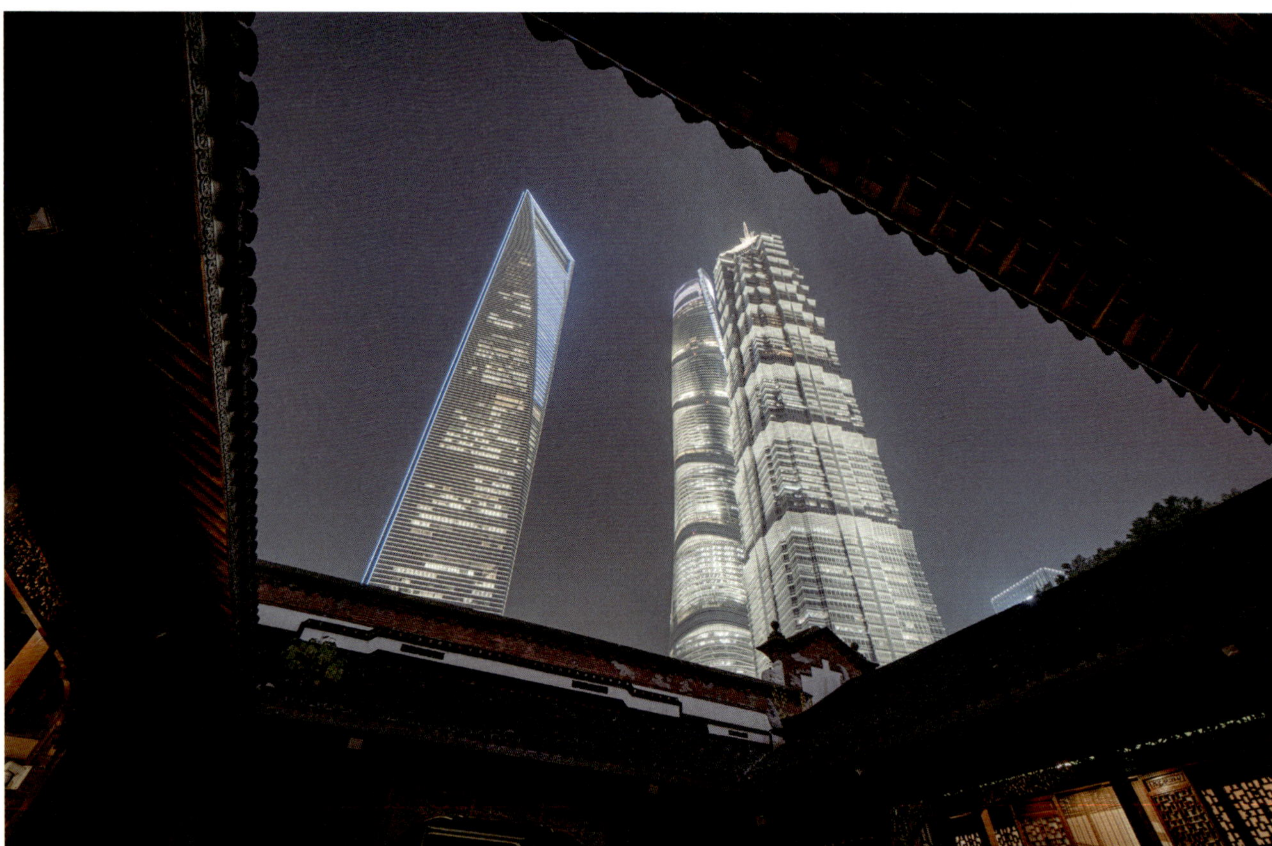

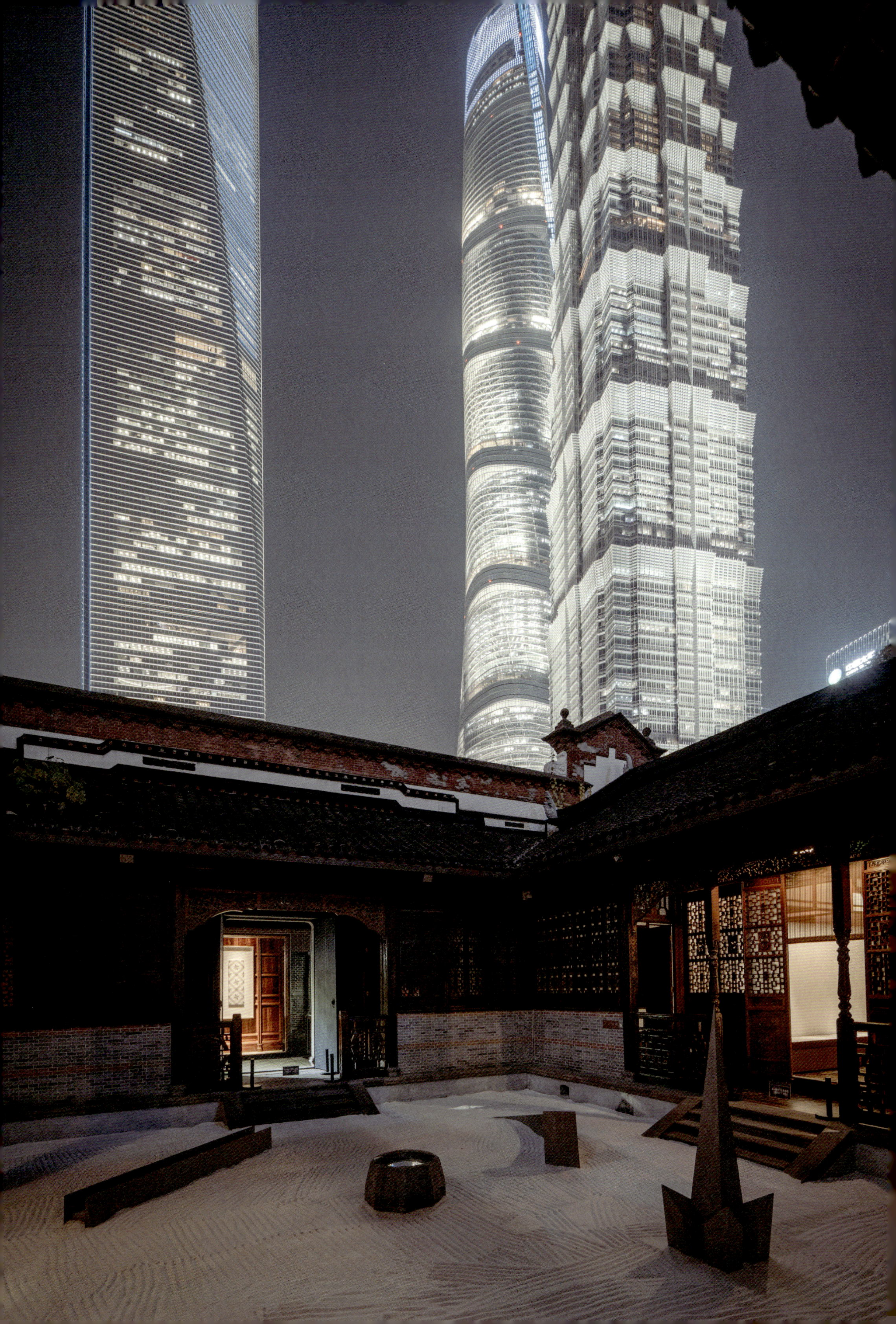

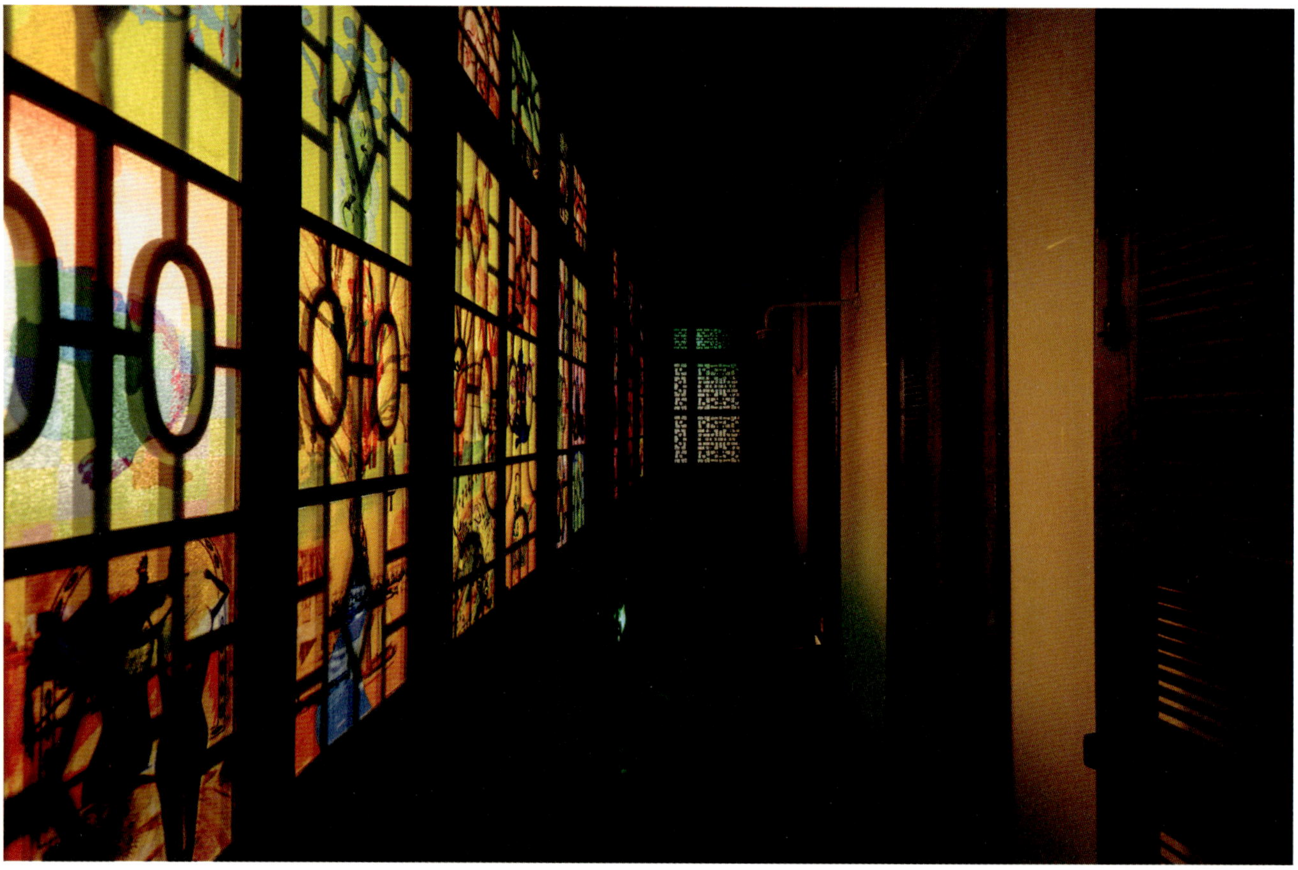

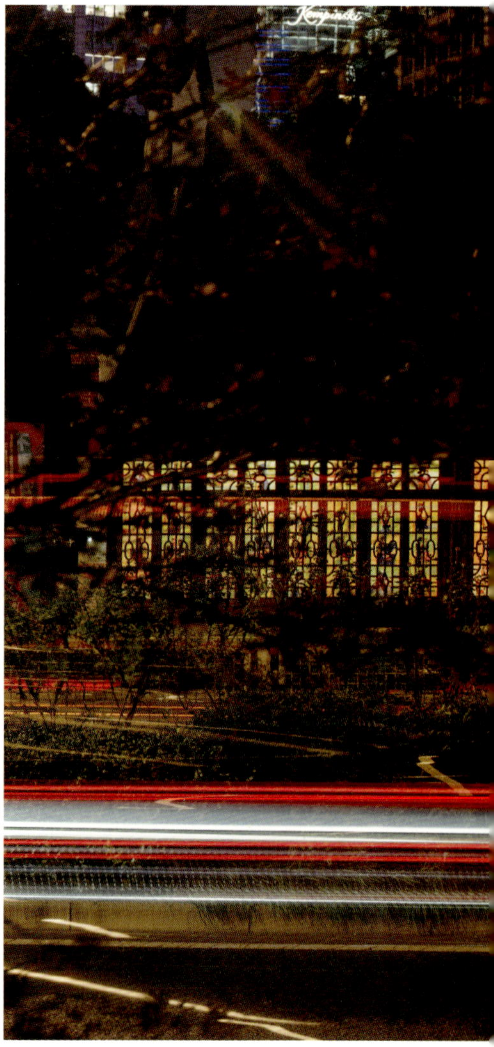

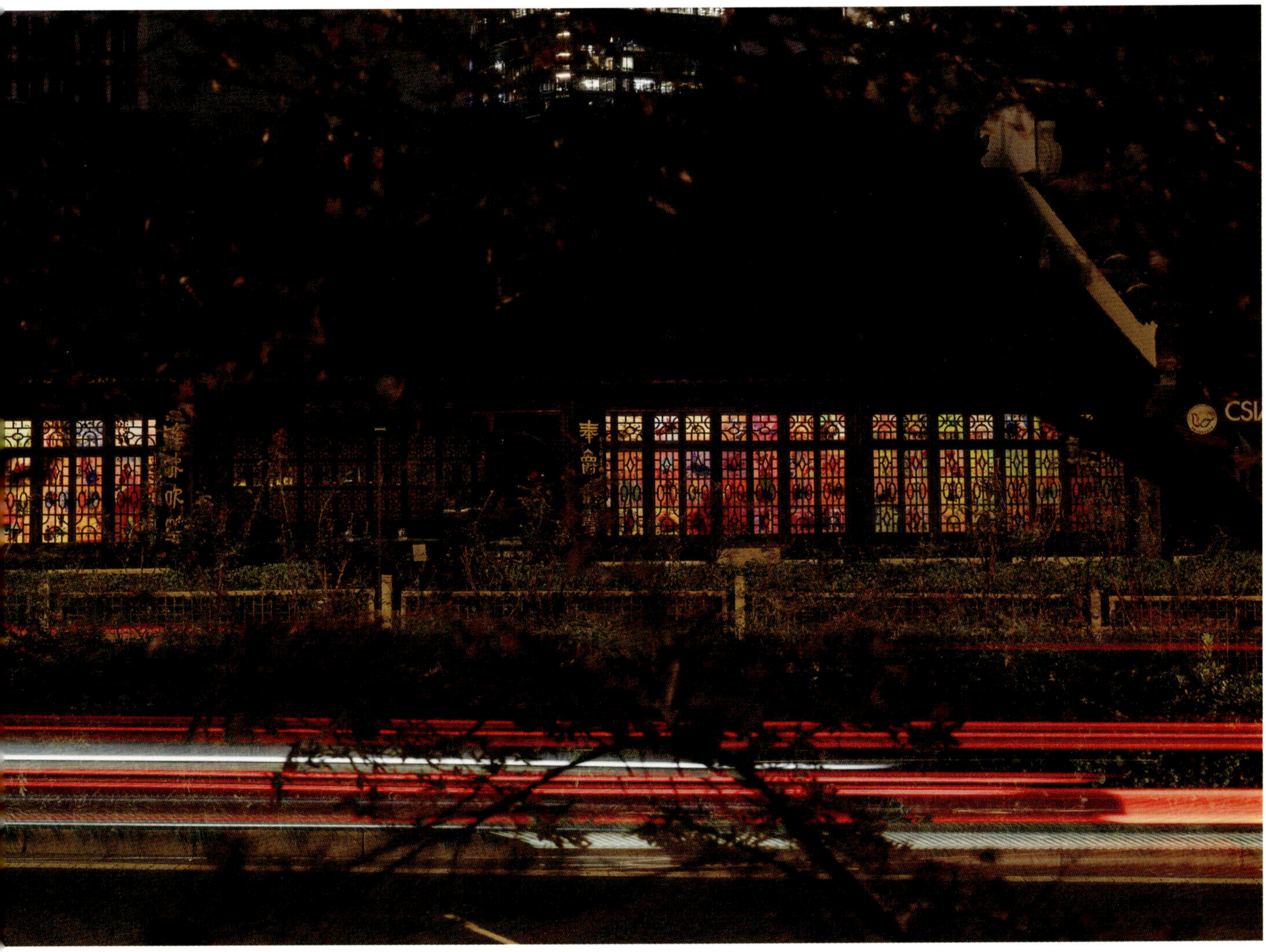

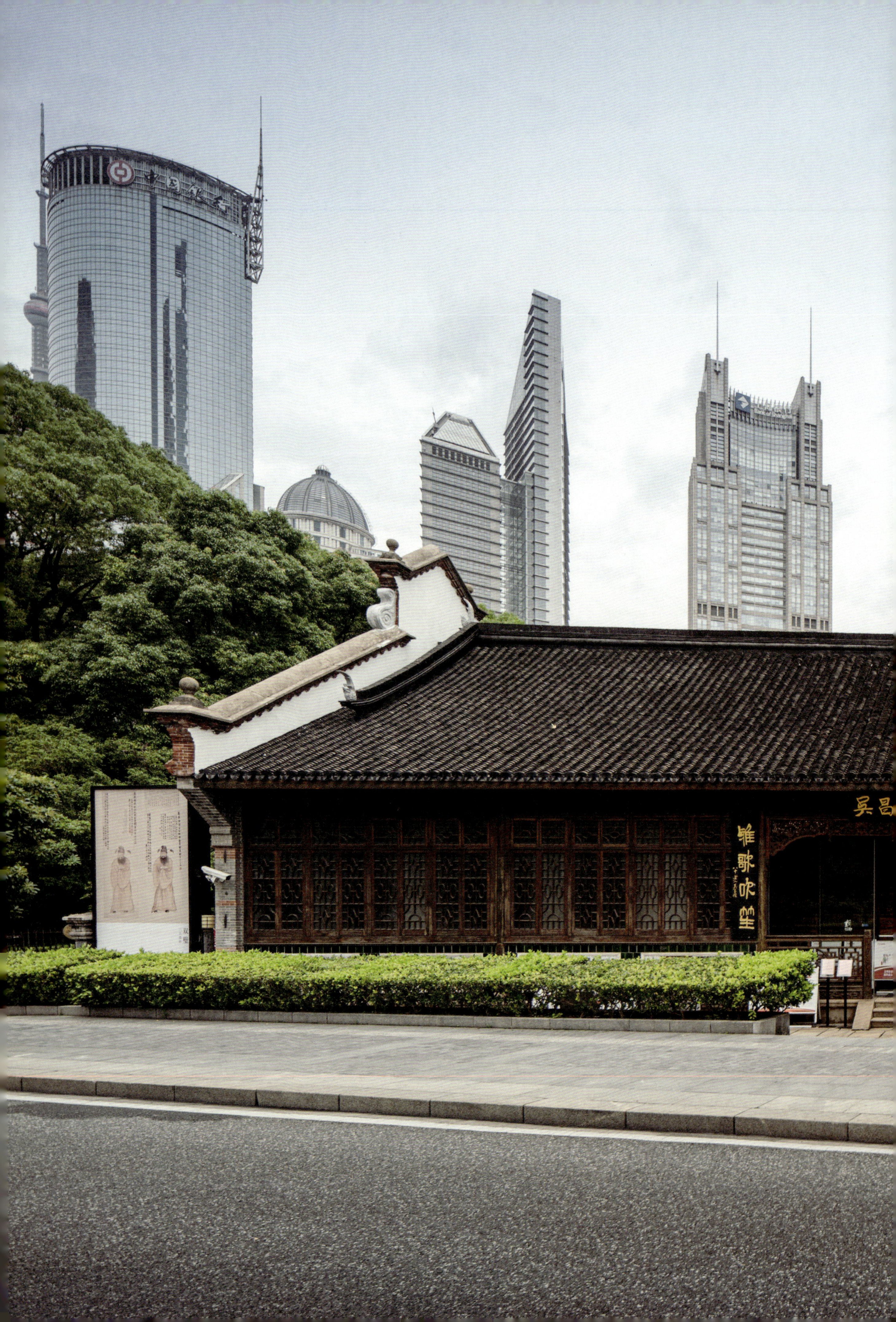

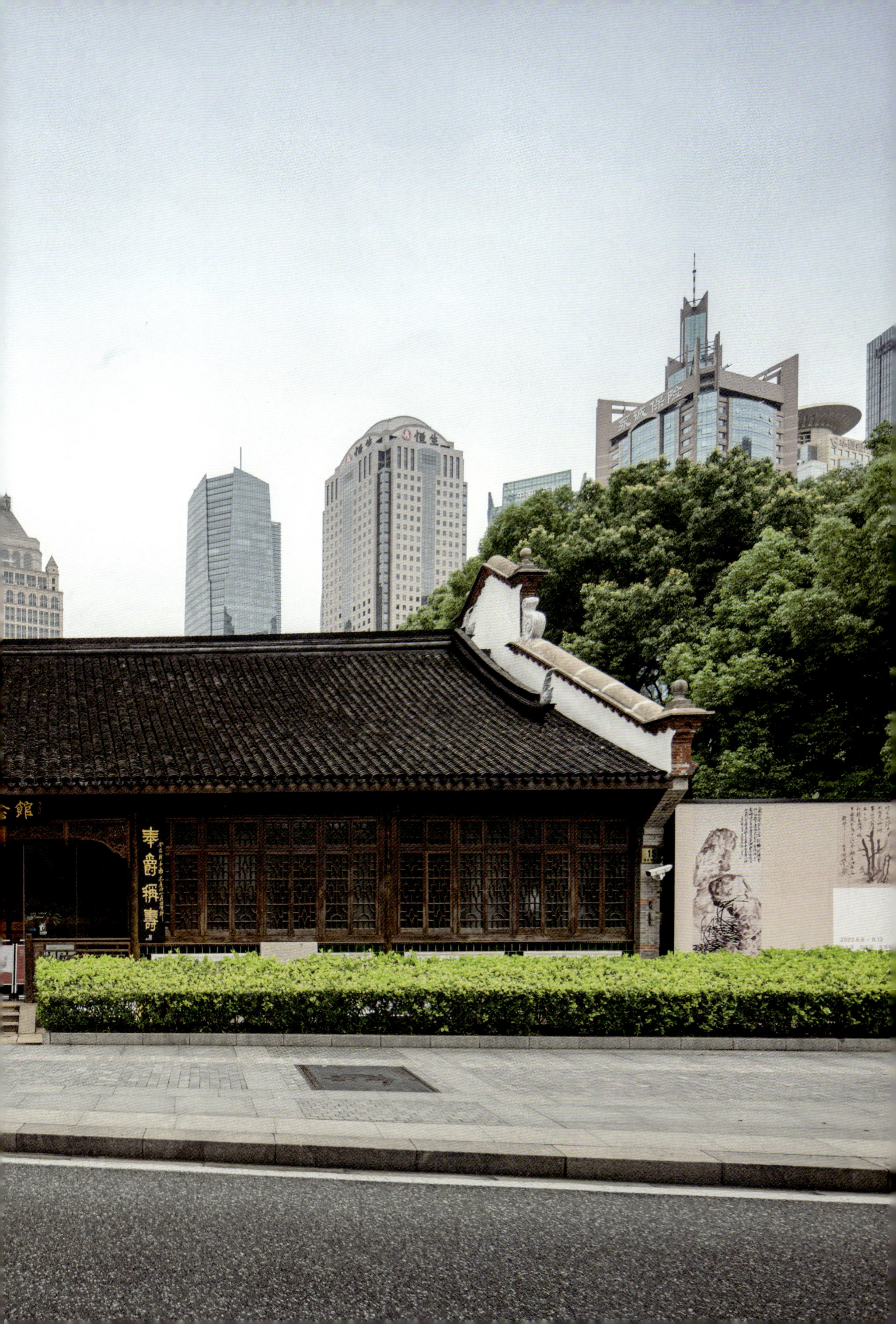
恒生
奉爵稱壽

Year of the Rabbit Inaugural Exhibition

12 June – 13 August 2023

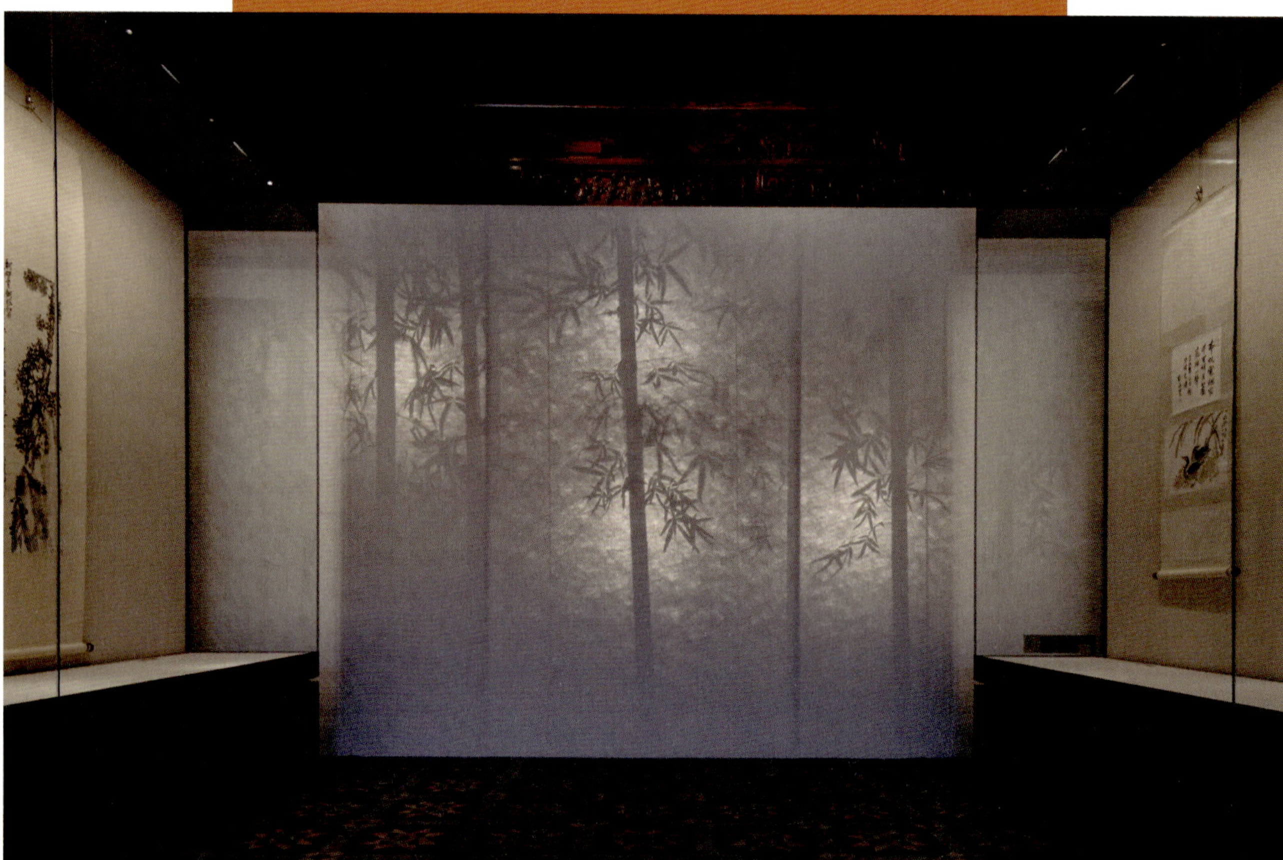

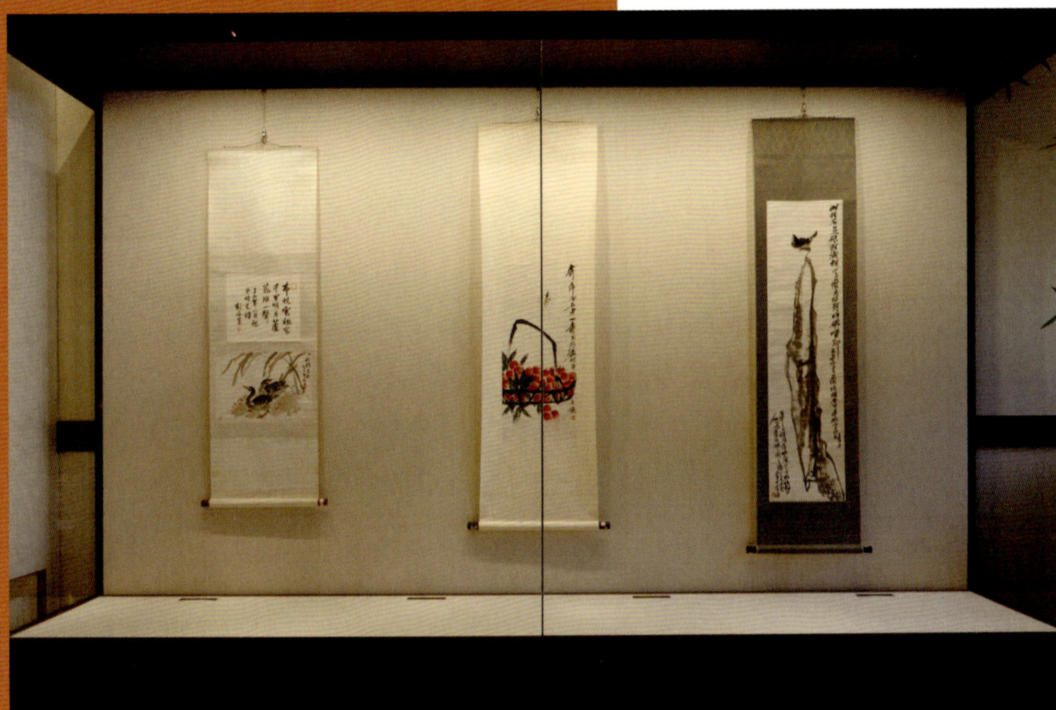

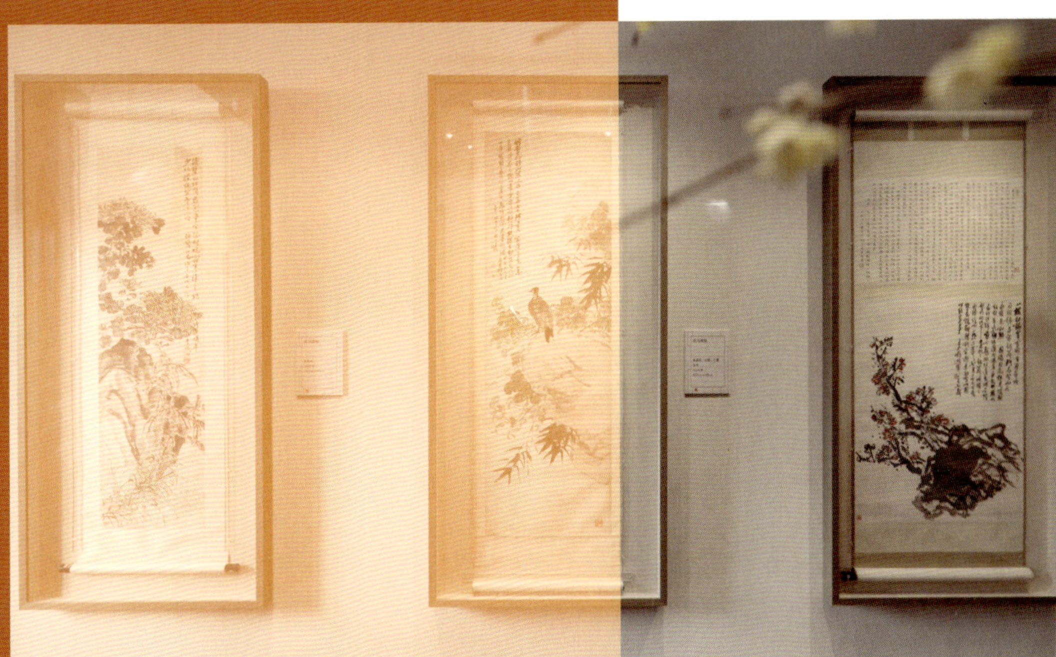

Splendid Contemporary Silk Tapestry Art Exhibition
7 March – 28 May 2023

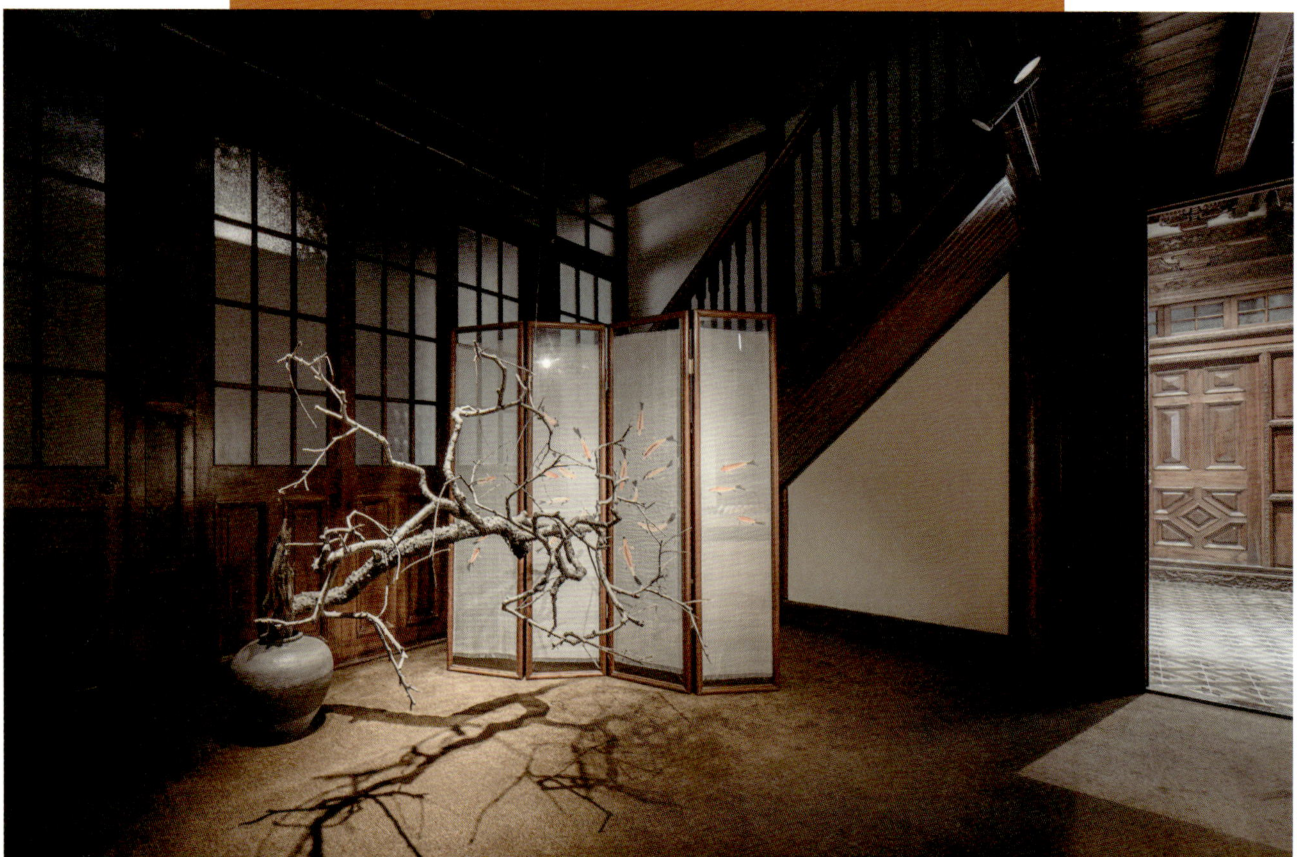

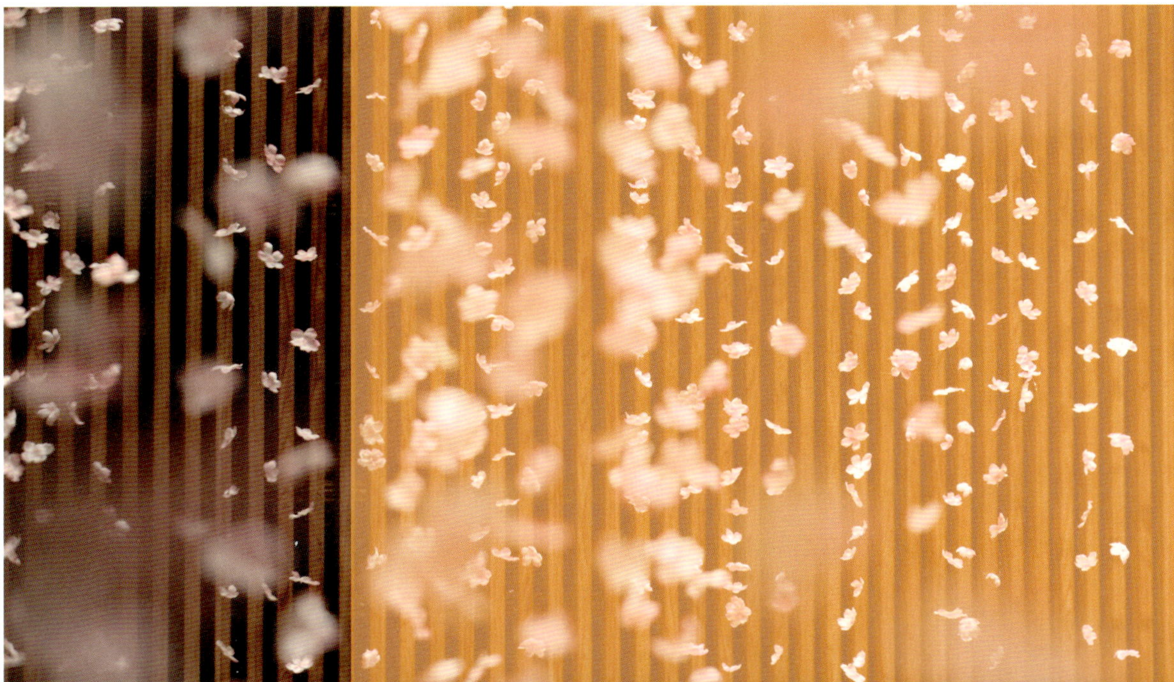

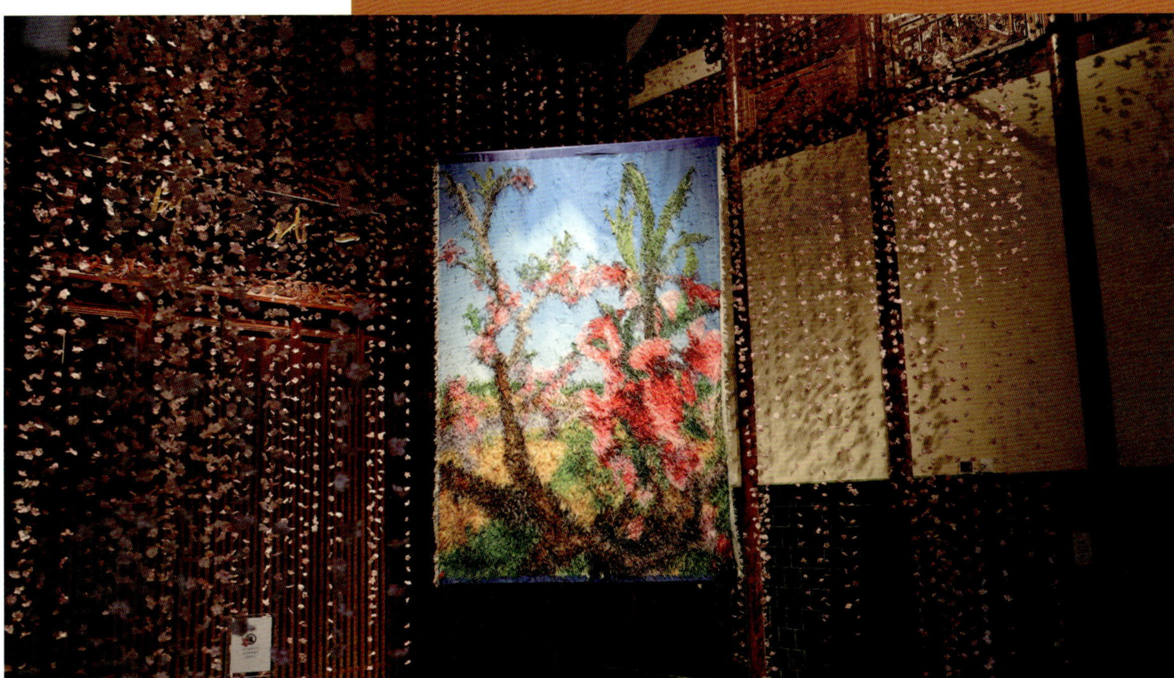

Documenta Wu Changshuo

7 March – 19 October 2023

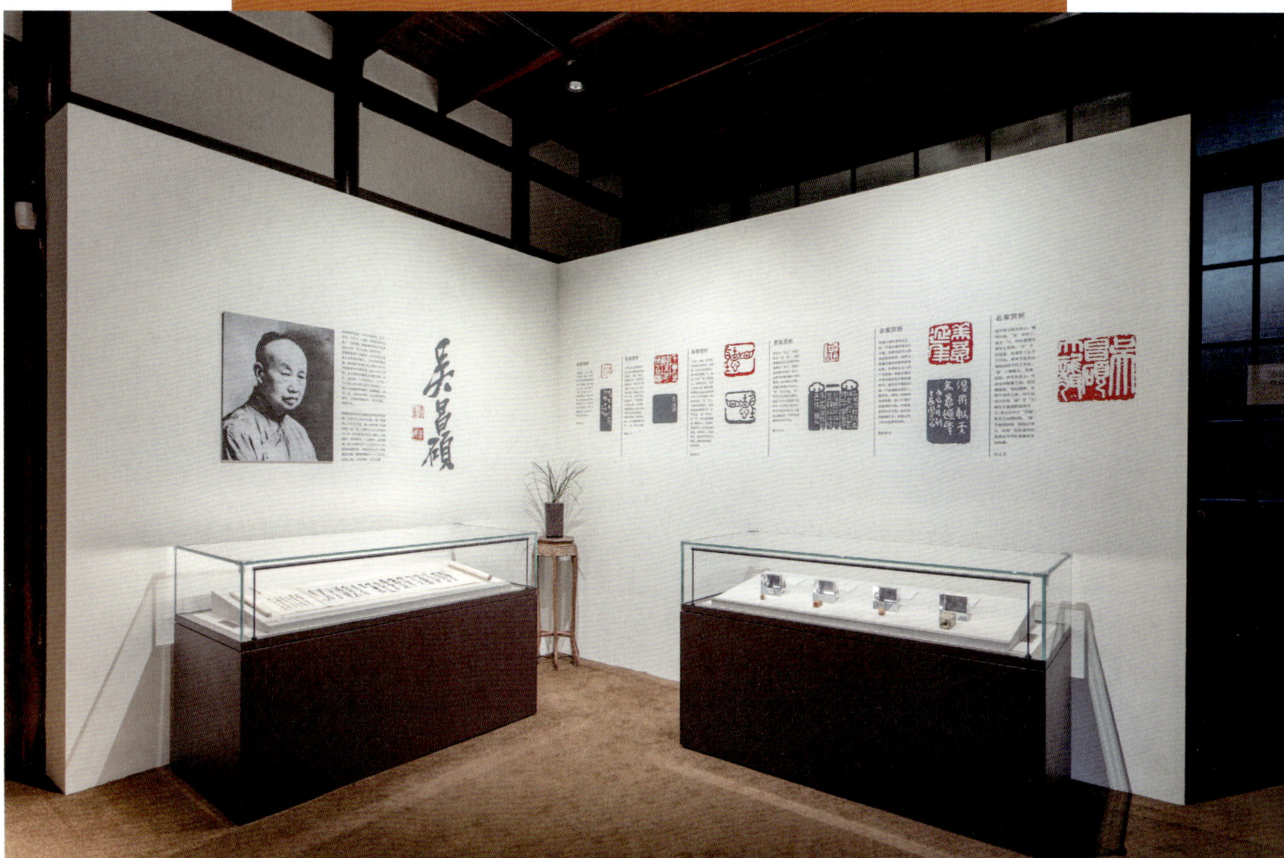

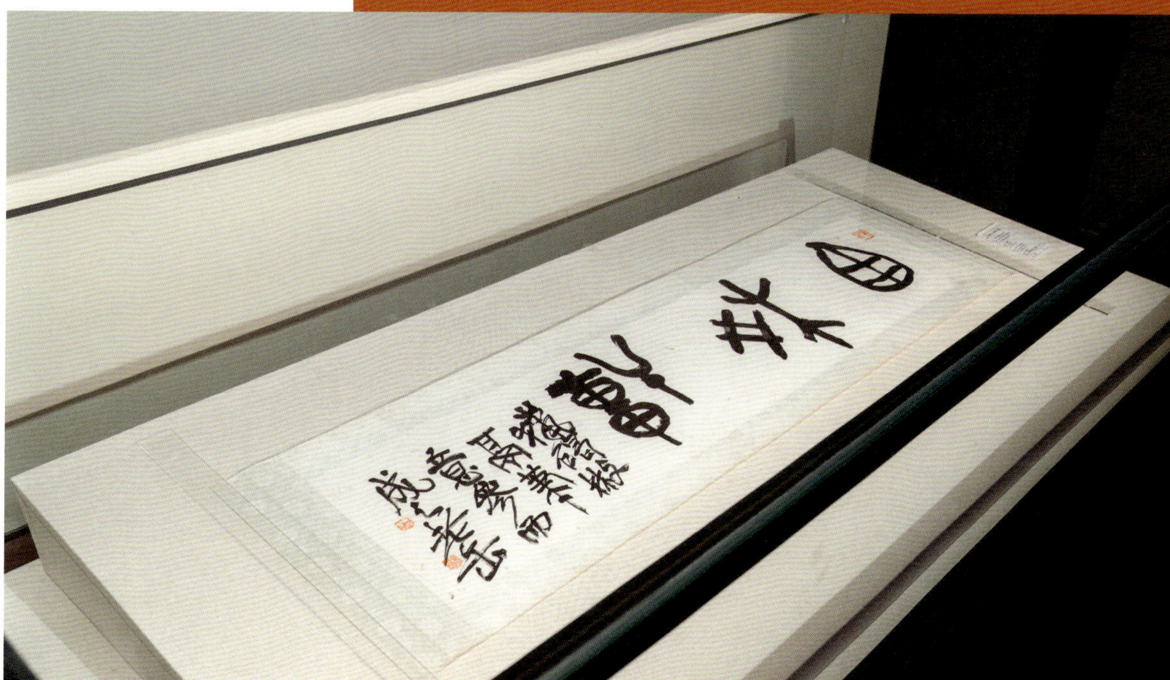

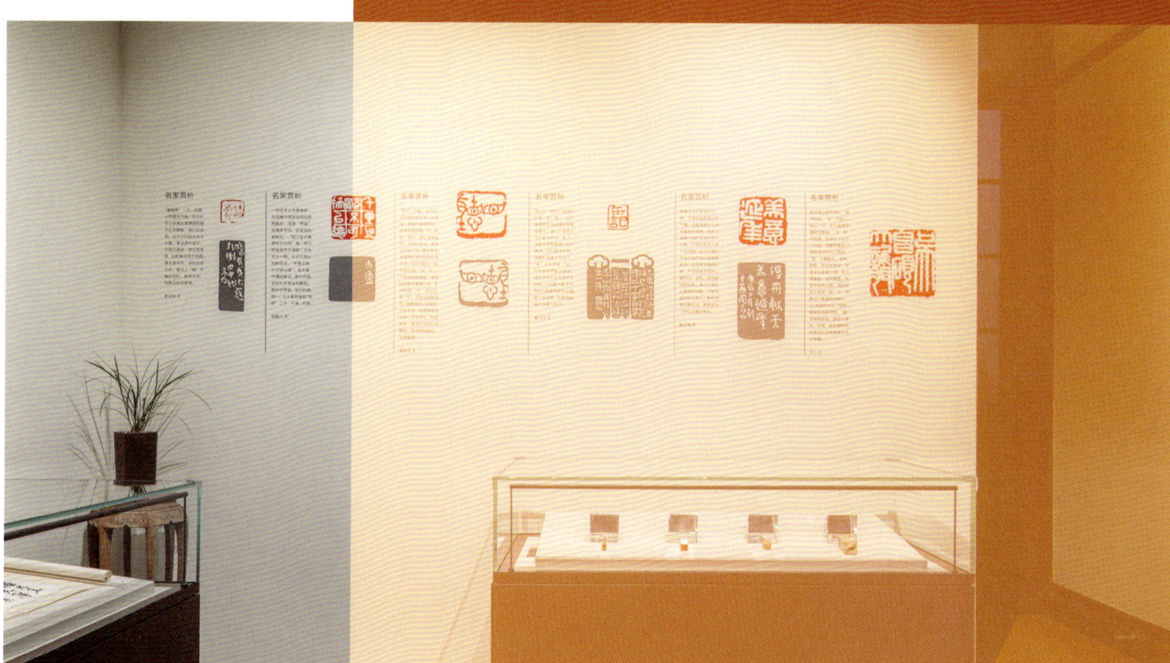

Wu Dacheng Wu Changshuo Wu Hufan—Exhibition of Authentic Paintings & Calligraphy

12 June – 13 August 2023

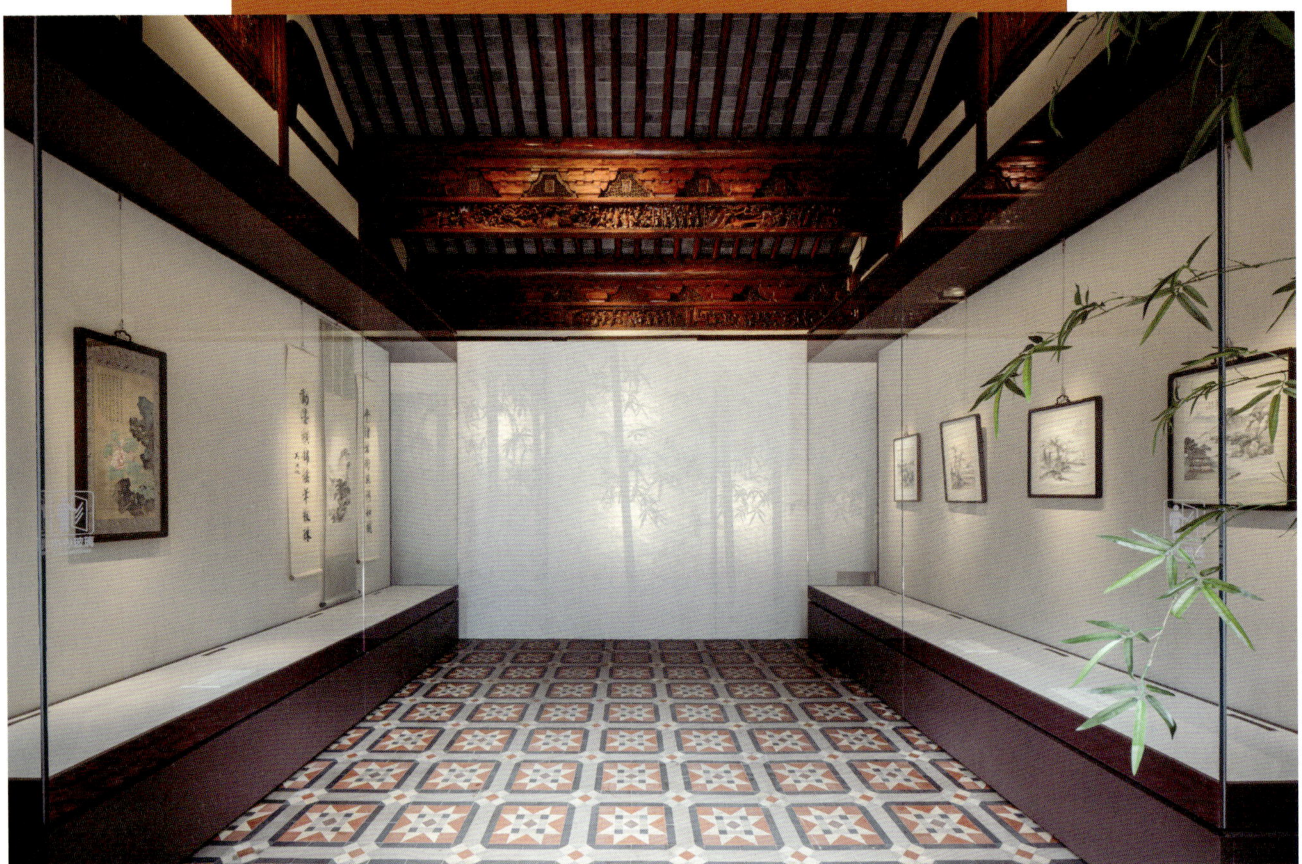

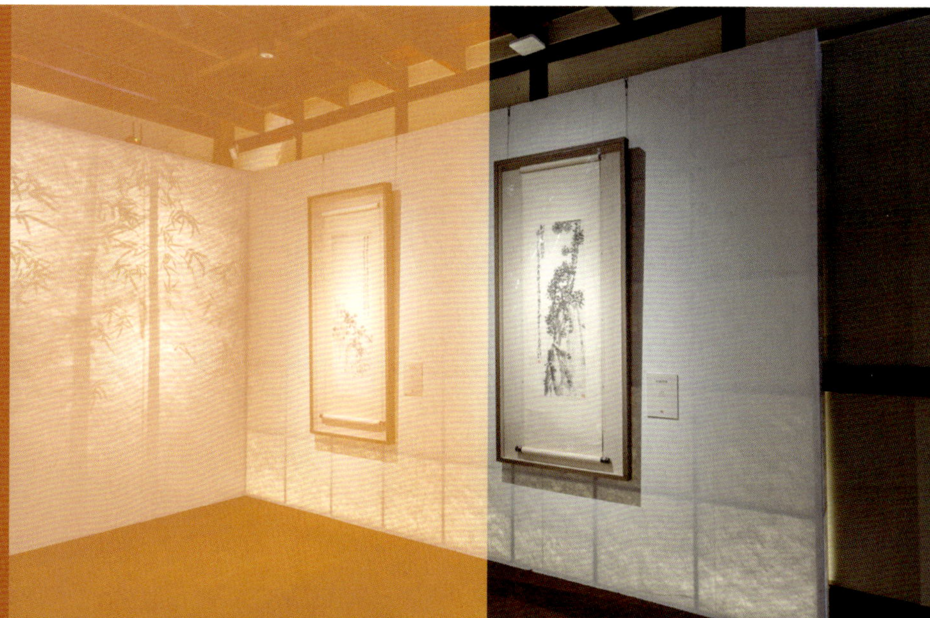

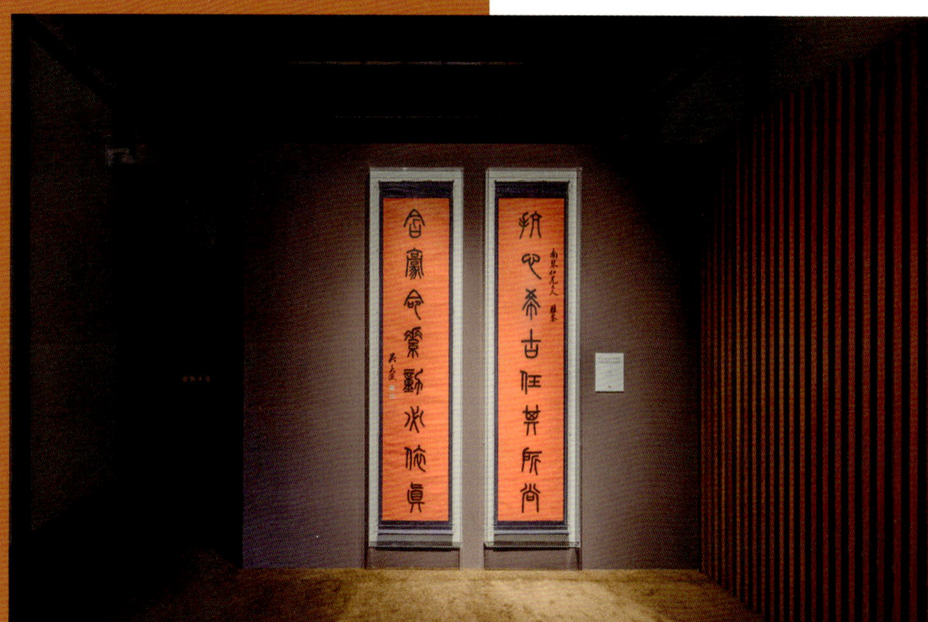

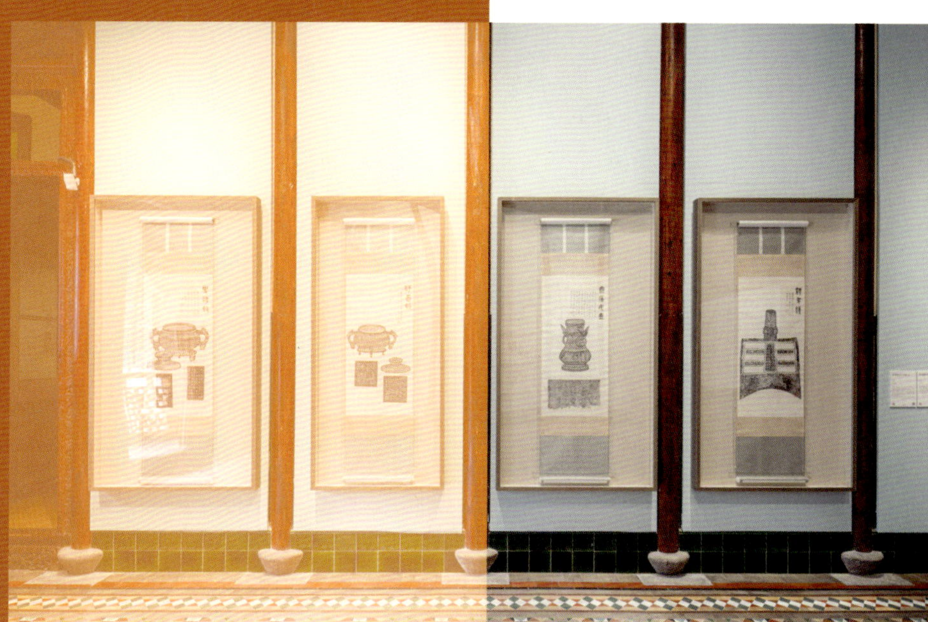

Ink·Mark—Paintings & Calligraphy Exhibition of Wu Changshuo & Members of Xiling Seal Engraver's Society in Early Stage

29 August – 19 October 2023

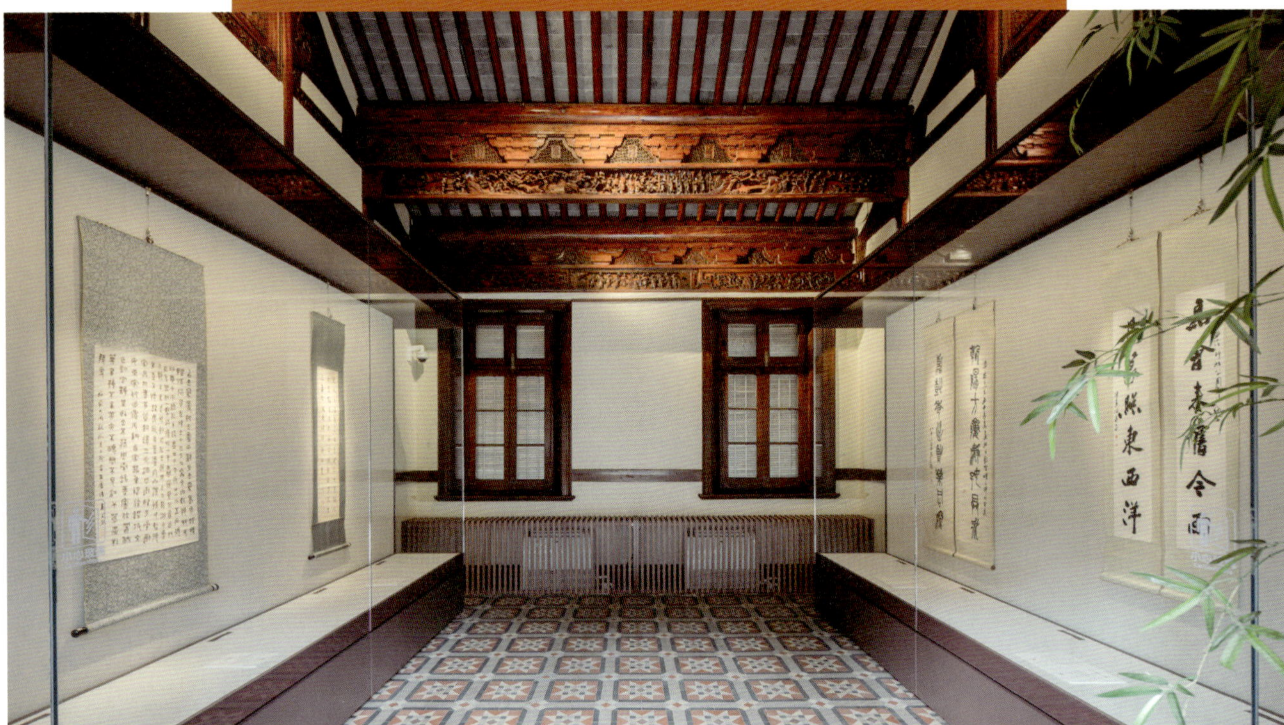

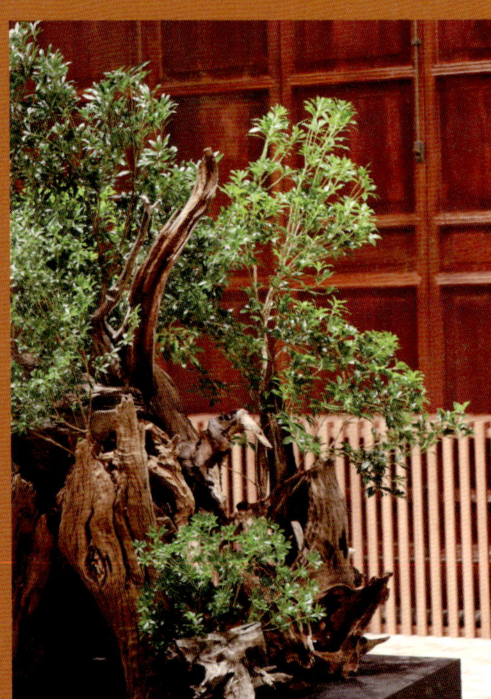

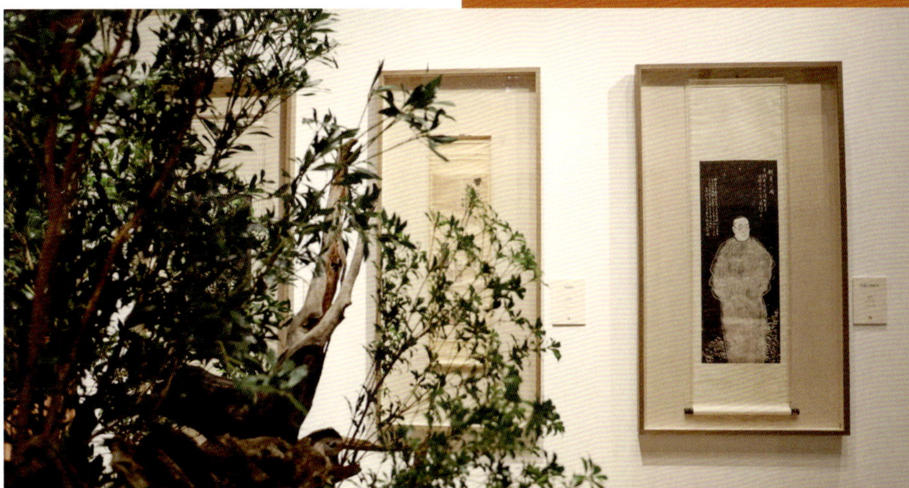

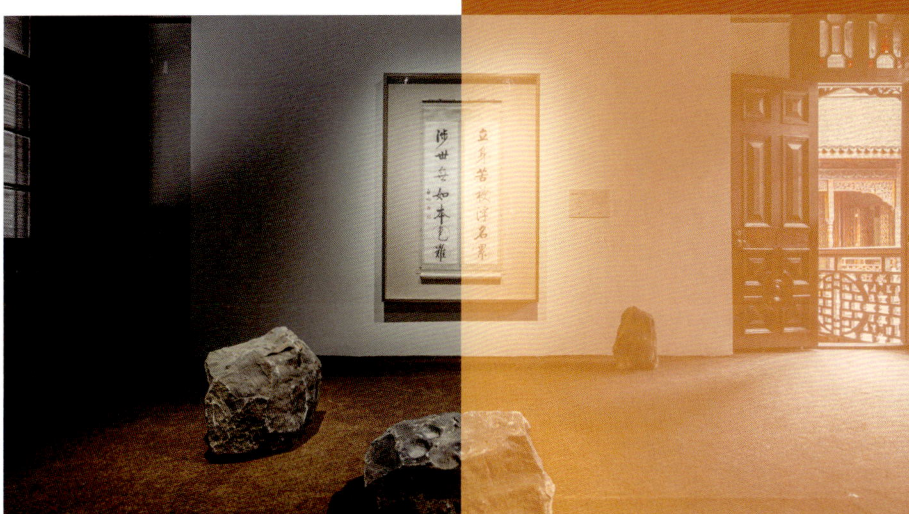

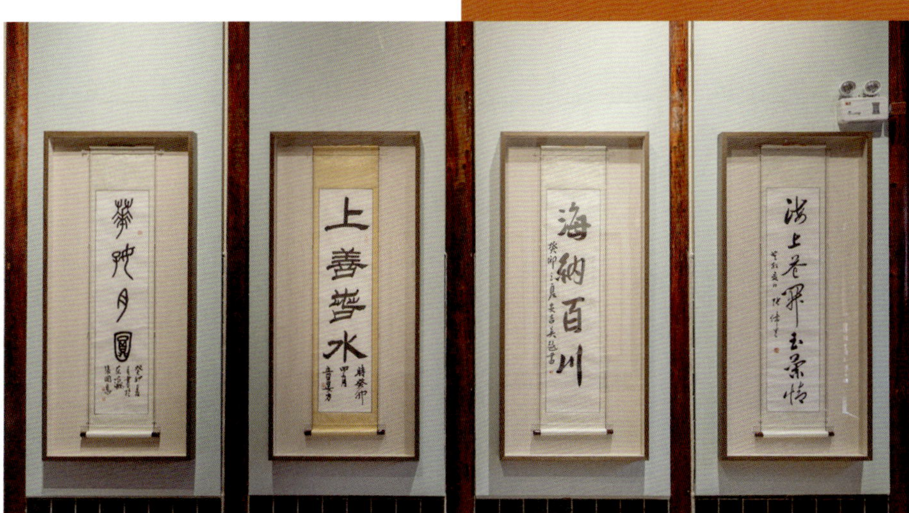
上善若水
海納百川

Lofty Mountains and Flowing Water—Ren Bonian and Wu Changshuo
3 February – 7 April 2024

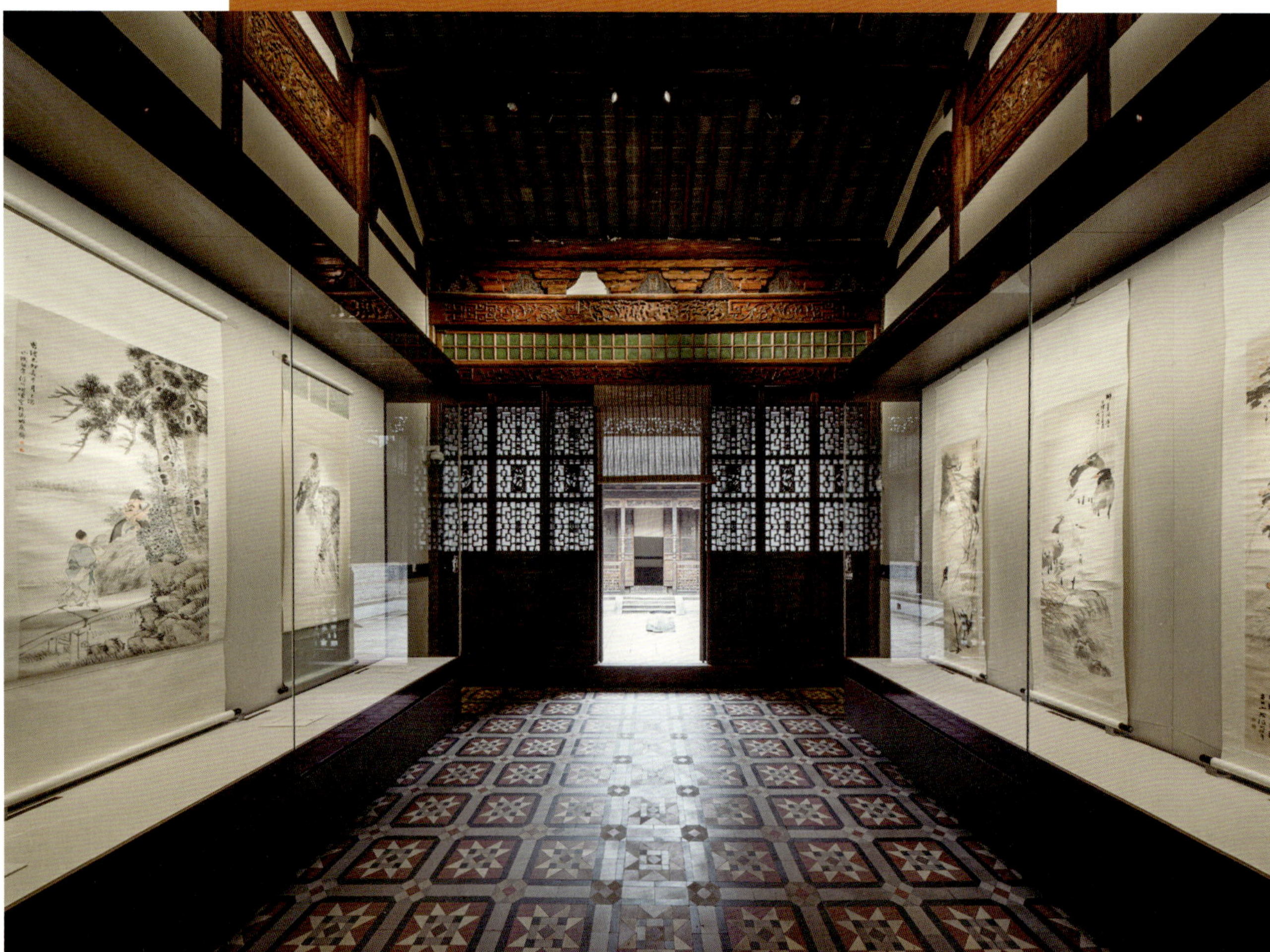

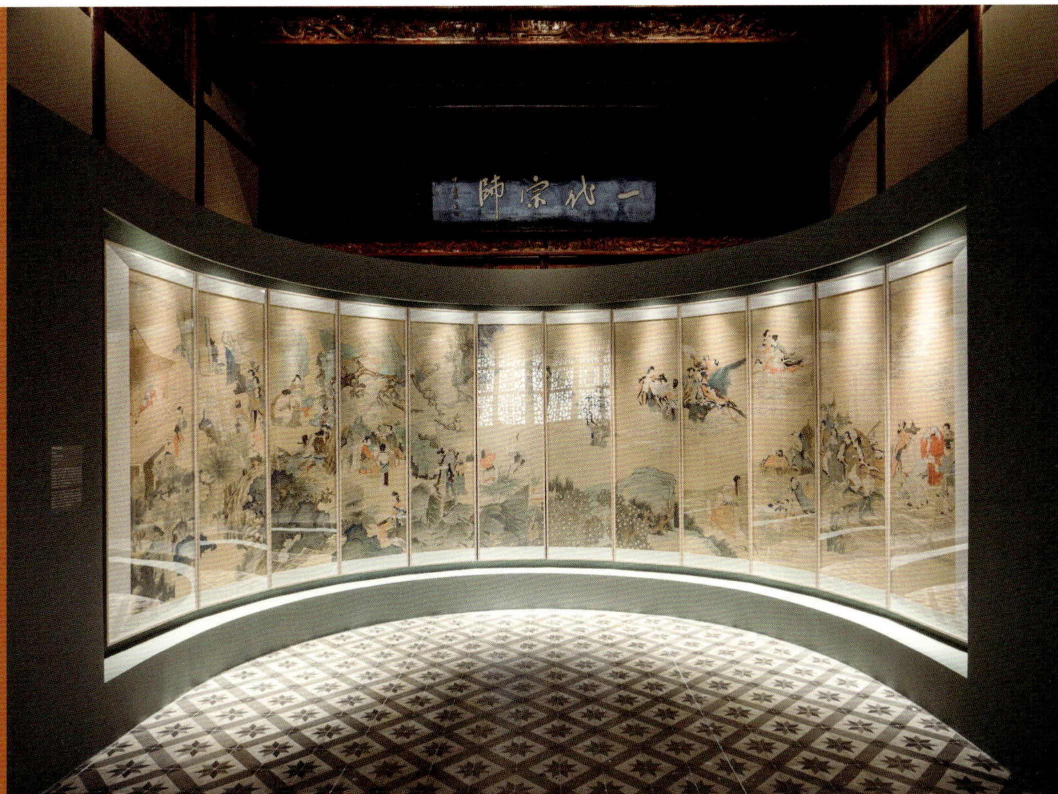
一代宗師

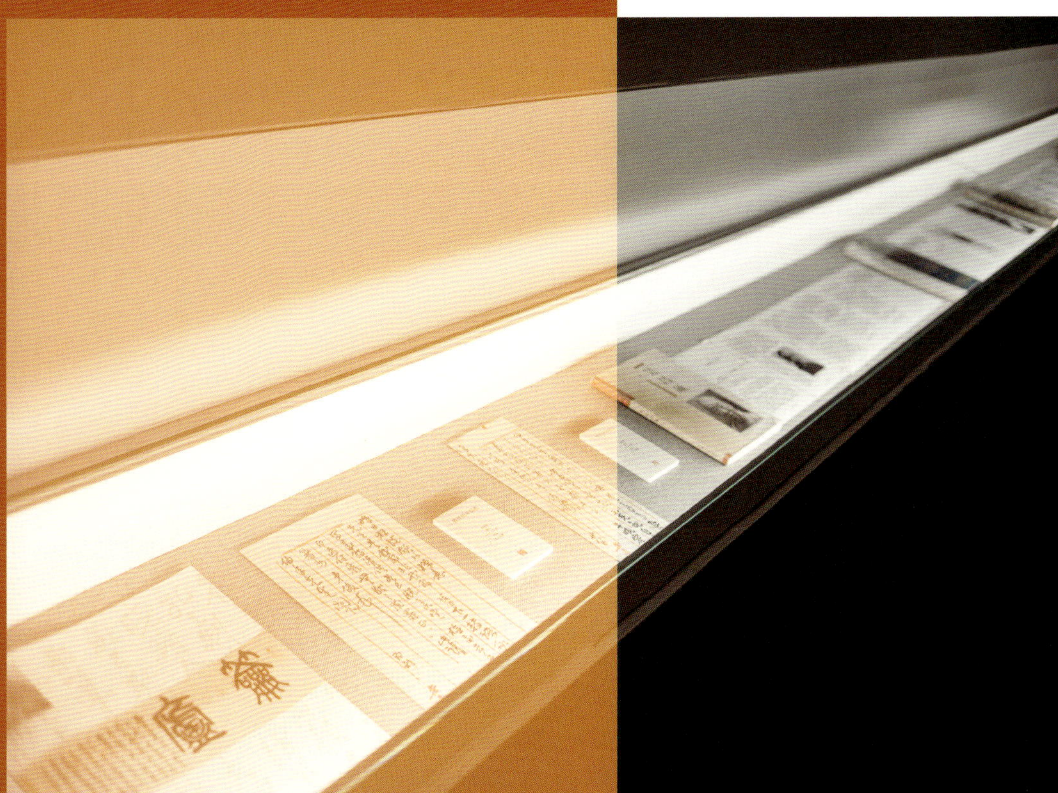

The Beauty of Lines—Exhibition of Wu Changshuo's Calligraphy Works

16 April – 16 June 2024

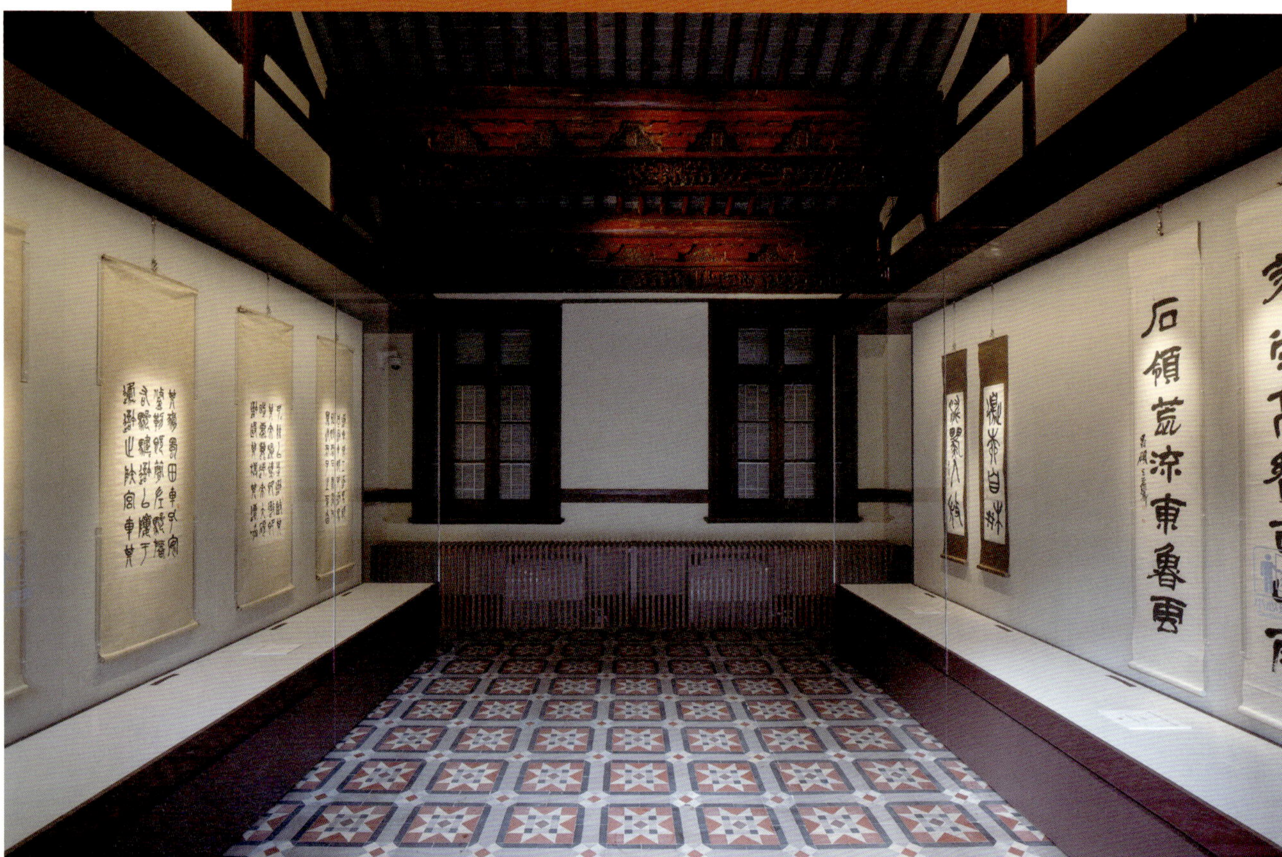

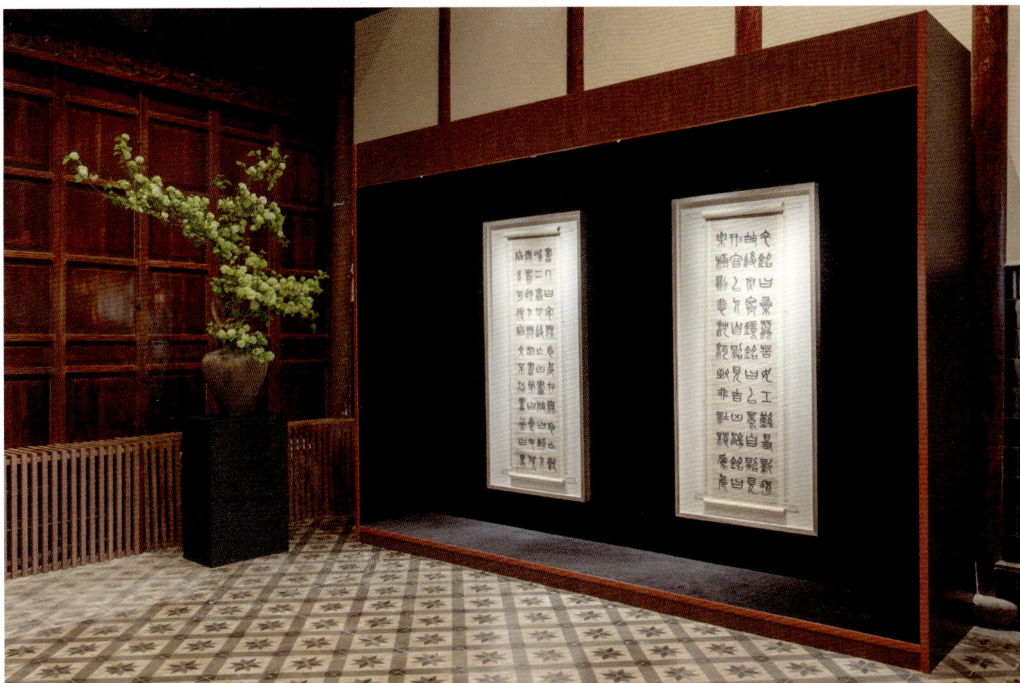

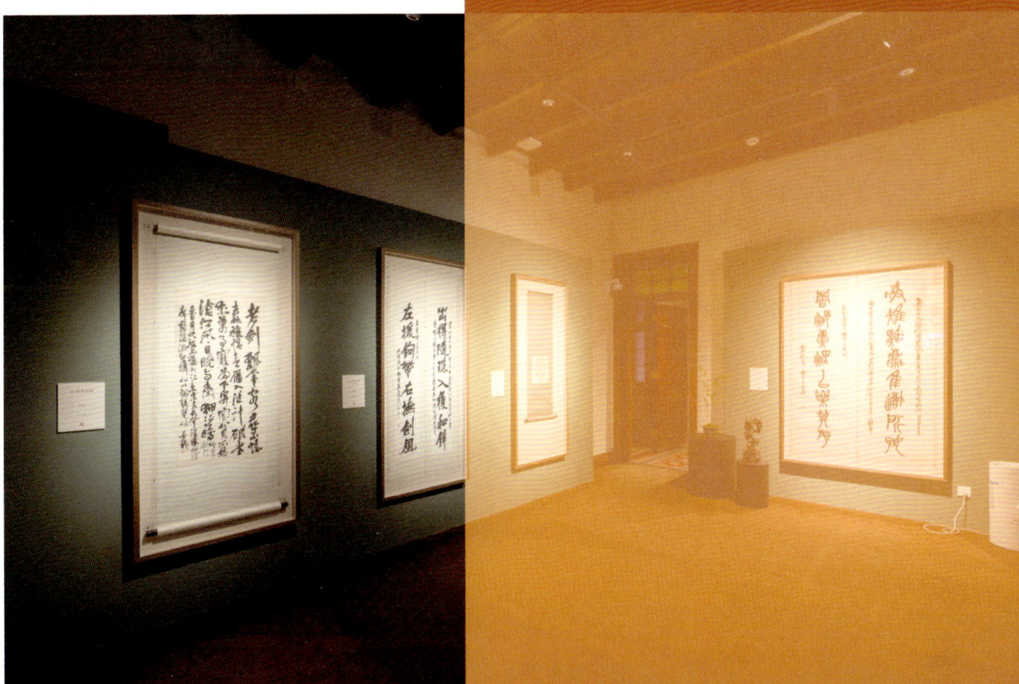

Artistic Brilliance, Shining on the Seas—Wu Changshuo: The 180th Anniversary of His Birth (Documentary Exhibition)

4 July – 22 September 2024

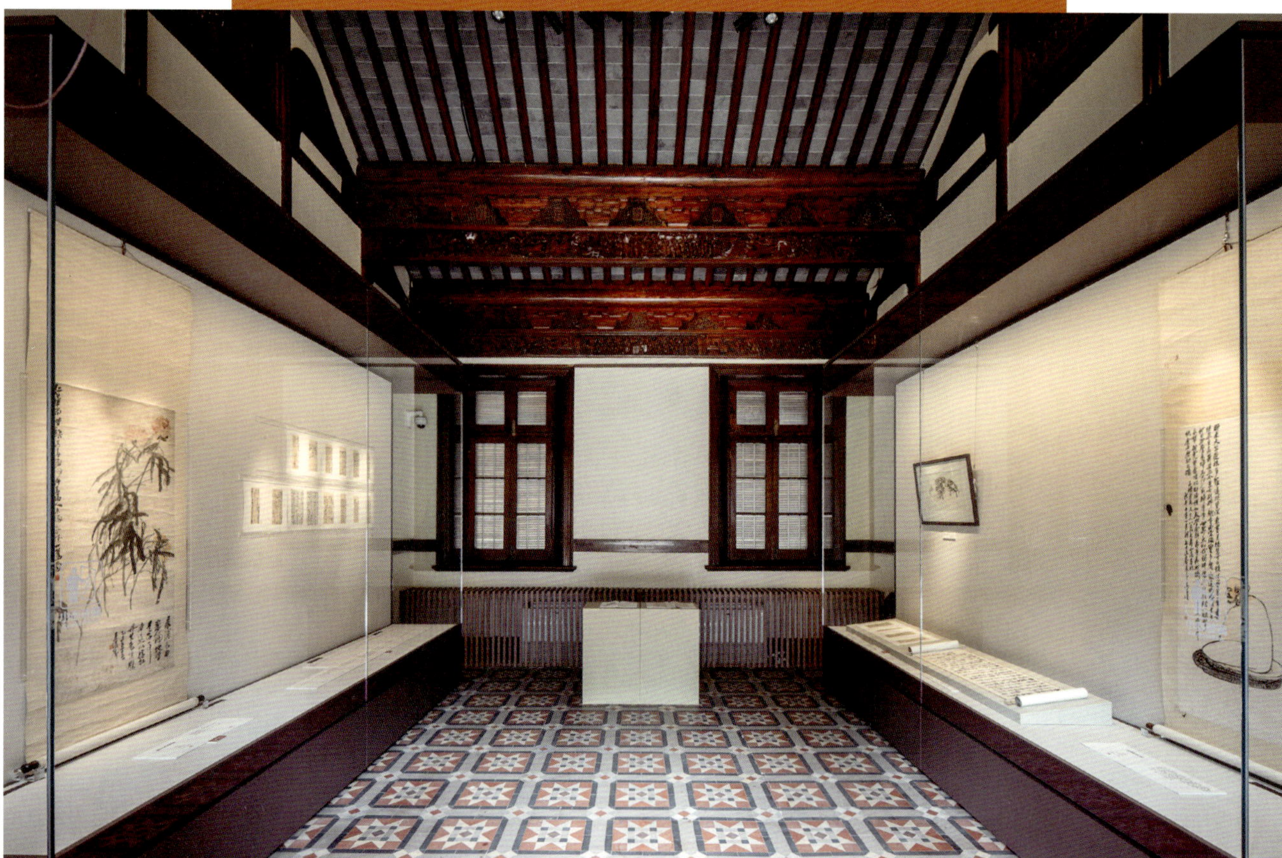

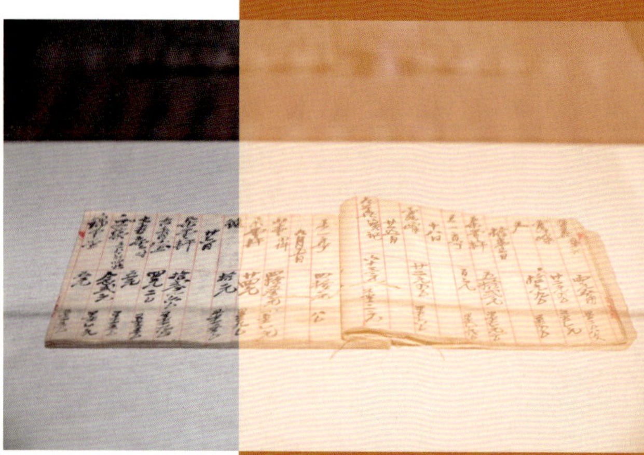

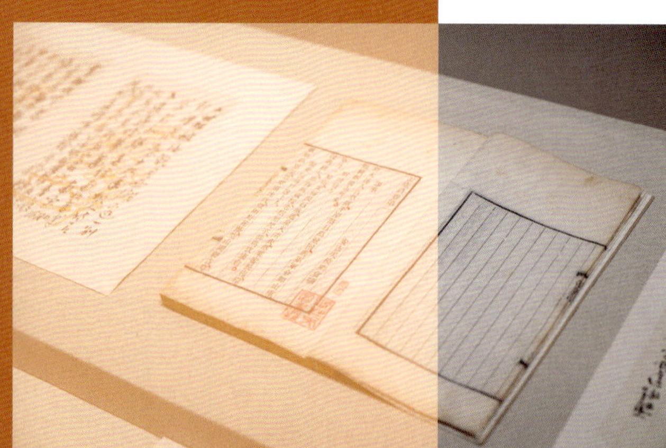

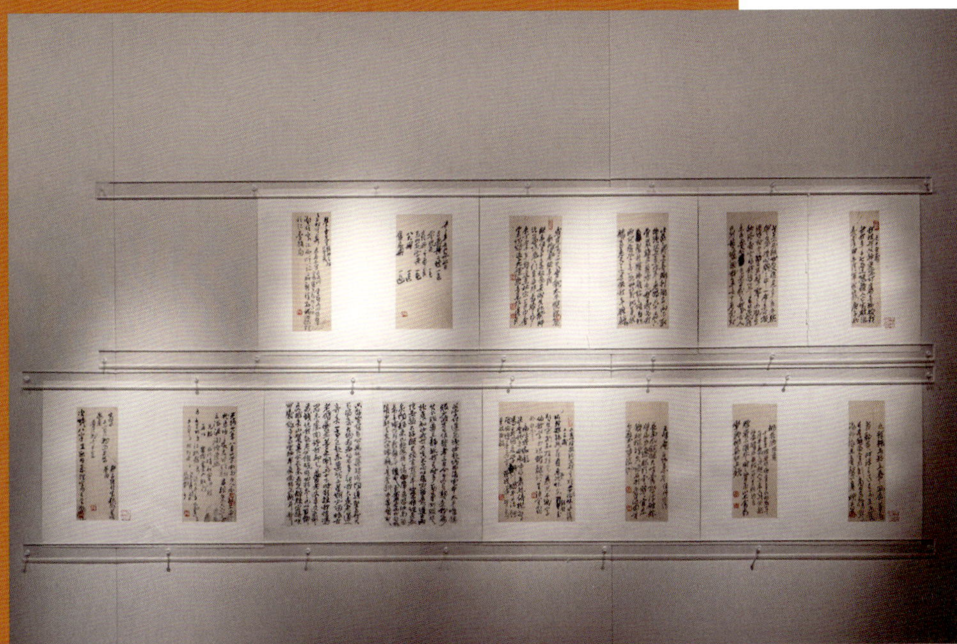

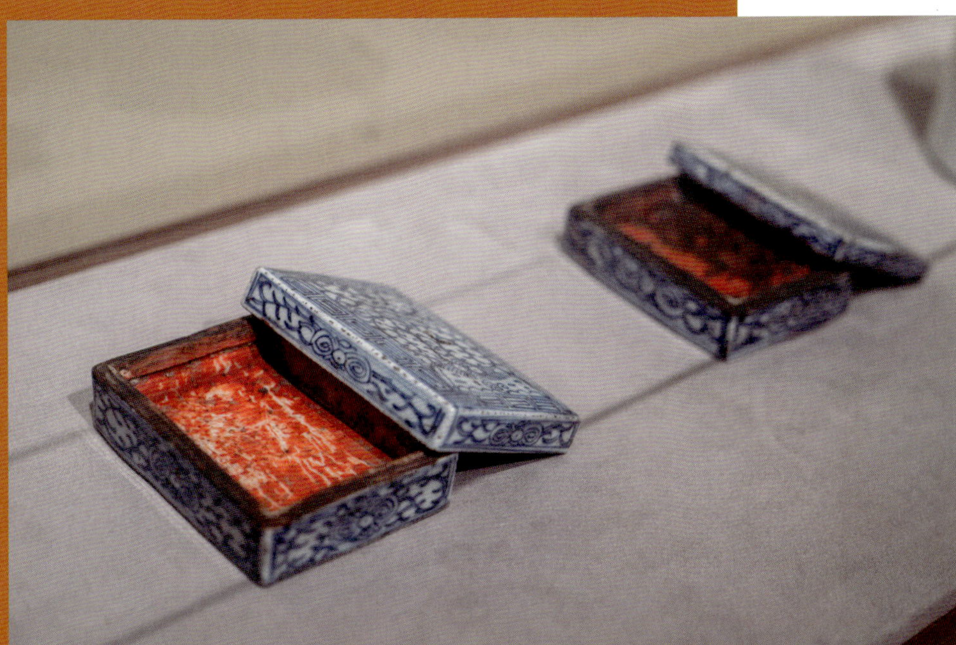

From Bronze and Stone to Ink and Brush—Wu Changshuo: The 180th Anniversary of His Birth Heritage Exhibition

1 October – 22 December 2024

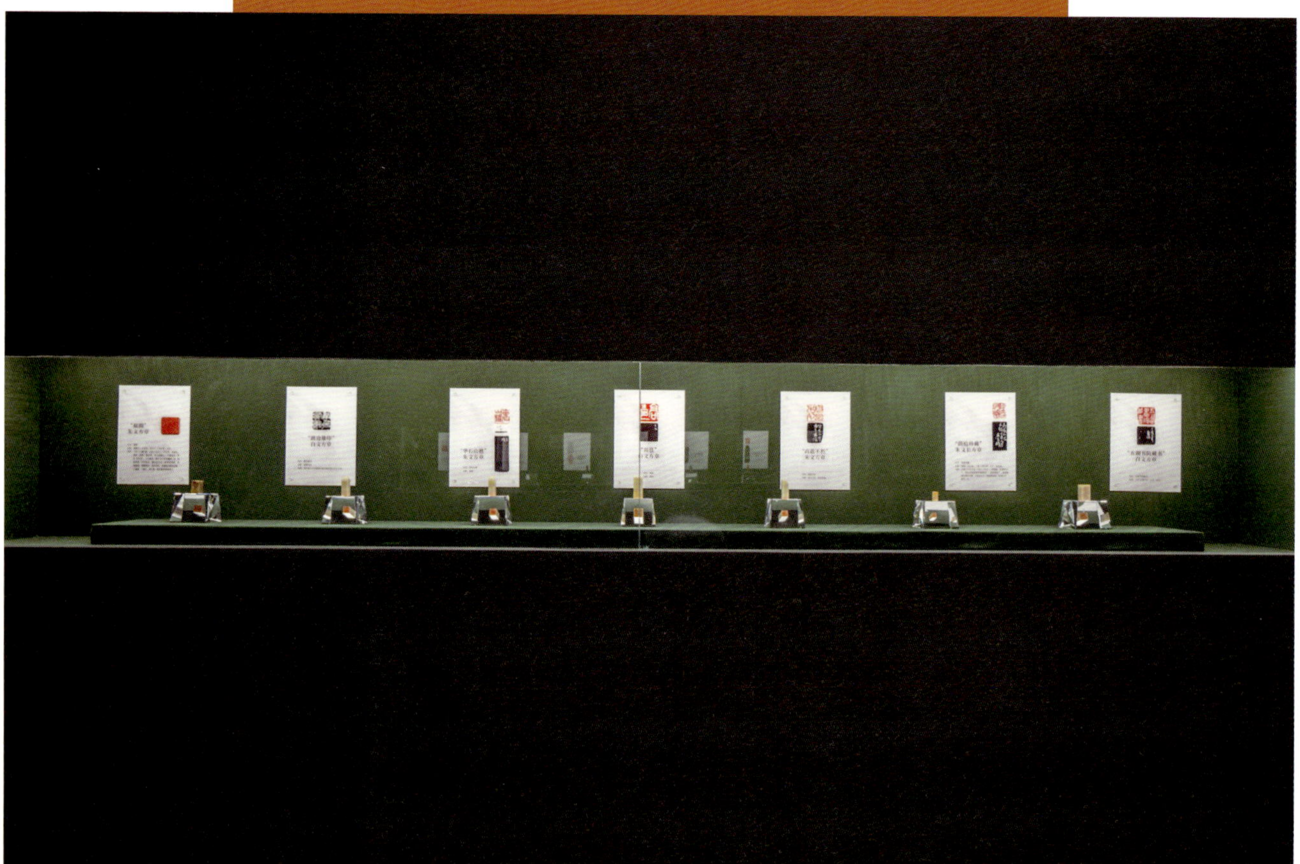

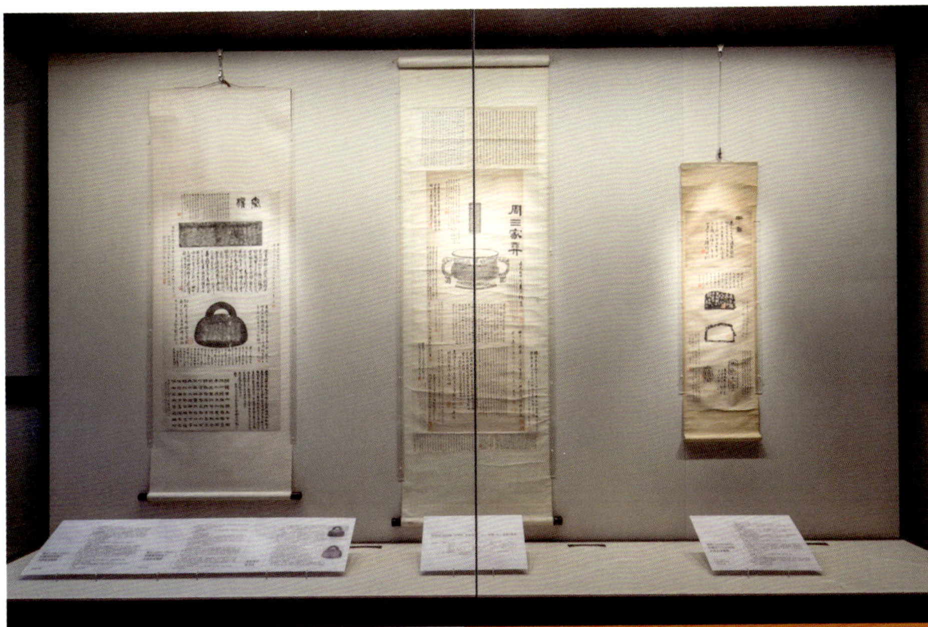

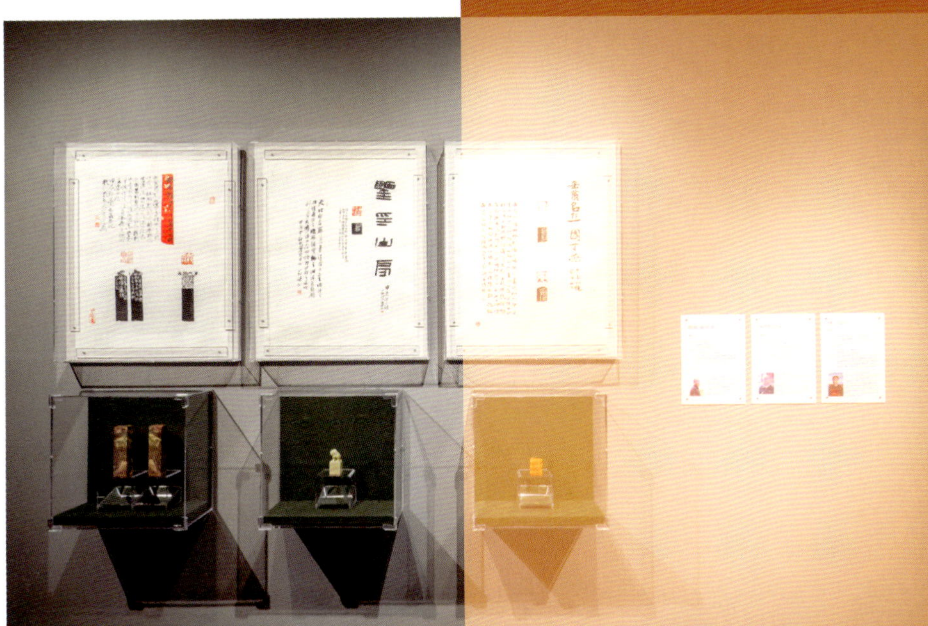

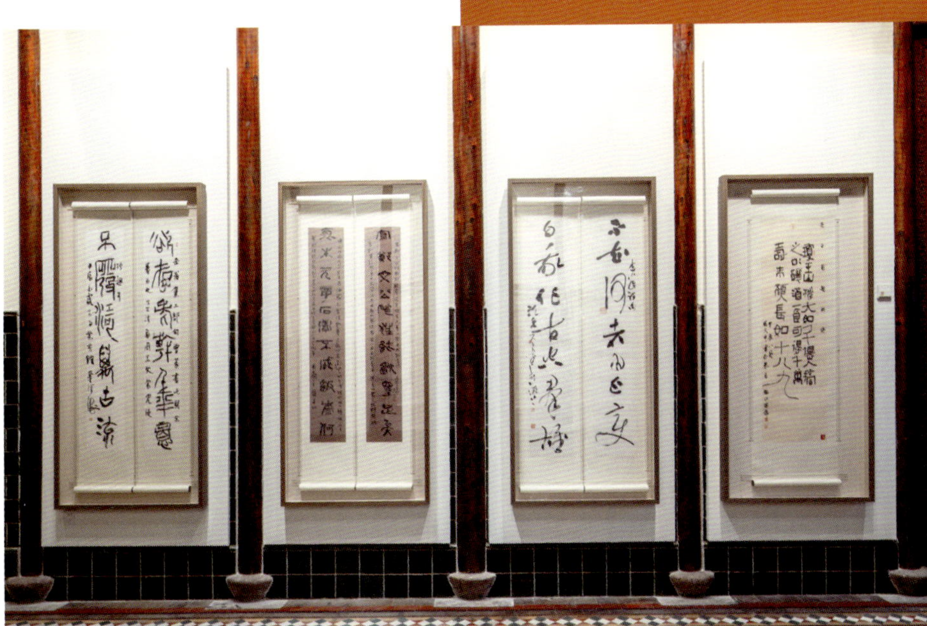

Guided by: The Culture, Sports and Tourism Bureau of Shanghai Pudong New Area
Organised by: Shanghai Wu Changshuo Art Museum
Produced by: Shanghai Pudong Media Group
Supported by: Shanghai International Culture Association
Wu Changshuo Memorial (Anji)
Shanghai Wu Changshuo Art Research Association
Shanghai Wu Changshuo Cultural and Art Foundation
Image Copyright: Shanghai Wu Changshuo Art Museum

ISBN: 978 1 78884 286 0

Published by ACC Art Books with Guangxi Normal University Press 2025

A CIP catalogue record for this book is available from the British Library

Editors: Alice Bowden, Ru Jingyu
Designer: Qu Zhonghua

Printed in China
for ACC Art Books Ltd., Woodbridge, Suffolk, UK

www.accartbooks.com
www.gxnu.edu.cn

ACC ART BOOKS